# ENCYCLOPEDIA

## OF BLACK COMICS

## SHEENA C. HOWARD

FULCRUM

Cover design by John Jennings

Edited by Larisa Hohenboken
Image credits: title page (Afua Richardson [left], Professor W. Foster [top], Nancy Goldstein [right], Comic Strip Archives [bottom]).

Library of Congress Cataloging-in-Publication Data

Names: Howard, Sheena C., author. | Gates, Henry Louis, Jr., writer of
    foreword. | Priest, Christopher J. (Christopher James), 1961- writer of
    afterword.
Title: Encyclopedia of black comics / Sheena Howard ; foreword by Henry Louis
    Gates, Jr. ; afterword by Christopher Priest.
Description: Golden, CO : Fulcrum Publishing, [2017] | Includes index.
Identifiers: LCCN 2017027581 | ISBN 9781682751015 (paperback)
Subjects: LCSH: Comic books, strips, etc.--Encyclopedias. | American
    literature--African American authors--Encyclopedias. | African American
    cartoonists--Encyclopedias. | African Americans in
    literature--Encyclopedias. | African Americans in popular
    culture--Encyclopedias. | Graphic novels--United States--History and
    criticism. | BISAC: LITERARY CRITICISM / Comics & Graphic Novels. |
    LITERARY COLLECTIONS / American / African American. | REFERENCE /
    Encyclopedias.
Classification: LCC PN6707 .H69 2017 | DDC 741.5/03 [B] --dc23
LC record available at https://lccn.loc.gov/2017027581

Printed in the United States of America

0 9 8 7 6 5 4 3 2 1

Fulcrum Publishing
4690 Table Mountain Dr., Ste. 100
Golden, CO 80403
800-992-2908 • 303-277-1623
https://fulcrum.ipgbookstore.com

# ENCYCLOPEDIA OF BLACK COMICS

# CONTENTS

# FOREWORD

## by Henry Louis Gates, Jr.

Pam Grier's star-turn in the 1974 Blaxploitation classic, *Foxy Brown*, is a cultural touchstone, as significant for Grier's badass performance as it is for her fashionable embrace of the Afro. But who still remembers "Torchy Brown"? A style icon in her own way, Torchy Brown, for those of you who like to win at trivia, was the star of *Dixie to Harlem*, the first comic strip by a Black woman about a Black woman. Long before Foxy Brown went out seeking vengeance in the Black Power era, Torchy's Depression-era rags-to-riches story featured a runaway from Mississippi who finds renown in Harlem's legendary Cotton Club alongside Bill "Bojangles" Robinson, Cab Calloway, and the one and only Josephine Baker, who calls Torchy "My baby!"

Torchy Brown image courtesy of Nancy Goldstein

Torchy first appeared in the *Pittsburgh Courier* in 1937. She flowed out of the pen of Zelda Mavin Jackson, known as Jackie Ormes, a twenty-six-year-old woman from Monongahela, Pennsylvania, who taught herself to draw by copying comics out of the newspaper. Like Torchy, Ormes was making her way in the North as part of a pioneering generation of professional African American women in politics, education, and entertainment. And the struggle they waged to represent – and uplift – the race was anything but easy, crowded out as it often was by decades of negative Jim and Jane Crow stereotyping.

How do I know about Ormes? She is a highlight in the ever-more fascinating pages of Sheena C. Howard's *Encyclopedia of Black Comics*, contained within the covers of this book. One of its defining features is the fact that fully one-third of the 106 biographies Howard has chosen for her pathbreaking volume are on African American women artists, publishers, comic convention founders, and other leading figures in the Black comics industry. In other words, Ormes is in good company here, illustrating the astonishing power of comic books and graphic novels to reflect the diversity that defines the Black American experience. The biographies of these artists, from the early twentieth century to today, also offer us a unique compass for charting the startling changes we've seen in that same span in African American culture and society and American race relations as a whole.

*Krazy Kat* image courtesy of Comic Strip Library

Without giving too much away, the first major Black, or "colored," cartoonist canonized in Howard's Encyclopedia is New Orleanian George Herriman. At least, that's how his 1880 birth certificate defined him, though when he moved to New York to ply his trade, he began identifying himself as French or Greek, the latter being his nickname, "Greek" Herriman, the genius behind the smash comic strip, *Krazy Kat*. The first self-identified Black cartoonists, emerging in the 1920s and 1930s, were Wilbert Holloway and Jay Jackson, who attended art colleges and wrote for major Black newspapers. In the *Chicago Defender*, Jackson's *As Others See It* lampooned the manners and mores of established Black urban dwellers as well as those who'd only arrived from the rural South by way of the Great Migration. Holloway's *Sunny Boy Sam* appeared in the *Courier* from 1928 until his death in 1969, and along the way he earned awards for his cartoons attacking lynching and the Ku Klux Klan, and for opposing Italy's invasion of Ethiopia before the start of World War II. As memorable, Holloway designed the indelible

"Double V" logo, which the *Courier* promoted to rally African Americans to press for victory at home and abroad during the war. Another "founding" Black cartoonist was Ollie Harrington, the son of an African American construction worker and a Jewish Hungarian mother in the South Bronx. The main cartoonist for the *New York Amsterdam News* in the 1930s, Harrington innovated *Dark Laughter*, later taken up by other Black papers, which was uncompromising in its vociferous critique of American racism. Harrington, who reported on the experiences of Black soldiers in Italy and North Africa for the US State Department, nevertheless found himself being investigated by the House Un-American Activities Committee (or HUAC) for his radicalism, to the point that he eventually settled in communist East Germany in the early 1960s.

The first self-identifying Black cartoonist to be featured in mainstream publications was E. Simms Campbell, who landed in New York at the tail end of the Harlem Renaissance. Among his numerous achievements: Campbell drew a Night Club Map of Harlem, illustrated poems by Sterling Brown, and, with luminaries Arna Bontemps and Langston Hughes, produced an illustrated children's book, *Popo and Fifina: Children of Haiti* (1932). From there, he began placing cartoons in *Esquire*, *The New Yorker*, and other trendsetting publications – even *Playboy*, home to that other influential Black cartoonist Buck Brown's risqué "Granny" character. Amazingly, few readers ever knew Campbell was Black.

*More Cuties in Arms* photo courtesy of Professor W. Foster

However haltingly, opportunities for African American cartoonists expanded beyond the Black press in the years after World War II. For example, Orrin Evans created the first Black comic book, *All Negro Comics*, in 1947, the same year Jackie Robinson broke the color barrier in professional baseball. Matt Baker achieved heightened success in what is now known as the Golden Age of the comic book industry drawing for Atlas Comics, forerunner of Marvel, though tragically, he died of a heart attack at thirty-seven in 1959. Later, in the mid-1970s, Billy Graham, an artist shaped by the Black Arts and Black Power movements, provided artwork for Luke Cage, the very first Black leading protagonist with his own signature Marvel comic (initially created by a team of white artists). Graham also penned another stand-alone and enduring Marvel Superhero, Black Panther, who will soon be dazzling moviegoers in his own stand-alone film, directed by Ryan Coogler and starring Chadwick Boseman, Michael B. Jordan, and Lupita Nyong'o.

Still, it was not until the mid-1960s that the first Black-themed comic strip created by a Black artist was syndicated in the mainstream American press. A watershed event in African American cultural history, Morrie Turner's *Wee Pals*, with its multiracial cast, first appeared in February 1965 in the shadow of the Selma voting rights campaign and Malcolm X's assassination, and it would be syndicated nationally in 1968, following the murder of Rev. Dr.

Photo of Morrie Turner courtesy of Kheven LaGrone

Martin Luther King, Jr., a development that dispirited Turner, even as it won him a wider readership and acclaim, while spurring white cartoonists like Charles Schulz to include more diverse characters in their work.

Without a doubt, the total number of Black cartoonists and comic book writers exploded in the 1970s, when Marvel and other leading producers began hiring a rising generation of Black talent. Among them was artist Ray Billingsley, who, inspired by Turner's *Wee Pals*, launched a career at Disney before creating his own *Lookin' Fine* in 1980 as one of the first syndicated comic strips to feature a Black family. Turns out, the strip only lasted two years before Billingsley tired of his editors' efforts to dilute the strip by suggesting that the family adopt a white baby to appeal to white readers. Next, in 1988, Billingsley created the still-published *Curtis*, based on his childhood in Harlem.

What was notable about the Black comic book and cartoon world of the 1970s and early 1980s was the increasing diversity of its themes and content, and we all can be grateful for their inclusion in Howard's *Encyclopedia* – from Vernon Grant, the first American cartoonist to be influenced by Japanese innovators in anime; to the Afrofuturist Tim Fielder, who undertook the concept design for Funkadelic's aborted sci-fi movie, *The Mothership Connection*; to Stanford Carpenter, who wrote African folktales drawn from anthropological interviews on the continent. Their output was strong; so, too, the pushback they sometimes received. At the height of the Black freedom struggle in South Africa in the 1980s, for example, Denys Cowan drew an anti-apartheid themed *Black Panther* series that faced resistance from the head of Marvel Comics, because, as we learn herein, "it look[ed] like all the white people are killing all the black people" (p. 59). After the series was pulled, Cowan went on to co-found the first Black-owned comics company to tackle the underrepresentation of Black people in the industry. A more positive development was the emergence of Christopher Priest, who at twenty-two became the first African American writer/artist assigned to a monthly title, *The Falcon*, in 1983. Two years later, Priest took over Marvel's coveted *Spider-Man* franchise and became a leading creative force at Marvel over the ensuing decades.

The emergence of hip-hop as a megacultural force in the 1980s would once again transform the Black comic book and cartoon world. Artists like Brooklyn's Andre LeRoy Davis were the contemporaries of the Sugarhill Gang and Grandmaster Flash and immersed themselves in the scene. With a freshly minted fine arts degree, Davis became the main artist at *The Source*, capturing LL Cool J, Sean Combs, Dre, and others, and his iconic image of DJ Quik of California's X-Klan would ignite a brief East Coast/West Coast war of words, although most rappers realized that being featured in Davis's "The Last Word" for *The Source* was a badge of honor.

By my lights, the best-known newspaper comic strip of the 1990s and early 2000s was the great Aaron McGruder's *The Boondocks*. *The Boondocks* had its origins in McGruder's work for the University of Maryland newspaper, where his characters Huey and Riley Freeman and Jazmine DuBois first appeared, in the early 1990s. Syndicated nationally in 160 newspapers – the largest-ever debut for a comic strip – *The Boondocks* caught hell from white critics who deemed it "racist," while some Black critics thought it derogatory in its portrayal of African Americans. It was the strip's criticism of the Bush administration after 9-11 that eventually caused some newspapers to pull it altogether, but none of them could take away from McGruder the visionary powers of his pen.

As you read and refer to this *Encyclopedia of Black Comics*, you will find that around one-quarter of its entries covers artists and writers born since the 1980s, what we "Boomers" refer to as "Millennials." And more than half of the more than thirty women featured in Howard's volume came of age in the early twenty-first century. Their work, like that of Jackie Ormes before them, has only made the comic book world more representative and exciting. At the same time, the expansion of the internet has played a major role in lowering the barriers to entry. Take Jamie Broadnax, a self-identified "social media geek," who has been the blogger and podcaster behind *Black Girl Nerds* since 2007, a site where "Black women and women of color [can] embrace their nerdiness and eccentricities" (p. 31). Then there is Shauna Grant, who, strongly influenced by Japanese manga and its "cute" subgenre, has created a biweekly webcomic, "Princess Love Pon," a Black character who is at once "happy and girly" but also a "strong woman."

The important, and growing, connections between the worlds of academia and Black comics are represented by, among others, Sheena Howard, the driving force behind this book and the first Black woman to be awarded an Eisner Award (the comic book equivalent of a Pulitzer or an Oscar) for *Black Comics: Politics of Race and Representation*. Among others connecting the worlds of Black comics and academia are Joel Gill, who leverages the graphic novel form to teach about lawman Bass Reeves and other neglected figures from Black history

Black Girl Nerds image by Asia Kendrick-Horton, courtesy of Jamie Broadnax

through his comics *Strange Fruit, Volume I* and *Strange Fruit, Volume II*; John Jennings, Jr., a Nasir Jones fellow at Harvard's Hutchins Center (where I serve as director), who has organized Black comic book conventions and scholarly conferences, and in 2017 adapted Octavia Butler's breakthrough work of science fiction, *Kindred*, as a graphic novel; and Mat Johnson, who set an installment of the long-running *Hellblazer* comic series during an eighteenth-century New York City slave conspiracy, and published *Incognegro*, a graphic novel that borrows from former NAACP executive director Walter White's story of traveling through the South disguised as a white man to expose the criminality of lynching. Last but not least, it is a testament to the power of the Black comic world that some of our leading intellectual and literary voices have embraced the genre, most notably with Marvel Comics' selection of Ta-Nehisi Coates to reboot its iconic *Black Panther* comic series in 2015.

*Strange Fruit* image courtesy of Fulcrum Publishing

I encourage every reader of this fantastic collection to explore in its pages the historical development of Black comics over more than a century, and to seize it as a jumping-off point for learning more, perhaps by examining the work of the pioneering Jamaican historian, Joel A. Rogers, whose iconic *My History* and *Facts about the Negro* were impressively illustrated in the *Pittsburgh Courier* by Sam Milai, from the 1930s to the 1960s. Rogers and Milai riveted me as a child growing up in the factory town of Piedmont, West Virginia, where comics were passed around as a way of educating ourselves outside the textbook world of our weekday classrooms. Sheena Howard's *Encyclopedia* is another classroom, anthologizing the lives of artists who redrew the rules.

On my tour through the entries included in this splendid volume, I often found myself thinking about what a sequel to it might look like in fifty or one hundred years. For now, that future is unwritten and undrawn, but we can be sure that, like the past, it will reflect the genius and creativity of African Americans shaping worlds within worlds within their minds and pens. A perfect starting point for this future begins here in these pages, in this classroom, and the artists of the future would do well to learn the deep history they contain as they contemplate adding their own gifts for expression to it. In these tense and divided times, we are counting on them, as we have since the days of Torchy Brown, to make America feel, think, laugh, and wonder.

## HENRY LOUIS GATES, JR.

Cambridge, Massachusetts
June 2017

# ACKNOWLEDGMENTS

The book you hold in your hands could not have been written without the contributions of various writers, researchers, and comic enthusiasts across various disciplines and fields. These are the many writers of the one-hundred-plus entries in this book. I am forever grateful for their time, support, and expertise.

Brigid Alverson

Skryb Anu

Barbara Brandon-Croft

Mora Byrd

Imani Cheers

Alanna D'Avanzo

Tara Donahue

Mark Dudley

Erika Ellis

Tea Fougner

Wesley French

Joel Christian Gill

Grace D. Gipson

Nancy Goldstein

Walter Greason

Chloe Hilla

Karama Horne

Amber Hubbard

Kyrié Kirkland

Christina M. Knopf

Kheven LaGrone

Tyler Lolong

Ajuan Mance

Erica Mason

Jeremiah Massengale

Jay Mattson

Anita McDaniel

Myron McGhee

Michael McGill

Shamika Mitchell

Carlos Morrison

Sherin Nicole

Joshua Phillips

Joshua Plencner

Jason Richardson

Caitlin Rosberg

Timothy Ross

Brandon Russell

Heide Solbrig

Scott Stalcup

Amitabh Vikram

Donnalyn Washington

Melvin Williams

Matthew Wood

Verdell Wright

Camilla Zhang

A special thanks to Barbara Brandon-Croft, Brigid Alverson, Alanna D'Avanzo, Karly Munoz, and William Foster.

Barbara, your willingness to dedicate your time, expertise and knowledge of the field means a lot. You went above and beyond to help in any way you could, and your support was invaluable.

Brigid, words cannot express how appreciative I am of your willingness to help with the details of this volume, including overseeing aspects of editing and stylistic nuances. Thank you.

Alanna, throughout the process of completing this volume, you were my right-hand woman. I am so grateful to have worked with you on this project. You were vital to completing various aspects of this book.

Karly, your work throughout the year with various aspects of this project really elevated this volume to the next level. Thank you.

Professor Foster, thank you for always supporting my work in the field of comics. Your breadth of knowledge and willingness to help me throughout the years has been unwavering. Thank you.

To my advisory board, Joel Christian Gill, Regine Sawyer, Barbara Brandon-Croft, John Jennings, and Juliana "Jewels" Smith, I admire the work that all of you do and I appreciate your support as well as the contacts you were able to provide across the field of comics. Your insight and advice was crucial, and I am forever grateful for your participation.

And a final thank you to Nancy Goldstein, for your assistance in sourcing rare images and hard-to-find facts.

# INTRODUCTION

## by Sheena C. Howard

In 2010, I graduated from Howard University with my PhD in intercultural and rhetorical communication. My dissertation is titled "The Continuity and Extension of African-American Communication Dynamics through Black Comic Strips"; it focuses on racial and gendered representations in the comic strip *The Boondocks*.

My dissertation required me to write a literature review on the history of Black comic strips and Black cartoonists, but I found that there were no comprehensive texts that provided a historical survey of either. Books that focused on the history of American comics seemed to leave out iconic Black comic artists such as Brumsic Brandon or Morrie Turner, and always failed to mention the first Black comic book, *All Negro Comics*. This was a glaring omission across both popular and academic literature.

Image courtesy of Barbara Brandon-Croft

To address this void, in 2013 I published the book *Black Comics: Politics of Race and Representation* to provide an introduction to the history of Black comics and Black American artists across the comics medium. My aim was to cover as much as I could in one volume, including both gendered and racial representations in Black comics and cartoons and the cultural barriers for Black cartoonists in the comics industry. In 2014, the book won an Eisner

Award for Best Scholarly/Academic work, making me the first woman of color to ever win an Eisner Award – the highest award one can receive in the comics industry.

There is a need to build upon and continue to document this history. As such, I felt that the *Encyclopedia of Black Comics* needed to be written, particularly because there is no such text currently available. It is my hope that future texts will build off of the work here as, with any such text, there will always be new editions and new people to include as the medium continues to evolve.

This encyclopedia focuses on people of African descent (African American, African, African/Black diaspora, Black peoples) who have published significant works in the United States. It contains more than one hundred entries on individuals both living and dead. Their published work(s) – including characters, content, books, and so forth, and their contributions are mentioned as a part of their entry. The text focuses on people in the following sectors in the field of comics: artists, creators, illustrators, inkers, writers, Black comic historians, convention creators, website creators, self-published comic creators, editors, archivists, and academics. It also includes individuals who may not fit into any of these categories, but who have made notable achievements in Black comic culture.

SHEENA C. HOWARD

June 2017

# Entries A-Z

## Anderson, Jiba Molei

Jiba Molei Anderson's creation *The Horsemen* served as the flagship property for his publishing house, Griot Enterprises, gaining inclusion in the permanent library of the Smithsonian Institution.

His first crack at comics came in 1995, when La Morris Richmond hired Anderson as an inker for his *Jigaboo Devil* comic. Anderson's creation *The Horsemen* began during work on his master's of fine arts thesis. This comic marked a shift from the concerns that normally occupied African-American superheroes at the time, such as drug dealing or other forms of inner-city crime. Anderson connected African American superheroes to African mythology, immersing himself in the study of Yoruba, which managed to survive the slave trade in Cuba and Haiti.

> **(Aug. 17, 1972– )**
> - **Born in Detroit, MI**
> - **University of Michigan, BFA in illustration and photography, 1994**
> - **School of the Art Institute of Chicago, MFA in visual communication, 1998**
> - **Illustrator, designer, writer, educator, and publisher**
> - **Creator of *The Horsemen***

The comic depicts Yoruba gods as superheroes, with each chapter named for a different divine entity. The team consists of seven orishas, or manifestations of the god Olodumare. These orishas inhabit a group of young Black professionals from Detroit who do combat with a corrupt group of multicultural orishas known as The Deitis, who are bent on seeing humanity worship at the feet of politics, organized religion, commerce, and other corrupting elements of the modern world.

The year after receiving his master's degree, Anderson founded Griot Enterprises publishing house and creative studio, with *The Horsemen* serving as its first major property. The first *Horsemen* comic saw release in 2002, receiving critical acclaim.

While the major comics publishers continued to focus on an audience it believed consisted solely of white, middle-class, adolescent

Image courtesy of Jiba Molei Anderson

males, Anderson and his contemporaries created stories about a wider range of humanity. His work includes positive images of people from a variety of ethnicities, working to dispel years of negative stereotyping.

Anderson's influences ran the gamut of popular culture. Along with the obvious influence of cartoons and comic books, Anderson draws inspiration from the works of Alphonse Mucha, Frank Frazetta—whose artwork was featured on numerous *Conan the Barbarian* covers and albums by Molly Hatchet—and Z-grade grindhouse films.

Anderson's other ventures into writing include the educational text *Manifesto: The Tao of Jiba Molei Anderson, Chronicle: The Art of Jiba Molei Anderson,* and his blog *The Afrosoul Chronicles,* where Anderson expounds on the subjects of race, politics, business, and popular culture. Anderson also served as the lead writer and art director of the comic *Crates: The Hip Hop Chronicles* with Christian Beranek.

Anderson has managed to straddle the fence between academic and corporate worlds during his career. As an educator, he has taught as an assistant professor at the Illinois Institute of Arts and as an adjunct faculty member at Sanford-Brown College and Chicago State University, and a visiting assistant professor at DeVry University. He has served in the capacity of graphic designer, production artist, and art director for the likes of KBA Marketing, Ryan Partnership, Cedar Grove Books, Landmark Sign Group, and Manga Entertainment. He has also worked as a graphic designer, animator, art director, and graphic novelist for institutions such as the Smithsonian National

Museum of African Art, the Chicago Academy of Music, and the University of Illinois at Chicago.

Anderson has taken part in both one-man and group shows and has had his work featured in the book *Black Comix*. He has also traveled the country as a public speaker, discussing comic books and graphic novels as a means to explore issues of race, identity, and culture in the classroom.

Anderson believes comics are a democratic medium with power to speak globally. Through his work, he hopes to develop what he calls "young warriors," people with strong viewpoints and the drive to succeed.

## ANDERSON, JULIE M.

A self-taught artist, Julie Anderson is the author of two webcomics, *Onyx* and *VE Dead Breed*. Many of her works engage with Afrofuturism, an international aesthetic movement that addresses concerns of the African Diaspora through science fiction.

> (July 30, 1987– )
> - **Born in New York, NY**
> - **Miami Palmetto High School, 2007**
> - **Illustrator, designer, and webcomic author**
> - **Creator of the webcomics *Onyx* and *VE Dead Breed***

Anderson has worked in a variety of creative fields, including modeling, illustration, and graphic design. She also illustrated two children's books: *It's Okay to Be Like Me!* written by Grace Zhang, and *Sir Frederick Squirrel of Canterbury*, written by Robenia McKinley.

In 2015 and 2016, Anderson developed two webcomics: *Onyx*, a post-apocalyptic story in which survivors face the threat of a catastrophic virus, and *VE Dead Breed*, about a group of assassins. She also created a series highlighting Black women in comic book–themed genres that appeared in the 2017 Black Comix Arts Festival in San Francisco.

In 2015, Anderson was a featured artist in the New York Public Library's *Unveiling Visions: The Alchemy of the Black Imagination*, an exhibit exploring Black speculative imagination surrounding Afrofuturism, science fiction, horror, comics, magical realism, and fantasy. She also did artwork for the 2014 documentary film, *The Czar of Black Hollywood*, chronicling the early life and career of African American filmmaker Oscar Micheaux.

Anderson describes her artistic style as "million-in-one multi-stylized work" that is influenced by fine art, anime, comics, and cartoons alike.

Image courtesy of Julie M. Anderson

IDEAL SUPERPOWER? "I'D LIKE TO BE ABLE TO LEVEL UP MY SKILL SETS LIKE AN RPG (ROLE-PLAYING GAME) PLAYER."

She most identifies with the story structures and character development of anime and manga, although her art itself does not have strong elements of the style.

## ANYABWILE, DAWUD

Although primarily known as a storyboard artist, Dawud Anyabwile is also the illustrator and cocreator of the comic series *Brotherman: Dictator of Discipline* and the illustrator of the graphic novel adaptation of Walter Dean Myers's *Monster*. He is a frequent collaborator with his brother Guy Sims, who wrote the scripts for both *Monster* and *Brotherman*.

(Feb. 6, 1965– )
- **Born in Philadelphia, PA**
- **Rutgers University, 1983–34; Temple University, 1984**
- **Storyboard artist, illustrator, and comic creator**
- **Illustrator and cocreator of *Brotherman: Dictator of Discipline***

In 1989, he began collaborating with Guy Sims to create the *Brotherman* series. This groundbreaking series showcased a hero of African American descent, Antonio Valor, working to combat social apathy in an embattled city. The series ran from 1992 until 1996, selling 750,000 copies without major distribution or publishing. It later won several Glyph Awards, including one for Best Artist.

The year the series ended, Anyabwile began working with Wanderlust Interactive on the *Pink Panther* computer games and with MTV on *Daria*. After moving to California, he worked in the animation department for Klasky Csupo for *The Wild Thornberrys* and *Rugrats*, later moving to Atlanta, Georgia, to do production design for Turner Studios, the owner of Cartoon Network, Nickelodeon, HarperCollins and Scholastic. His credits include *Harvey Birdman, Attorney at Law* (2004), *Level Up* (2011), and *Diary of a Wimpy Kid: The Long Haul* (2017). In 2014, Anyabwile was the art director for the short *Charged*, which he both wrote and directed.

In 2015, Anyabwile and Sims adapted Walter Dean Myers's *Monster*, a novel about a teenager awaiting trial for murder, to graphic novel format. The work received praise for both its writing and illustration.

Dawud Anyabwile has also developed an instructional video, *Drawing From the Soul*, to help artists unlearn the "proper" way to make art and focus on genuine expression. He developed this philosophy as a young man when he was challenged by his father to draw more Black people. Anyabwile couldn't understand why his drawing of African Americans looked so white until he realized that his primary education in drawing, *How to Draw Comics the Marvel Way*, had encouraged white-centric drawing styles that reflected neither himself nor his culture.

Dawud Anyabwile is the recipient of numerous comic and community service awards. In 1992, he was nominated for an Eisner Award for Best Comic Book Artist at the San Diego Comic-Con, the same year he was granted the key to Kansas City, Missouri, for outstanding service to children. In 2008, he won an Emmy for conceptualizing a PSA for the Dalai Lama, and he won the Lifetime Achievement Award from the East Coast Black Age of Comics Convention in Philadelphia in 2015. He has an artist archive at the Auburn Avenue Library on African American Culture and History in Atlanta, Georgia.

Image courtesy of Professor W. Foster

# ARMSTRONG, ROBB

Robb Armstrong is the creator of *JumpStart*, a comic strip that has appeared in more than 400 publications. Entered into syndication in 1989, *JumpStart* can be seen as a living memoir; the characters Joe Cobb, Marcy Cobb, and their children are a reflection of his family life. Part of his motivation, he has said, was to create a comic that depicts middle-class life, as Black youth in the media are so often depicted as poor and underserved.

**(March 4, 1962– )**
- **Born in Wynnefield, PA**
- **Syracuse University, BFA**
- **Cartoonist and public speaker**
- **Creator of *JumpStart***

Robb Armstrong grew up using cartooning as an escape from difficult realities. He witnessed many tragedies in his early life: Armstrong's father abandoned the family when he was only six, and the five fatherless children were brought up with little money to spend and little space to live in. His older brother was killed in an accident when he was still just six years old, and soon thereafter his mother died of cancer and his brothers suffered police brutality. By creating funny and light-hearted cartoons, he was able to live vicariously through his characters' easier lives.

Robb Armstrong published his autobiography, *Fearless*, in 2016. It offers cartooning tips as well as lessons from his upbringing. In a 2016 interview with the *Hartford Examiner* he said, "Suffering is the only thing we all have in common, but not everyone learns useful lessons from suffering. My book explores the value of hardship, and demonstrates how to use it for personal empowerment."

**"SUFFERING IS THE ONLY THING WE ALL HAVE IN COMMON, BUT NOT EVERYONE LEARNS USEFUL LESSONS FROM SUFFERING."**

Besides being an accomplished cartoonist, Armstrong is also a public speaker. He has addressed the Smithsonian Institution, the Library of Congress, and numerous educational institutions and large companies. He has also served as a visiting professor at the Savannah College of Art and Design in Georgia.

In 1995, Armstrong received the Wilbur Award for *JumpStart* from the Religion Public Relations Council and was honored with Nestlé's Men of Courage award. In 2012, the Holy Family University in Pennsylvania awarded him *Honoris Causa*, an honorary doctor of humane letters.

As of this writing, Robb Armstrong resides in Los Angeles, California, with his wife, Crystal D. Armstrong, and two children.

# AYALA, VITA

**(March 1, 1985– )**
- **Born in New York, NY**
- **State University of New York, Potsdam**
- **Comics and fiction writer**
- **Alumna of DC Comics Writers Workshop, 2016**

Vita Ayala is the coauthor of the independent comic *Our Work Fills The Pews* and has contributed scripts to several DC Comics titles.

She and her brother were raised in Alphabet City, also known as Manhattan's Lower East Side, in a blended home that hosted a number of neighborhood children, seven of whom she considered siblings. Ayala's early life helped her understand the complex dynamics of big groups, making her adept at writing about the arguments and compromises that arise from many clashing personalities. Her experience growing up in a predominantly Latino and Black neighborhood also influenced the development of her original story protagonists, all of whom come from diverse backgrounds.

As a person and an artist, Ayala was deeply influenced by her mother, Doris, and Doris's best friend, Ben Soto, who acted as a father figure to Ayala. Both were poets, bibliophiles, and storytellers who supported Ayala's creative pursuits.

Ayala first experienced racism at age five, when she was called the N-word for the first time. This experience, according to a 2016 interview, was also the first time Ayala "realized that an adult could be filled with disdain for [her] and not know [her] at all." This moment had a significant influence on Ayala's life and work.

Around the same time, Ayala was given the Fisher-Price version of *1,001 Arabian Nights*. She was fascinated by how Scheherazade was such a powerful storyteller, "so powerful that she could tame the bloodlust of a man who singlehandedly murdered every woman in his kingdom and still wasn't satisfied," Ayala recalled in a 2016 interview. Ayala regarded Scheherazade as the real hero of *1,001 Arabian Nights*, particularly appreciating that both Scheherazade and the other characters, like her, were brown.

Ayala procured her writing ability through sheer force of will, as she was at a kindergarten reading level until the fifth grade. At the time, she had just transferred from public school to Mary Help of Christians. Determined to catch up to the rest of her class, Ayala taught herself how to read *The Giver*, *Bridge to Terabithia*, and *The Little Prince* in a matter of three weeks. A few months later, she wrote her first story, a *Xena: Warrior Princess* fanfiction.

At age fifteen, Ayala was reinspired to write after her humanities teacher introduced her to Octavia Butler's *Dawn*, a book she cited in a 2016 interview as having "saved [her] life and forever changed how [she] looked at fiction and writing." That same year, Ayala realized she was gay, a pivotal moment in her personal and creative life. Up until then, she said, she "had a lot of trouble writing interpersonal relationships." After realizing this part of herself, she was able to "write from a truer place."

Around the same time, Vita Ayala met Erica Henderson, whose father's writing critiques would prove hugely influential to her. C. J. Henderson, a professional writer, was the first person to read her stories and offer constructive criticism.

As a college student at SUNY Potsdam, she was made acutely aware of her race as one of only fifty-four nonwhite students university-wide. This pushed her even further in her desire to write stories that represent herself and other people of color.

Ayala's identity as a queer woman of color permeates all of her non-franchise stories. In *Our Work Fills The Pews*, to be published by Black Mask Studios in 2018, Ayala and cowriter Matt Rosenberg created the main character, Marcus Melville, a gay Black man. Ayala states that

> ON SCHEHERAZADE'S STORYTELLING:
> "SO POWERFUL THAT SHE COULD TAME THE
> BLOODLUST OF A MAN WHO SINGLEHANDEDLY
> MURDERED EVERY WOMAN IN HIS KINGDOM
> AND STILL WASN'T SATISFIED."

"[Marcus's] queerness is not just a part of his character, but an integral aspect of what drives the plot and informs how he navigates his strange and dangerous world." Marcus Melville's character arc illustrates what Ayala had seen and experienced as a queer person of color: frustration, oppression, and learned helplessness.

Ayala is also a 2016 alumna of the DC Comics Writers Workshop. This led to her work on *Suicide Squad Most Wanted: El Diablo and Amanda Waller*, *The DC Talent Showcase*, and *The 2016 DC Holiday Special*.

# BAKER, CLARENCE MATTHEW (MATT)

**(Dec. 10, 1921–Aug. 11, 1959)**
- **Born in Forsyth County, NC**
- **The Cooper Union for the Advancement of Science and Art**
- **Cartoonist and illustrator**
- **Illustrated *Phantom Lady*, *Canteen Kate*, *Tiger Girl*, and many others**

Matt Baker was a Golden Age (1940s–50s) comics artist who is best known for his drawings of beautiful women, including the Golden Age character Phantom Lady, and as the artist for the early graphic novel *It Rhymes with Lust*. He is often credited as the first known African American artist to achieve heightened success in the Golden Age comic book industry.

Baker, born Clarence Matthew Baker, suffered from rheumatic fever as a young child, which weakened his heart. His older sister, Ethel Viola, died in 1922, and his father died in 1925. In early childhood, Baker moved with his family to Pittsburgh, Pennsylvania, where his mother remarried. The family lived in the Homewood-Brushton neighborhood, which at the time was ethnically diverse, with Irish, German, Italian, and Black residents.

After graduating from high school around 1940, Baker relocated to Washington, D.C., where the onset of World War II had created many government jobs that were open to African Americans. Due to his heart condition, he was ineligible for the military draft. He then settled in New York City, where he studied art at The Cooper Union for the Advancement of Science and Art. At the time, the school offered full scholarships to all its students, and classes were taught at night so they could work during the day.

Baker secured his first comics-related position at Jerry Iger's S. M. Iger Studio, which was founded as a partnership between Iger and comics legend Will Eisner in 1936. The studio was one of the first comics "packagers," supplying outsourced comics to publishers that had recently begun engaging in the field. According to Iger's later recollection, Baker showed up at the studio looking for work and was hired on the strength of a single sketch of a beautiful girl. He quickly became known for his drawings of attractive women, known as "Good Girl" figures.

Baker's earliest confirmed work was the pencilling and inking of female characters in "Sheena, Queen of the Jungle," part of Fiction House's *Jumbo Comics* #69 (Nov. 1944). He soon became the lead artist on another *Jumbo Comics* story, "Sky Girl," which featured red-headed pilot Ginger Maguire (supposedly modeled on actress Ann Sheridan), who worked for the military during World War II and then unwillingly left the pilot's seat after the war ended. As in many other Matt Baker comics, Ginger's hijinks and acrobatics offered many opportunities to show off her shapely legs.

During the 1940s and '50s, Baker's work appeared in periodicals for Atlas/Marvel, Dell Comics, Fiction House, Fox Comics, Harvey Comics, Quality Comics, St. John Publications, and other publishing houses. Later, he completed collaborative projects with inker Jon D'Agostino (best known for his Archie Comics work), using the name "Matt Bakerino," at Charlton Comics. He often worked as a penciller, with other artists handling the inks.

His art appeared in "Tiger Girl" (1945–48) and "Camilla" (1945) for *Jungle Comics*, "Glory Forbes" for *Rangers Comics* (1947), and "Mitzi of the Movies" for *Movie Comics* #2–4 (1947). He also worked on some stories with male leads, including "The Skull Squad" for *Wings Comics*, "Kayo Kirby: Boxer" for *Fight Comics* (1946–48), and "Ace of the Newsreels" for *Crown Comics* (1945–47). He drew all the "South Sea Girl" stories for *Seven Seas Comics*, which was published by Iger's own company, Universal Phoenix, and assisted on another story for the same publication, "Tugboat Tessie." In 1946, he was the artist for the *Classics Illustrated* adaptation of R. D. Blackmore's *Lorna Doone*.

At Fox Comics, Baker transformed the Phantom Lady character into its most recognizable representation. Baker's lyrical rendering, with writing often attributed to Ruth Roche, first appeared in Fox's *Phantom Lady* #13 (August 1947). His cover for *Phantom Lady* #17 was later singled out by anti-comics crusader Dr. Fredric Wertham in his 1954 book *Seduction of the Innocent* as an example of the excessive sexualization of women in comics.

In 1947, Iger began syndicating newspaper strips based on Baker's comics, and he returned to the Iger Studios as a freelancer to draw *Flamingo*, an action story staring a gypsy dancer, from February to July 1952. In 1948, Baker began working for St. John Publications, starting with *Northwest Mounties* #1 (1948). In the late 1940s and early 1950s, he contributed cover and story art to a number of St. John romance and crime comics, including *Crime Reporter, Teen-Age Romances, Teen-Age Temptations, Wartime Romances, True Love Pictorial*, and *Authentic Police Cases*. He also drew all twenty-two issues of the screwball comedy *Canteen Kate* (1951–53).

In 1950, Baker illustrated the early "picture novel" *It Rhymes with Lust*, which was cowritten by Arnold Drake and Leslie Waller under the combined pen name "Drake Waller." *It Rhymes with Lust* has gained increasing attention in recent scholarship due to its transformative impact as an early precursor to the graphic novel and, hence, its expansion of the comics genre.

Baker stopped working regularly for St. John in 1954, although he continued drawing covers for them until 1958. In the aftermath of Wertham's book and the anti-comics movement that followed, many publishers went out of business and comics work grew scarcer. His work in the mid- to late-1950s included *Lassie* #20–22 (1955) and *King Richard and the Crusaders* (1954), published by Western Printing; a number of western stories (some of them written by Stan Lee) for Atlas Comics, which would later become Marvel; romance comics and some stories for *Robin Hood Tales* published by Quality Publications; more romance tales for *Harvey Comics*, and sci-fi stories for *Charlton Comics*. His last confirmed work is the first page of a tale titled "I Gave Up the Man I Love!" in Atlas/Marvel's *My Own Romance* #73 (Jan. 1960).

Baker died unexpectedly at the age of thirty-seven from a heart attack. He was inducted into the Will Eisner Award Hall of Fame in 2009.

# BARBEE, KIA TAMIKE

Kia Barbee is a woman of many creative passions. Her producing credits include *I'm Not Me* (2011), a psychological drama featured at the Project Forum during Independent Film Week in New York City; the award-winning short film *Taharuki* (2011), a fictional account based on true events of a man and woman from opposing tribes in Kenya; *Judo Girl* (2010), a redemptive story of a teenage girl coming back from a Judo injury; and the supernatural/sci-fi digital series, *Evolve* (2013). Two of her scripts, *Pathways Often Crossed, But Seldom Walked* and *Dare Me*, were featured at the NBC showcase, National Black Theater Festival and Here Theater. She has also served as a script analyst for numerous international film festivals.

**(August 5, 1973– )**
- **Born in Elmhurst, Queens, NY**
- **State University of New York, BFA in cinema/theater, 1996**
- **Long Island University, MS in education, 2005**
- **Writer, filmmaker, and web series producer/director**
- **Creator of the digital sci-fi series *Evolve***

Image courtesy of Kia Barbee

*Evolve* marked Barbee's directorial debut and serves as her best known contribution to the comics universe. Produced under her company Elmhurst Entertainment, *Evolve* is a riff on the superhero version of Joseph Campbell's monomyth, a story about the central character's journey to becoming a hero. Like *Spider-Man*'s Peter Parker, the Black female lead is not eager to embrace the role of hero, but unlike him, she adapts her situation to her will rather than being transformed by it.

The first five webisodes chronicle the first of the three stages of the monomyth: her separation from the normal world, in other words, the onset of and experimentation with her superpowers. Vanessa Martinez, a writer for IndieWire, describes *Evolve* as a story about "acceptance of self and responsibility seen through the eyes of a reluctant heroine and sheltered teenager Donia Reyes who inherits super abilities. Throughout the series Donia struggles to maintain a balance between what she wants and what she's destined to become." Cast in the tradition of *Star Wars*, the web series starred unknowns, which proved to be both a blessing and a curse. While some of the acting lacks polish, *Evolve* is a refreshing depiction of a Black female lead character in the live-action superhero genre. Barbee intended the web series to be the first step for this project, followed by a graphic novel and feature film or television series. After producing the latter, it received recognition in Austin Film Festival's AMC One-Hour TV Pilot competition (2015).

When asked why her characters reflect so much diversity, Barbee replied that it was merely a representation of the environment in which she was raised. Through her production company, she intends to create a space for "relatable characters with diverse voices and entertaining stories that live outside the box."

A self-described believer in hard work, good energy, and perpetual drive, and a supporter of all things creative, Kia Barbee has appeared at events featuring the work of Black storytellers such as 2nd Annual Black Comic Book Festival, East Coast Black Age of Comics Convention, and the Women in Comics panel at the Bronx Heroes Comics Convention. Women in Comics celebrates the contributions women have made in the comic industry as artists, writers, filmmakers, animators, characters, and self-publishers.

Kia Barbee is based permanently in Los Angeles, California.

# BATTLE, ERIC

(1967– )
- **Born in Philadelphia, PA**
- **University of the Arts, BFA in illustration**
- **Illustrated *Green Lantern*, *Batman*, *Vampire Huntress Legends*, and *Tales of the Unexpected***

Eric Battle's illustrations have been featured in several prominent comic series, including *Green Lantern* and *Batman*.

As a young boy, Eric Battle watched his single mother work hard to raise her children. "She tried to give us as well-rounded an upbringing as possible, with a very balanced view of the world,"

Image courtesy of Eric Battle

he says. Battle was a typical middle child: happy, quiet, and, at times, moody, painfully shy, and stubborn. These attributes helped him learn and hone his powers of observation, spending many hours watching people interact with one another, reading body language and noting their mannerisms.

Battle learned to appreciate reading from his mother's involvement in a local book club. He became particularly entranced with horror novels, saying, "If I didn't feel a knot in the pit of my stomach while reading a story, that book was not doing its job!" He also appreciated the work of illustrators from an early age. He remembers feeling mesmerized by the painting of a dog's rabid snout on the cover of Stephen King's novel *Cujo*.

After seeing *Close Encounters of the Third Kind* at age ten, he recalled, "I was so awestruck that I sat out on the porch of our fourteenth floor apartment all night, with my sketchbook and charcoal pencils, drawing the aliens and whistling the musical alien code from the movie, waiting for them to recognize where I was and to come and get me. For some odd reason, they never showed. They must have taken a wrong turn at Albuquerque."

The onset of Battle's professional career as an illustrator came in 1992 with a short stint doing editorial illustrations for *The Philadelphia Inquirer*. Since then, he has worked as freelance illustrator on projects such as *Batman* and *Green Lantern*. His collaboration with the *Vampire Huntress Legends* author, the late L. A. Banks, was a significant project;

## CREATIVE TIPS

For many, the most difficult parts of being an illustrator include navigating the freelance market and brainstorming new ideas. Eric Battle keeps his inflow of work steady by setting up the next project while at work on the current one. His goal is to maintain a constant supply of jobs and to offset his deadlines so they don't all hit at once.

When a deadline is looming, music "becomes as essential a tool to the artwork as the pencil. The right music, for me, helps to motivate and energize the construction of ideas and the movement of the pencil across the page." Exercise and physical activity are also essential staples for Eric to create his best work. "I have to trust that the idea will present itself, and trust myself to recognize it when it does. When all of that fails, it's time to go dancing!"

he was honored that she trusted him to create visuals for her iconic characters.

Battle has worked on a wide range of projects, from children's books to adventure comics. The first child-oriented illustration work he completed was for an exhibit at Philadelphia's Please Touch Museum, an interactive museum for children three years old and younger.

> "IF I DIDN'T FEEL A KNOT IN THE PIT OF MY STOMACH WHILE READING A STORY, THAT BOOK WAS NOT DOING ITS JOB!"

He created and illustrated poems and short stories as well as environmental murals for an interactive exhibit called *Nature's Nursery*. A few years later, he worked on *Br'er Rabbit* for Just Us Books.

Recently, Eric Battle participated as a panelist at the acclaimed Black Age of Comics Convention and has done several interviews with WHAT 1340 AM. He has also been interviewed by *Hard Knock Radio*, *The Philadelphia Inquirer*, and *Black America Web*. He also recently collaborated with writer Ivan Brandon on a comic book titled *Seeking the Black Panther*, which was a free companion to the photography exhibit *Pictures and Progress: The Black Panther 1966–2016* at the University of California–Santa Cruz McHenry Library.

Battle is presently curating and art directing a coffee-table book for the Philadelphia Jazz Project, which has assembled a diverse group of visual artists to create original illustrated profiles of Philadelphia-based musicians and singers.

# BELL, DARRIN

Darrin Bell is the first Black cartoonist to have two nationally syndicated comic strips, *Rudy Park* and *Candorville*.

While attending junior high and high school, Bell enrolled in gifted programs, where he developed an interest in civics and history. After seeing Pat Buchanan on television providing political commentary on the Clinton-Bush campaign, Bell decided that he too wanted

(Jan. 27, 1975– )
- **Born in Los Angeles, CA**
- **University of California–Berkley, BS in political science, 1999**
- **Comic strip creator, editorial cartoonist, and storyboard artist**
- **Creator of *Candorville***

to provide commentary on a national platform. With the encouragement of his high school guidance counselor and his older brother, he joined the school paper and went on to pursue civics and history in college.

Darrin Bell's editorial cartooning career began during his freshman year of college with the school paper, the *Daily Californian*. As a part of a homework assignment, Bell created a comic strip called *Lemont Brown*. *Lemont Brown* became a staple piece for *The Daily Californian*, running the strip from 1993 to 2003. It would provide the foundation for his later nationally syndicated work, *Candorville*.

Bell's work as an undergraduate garnered him many accolades, winning several Californian Intercollegiate Press Association Awards and the Society of Professional Journalists Mark of Excellence Award. He was also a runner-up for the Locher and Charles M. Schulz Awards.

During his studies, Bell sought to expand his readership by faxing his cartoon strips to various California papers, such as the *Oakland Tribune* and *San Francisco Chronicle*. However, it was *The LA Times* that provided him with his first sale and would go on to appoint him as a biweekly contributor to the paper's cartoon section.

After graduation, Bell continued to write cartoons for the *Daily Californian* while casting the net to various other newspapers for provide sustainable work. In 2001, during another round of cold faxing, Matt Richtel came across his artwork at the *Oakland Tribune*. At the time, Richtel had his own comic in the works, but his financiers hated his artwork. Recognizing Bell's skill, Richtel approached him to see if he could adapt his drawings to a four-panel comic strip. These collaborative efforts would go on to birth *Rudy Park*.

Also in 2001, Darrin Bell was thrust into the national spotlight. After the events of the September 11, 2001 attacks on the World Trade Center, many illustrators, writers, and cartoonists responded to the tragic event through their art. However, Bell's caricatured depiction of Muslims was not well received by the Muslim-American community. These editorials, along with his previous work on *Lemont Brown*, would give rise to the *Candorville* comic strip.

*Candorville* was launched in 2003 by the Washington Post Group. The comic depicts urban Black and Latino characters making social and political commentary on modern America. *Candorville* provides frank and honest conversations among persons of color, providing a perspective that may not be shared by the majority culture in the United States. As of 2016, six *Candorville* collections had been published.

Darrin Bell lives in Los Angeles with his wife, Laura Bustamante, who also translates the *Candorville* comics into Spanish. The internationally syndicated *Candorville* and *Rudy Park* comic strips are distributed by the Washington Post Group and can be found in most American newspapers.

# BENTLEY, STEPHEN

Stephen Bentley is the creator of *Herb & Jamaal*, a syndicated comic strip about family life.

Bentley's first job was for the US Navy, where he illustrated the comic panel *Navy Life* for the newspaper of the hospital base where he was stationed. He later enrolled in a professional illustrator course at Pasadena City College.

**(Aug. 19, 1954– )**
- **Born in Southern California**
- **Pasadena City College and Rio Hondo College, 1972**
- **Cartoonist and comic creator**
- **Creator of *Herb & Jamaal***

Working as a freelance illustrator, Stephen has created comic strips such as "Hey Coach" for *Swimming World* magazine and "Squirt," about a female firefighter, for *Weekly Features Syndicate*. As a commercial cartoonist, he has worked for many advertising agencies, including *Playboy*, Universal Studios, Wham-O Toys, the Playboy Channel, *Skateboard World* magazine, and the Los Angeles Dodgers. He has also served as president for the Comic Art Professional Society.

The comic strip *Herb & Jamaal* started in 1989 for Creators Syndicate. It now appears in more than one hundred newspapers, including *The Seattle Times*, the *Chicago Sun-Times*, and the *Los Angeles Times*.

"SOME OF THE CHARACTERS IN HERB & JAMAAL PARTIALLY COME FROM MYSELF AND PEOPLE THAT I KNOW, BUT THE FULL STORY IS JUST A FANTASY."

The strip's eponymous characters, Herbert and Jamaal, are two old high school friends, now adults and partners in an ice-cream parlor business. Herb, a stout fellow, lives with his wife, Sarah Louie, and his daughter, Uhuru (similar to the name of a character on the television show

*Star Trek*, although spelled slightly differently), his son, Ezekiel, and his mother-in-law, Eula. Herb's friend Jamaal, a former basketball player, is single, tall, and bald, with an independent-minded girlfriend, Yolanda, who often causes him grief.

*Herb & Jamaal* addresses the experiences of urban families of color with entertaining characters and storylines. He notes, "Some of the characters in *Herb & Jamaal* partially come from myself and people that I know, but the full story is just a fantasy." The strip also features frequent quotations from Langston Hughes's poetry.

There are many African American illustrators presently working in the comics industry, but only six are currently working with nationally distributed major syndicates. Bentley sees this as evidence that the comic industry is unwelcoming to Black writers and artists.

Early on, he says, his work was rejected by many syndicates without providing any justification. Bentley argues that this happens because editors assume white readers will ignore comics created by nonwhite illustrators. Such a biased attitude is not only unjust but also limits the scope of success, growth, and development for marginalized illustrators. He says of his characters, "Had they been white, I would be much more successful than I am now."

As of 2017, he lived in Northern California and is the single father of a teenage daughter, Natalie. In addition to cartooning, he is also actively engaged with the Episcopal Church.

# BETANCOURT, DAVID

(May 22, 1978– )
- **Born in Washington, DC**
- **Radford University, degree in media studies**
- **Comics commentator at the *Washington Post***

David Betancourt is a comics commentator for the *Washington Post's* Comic Riffs section, where he reports on recent developments in comics publication and culture.

Betancourt first fell in love with superhero comics by way of 1989's *Batman*. He then began reading *Batman*, *Superman*, and *The All New X-Men* by Chris Claremont and Jim Lee and watching the *X-Men* animated series. The 1992 story arc "The Death of Superman" prompted him to start seriously collecting comics as well.

After eight years as a contributing writer with the *Washington Post*, David Betancourt began writing for the Comic Riffs section in 2008. He transitioned to writing about comic book culture full-time in 2012.

David is passionate about diversity not only in comic characters, but in the comics business overall. He looks forward to the creation of new characters of color and to diverse new talent entering the industry.

As of 2016, David planned to continue reporting on comics and comic culture at the *Washington Post*. As a prestigious journalist of color working for an iconic news source, David is an important figure in bringing comics and heroes of color to the mainstream.

> "SOCIAL MEDIA HAS REALLY GIVEN A VOICE TO THE FACT THAT THERE IS A VERY DIVERSE GROUP OF READERS OUT THERE WHO APPRECIATE HEROES THEY CAN RELATE TO. WHAT I THINK IS MOST IMPORTANT IS THAT THE BIGGEST MAINSTREAM SUPERHEROES OF COLOR, WHEN IT COMES TIME FOR THEM TO BE ADAPTED TO LIVE-ACTION ENTERTAINMENT, WHETHER IT BE LUKE CAGE OR BLACK PANTHER, THEY ARE PUT IN THE HANDS OF BLACK PRODUCERS, DIRECTORS AND WRITERS AND GIVEN AN AUTHENTIC VOICE PLEASING TO THOSE WHO HAVE WAITED A LONG TIME TO SEE THESE CHARACTERS IN LIVE-ACTION."
>
> — DAVID BETANCOURT

# BILLINGSLEY, RAY

Ray Billingsley, the author of popular syndicated comic strip *Curtis*, was first discovered while working on a school art display for a recycling drive. He was initially hired to work as a freelance artist and then on staff at *Kids* magazine, which featured work for children, by children and was published during the 1970s. His starting pay was five dollars per artwork.

> **(1957– )**
> - **Born in Wake Forest, NC, and raised in Harlem**
> - **School of Visual Arts**
> - **Cartoonist and creator of *Curtis***

Ray attended the celebrated LaGuardia High School of Music & Art and Performing Arts in Manhattan while continuing his freelance illustration work and earning a promotion to associate editor at *Kids*.

Ray established himself as a professional child cartoonist and earned freelance work for adult publications and national advertisers while he was still a teen. In one famous anecdote, Ray disguised himself as a messenger boy in order to sneak past a reception desk to meet an art director and successfully landed freelance work for his efforts. During this time, he met many famous professional cartoonists, including Mort Walker of *Beetle Bailey* fame, who gave him the moniker "The Kid," a nickname that stuck with him well through adulthood.

During his high school years, he experimented with many different concepts for a daily comic strip, but all of his efforts were rejected.

Ray resigned from his staff position at *Kids* at the age of eighteen in order to attend college at the School of Visual Arts (SVA) in Manhattan on full scholarship. It was during his time at SVA that he studied under the famed comic writer and artist Will Eisner, creator of *The Spirit*, among many other works, who pushed Ray to improve his art, and whom Ray considered to be a great influence on his work.

Upon graduation, Ray was hired to work as an assistant animator for Disney, where he remained only a short while until United Features Syndicate offered him a syndication contract for his first daily comic strip, *Lookin' Fine*. *Lookin' Fine* related the experiences of an African American family, with a focus on a group of friends in their twenties – contemporaries to Ray himself.

Ray expressed displeasure at the syndicate's handling of his work, largely in the form of frustration with an all-white staff's attempts to market a strip by a Black artist, created for and about Black people. He claimed that his editors wanted him to include more white characters in order to boost sales, even suggesting that the Black family featured in the strip adopt a white child to make the strip more appealing to white

readers. The strip only lasted two years, from 1980 until 1982, at which point Ray returned to freelance artwork.

Ray's ability to adapt his artistic style made him an extremely successful freelance commercial artist, and for six years he worked in a variety of different mediums. During this time, he worked in advertising, animation, clothing design, greeting card illustration, and a number of other fields. He also published cartoons in numerous monthly humor magazines, as well as *Ebony* magazine's "Strictly-for-Laughs" section, where Ray was a featured regular from 1978 until 2009.

In 1988, Ray returned to syndication with the birth of *Curtis*, a comic strip distributed by King Features Syndicate.

Image courtesy of Ray Billingsley

*Curtis* follows the antics of an eleven-year-old boy, Curtis Wilkins, who lives with his parents and younger brother, Barry, in Harlem, New York.

*Curtis* draws heavily from Ray's own childhood in Harlem, while updating the characters to feel contemporary to the time in which it is written. Ray also credited Morrie Turner's *Wee Pals* as a significant influence in his work on *Curtis*. The comic strip deals with many subjects typical to urban childhood and African American life, from home and family stories to school, friendship, and bullying, and in churches, local businesses, and tight-knit urban communities. Each year, the strip detours briefly from exploring the exploits of the Wilkins family as Ray tells a story focusing on Kwanzaa, varying his artistic style significantly for the duration of his Kwanzaa storyline.

Image courtesy of Ray Billingsley

Over the years, Curtis and Barry's interests evolved to stay up-to-date with children of the era. Ray watched popular family television shows and paid attention to technological milestones to keep *Curtis* current, retiring some popular jokes as technology shifted. For example, in the 1980s and 1990s, many jokes revolved around Barry listening in on Curtis's phone calls, but with the rise of mobile technology, those jokes were phased out of the strip. Other trends and technological advancements have been a key influence on Curtis over the years.

Ray's work on *Curtis* has received the NAACP Arts & Entertainment Achievement Award, as well as awards from the Society for Public Health Education and the American Lung Association. The latter two were awarded for his use of the strip to address issues surrounding smoking and lung cancer in a story line where Curtis attempts to convince his father to quit smoking.

# BRANDON-CROFT, BARBARA

(Nov. 27, 1958– )
- **Born in Brooklyn, NY**
- **Syracuse University, BFA in Illustration**
- **Creator of *Where I'm Coming From***

Barbara Brandon-Croft's cartoon *Where I'm Coming From*, along with her father Brumsic Brandon's comic strip *Luther*, make them the only daughter-father cartooning duo of any color to be nationally syndicated. Brandon-Croft is also the first nationally syndicated African American woman cartoonist in the mainstream press, a distinction that separates her from pioneering cartoonist Jackie Ormes, who enjoyed syndication in the Black national newspapers throughout the 1930s and '40s.

Brandon-Croft's first memories of the comics as an art form are of her father drawing. Her father is best known for his comic strip *Luther*, which ran in newspapers nationwide from the late sixties to the mid-eighties. Watching her father create original works throughout her childhood colored her destiny. She even sometimes assisted him on *Luther*, inking in silhouettes and applying the Zip-a-Tone. While she confesses she was never a "comic book kid," she would still take the opportunity to read her siblings' comic books, and enjoyed thumbing through the pages of *Archie* and *Richie Rich*. Her true obsession, however, was with *MAD* magazine. Later in life, she was honored when the editors of *Mad* featured *Where I'm Coming From* on three full pages.

After graduating from Syracuse University, Brandon-Croft moved back home and began a career as a fashion reporter and illustrator in 1981 for *Retail News Bureau* in Manhattan. She soon approached a new Black women's magazine, *Elan*, which was positioned to rival *Essence*, the premier publication for Black women, for a job. During her interview, *Elan*'s editor in chief, Marie Brown, wondered if Brandon-Croft would be interested in developing a cartoon feature for the magazine. She jumped at the opportunity. Unfortunately, *Elan* folded after only two issues, before Brandon-Croft's work was published. Undeterred, she was resolved to find a home for her new comic strip.

Next, she sent her strip to *Essence*. While her feature didn't meet their editorial needs, she was asked to join their fashion/beauty team as a writer in 1983. For more than five years, she wrote the fashion and beauty copy, often traveling the world for the magazine, visiting West Africa, Europe, and the Caribbean.

Image courtesy of Barbara Brandon-Croft

In 1988, her father, Brumsic Brandon Jr., won a CEBA Award for his work as a pioneering Black cartoonist. In a congratulatory letter, Marty Claus, the managing editor of the *Detroit Free Press*, asked Brandon if he knew of any other Black cartoonists the paper could feature in their comics pages. This prompted Brandon to challenge his daughter again: "Are you going to talk about being a cartoonist or are you going to be one?" Encouraged, she sent the *Detroit Free Press* the very strips she had created for *Elan* and sent to *Essence* magazine years before. The paper offered her a deal to produce a weekly strip, and *Where I'm Coming From* made its debut in 1989. Shortly thereafter, Brandon-Croft quit her magazine job to become a full-time cartoonist.

*Where I'm Coming From* was groundbreaking, not only because Brandon-Croft was the first African American female cartoonist to emerge in the mainstream press, but also because of the strip's content. The comic strip filled a void for people who longed to have their lives represented on the funny pages. It followed nine Black women and their daily musings on living life in America. The characters, based on Brandon-Croft and her friends, reflected on myriad topics, from racism and sexism to nail color and facial hair. *Where I'm Coming From* resonated with a wide variety of readers, especially Black women.

As a cartoonist, Brandon-Croft made the deliberate creative decision to exclude her characters' bodies. She started with floating heads and then added hands and arms to amplify their emotions through expression. Brandon-Croft was tired of women in general and Black women in particular being objectified by their bodies. With minimalistic artwork and the absence of backdrop art, the focus remained on their heads – and their minds.

Image courtesy of Barbara Brandon-Croft

Having learned from her father's experience that syndication is often the difference between a comic's failure and success, Barbara Brandon-Croft worked hard to acquire a syndication deal. Using the syndicates' sales protocol of sending press kits to newspapers, Brandon-Croft made press kits of *Where I'm Coming From* and sent them to prospective syndicates. After many rejections, she ultimately received a positive response from Universal Press Syndicated. *Where I'm Coming From* was signed to a development deal in 1991, and soon after was picked up for national syndication.

At its height, *Where I'm Coming From* was in more than sixty newspapers nationwide and internationally, appearing in *The Gleaner* in Jamaica, South Africa's *Drum*, and newspapers throughout Canada. Both Brandon-Croft's and her father's work are represented at the Library of Congress as well as featured in several editions of *Best Editorial Cartoons of the Year* by Pelican Publishing.

The steady decline of the print industry and dwindling circulations contributed to the demise of *Where I'm Coming From*, whose syndication ended in 2005. Currently Brandon-Croft is busy preserving her father's legacy by exhibiting both of their works across the country. She has been the research director for *Parents* magazine for twelve years and has been married to musician Monte Croft since 1997. The couple have one son, Chase, and reside in Queens, New York.

# BRANDON, BRUMSIC, JR.

Brumsic Brandon Jr. attended the segregated public schools in Washington, D.C., and graduated as valedictorian from Armstrong High School in 1945. His intellectual acuity earned him the attention of Adam Clayton Powell Jr., then the congressman representing Harlem, New York, who recommended Brandon for appointment to the United States Naval Academy. The

> (Apr. 10, 1927–Nov. 28, 2014)
> - **Born in Washington, DC**
> - **Served with the US Army occupation in Germany**
> - **Cartoonist, columnist, animator, painter, sculptor, civil rights activist, and humanitarian**
> - **Creator of *Luther***

teenager, acutely aware of the country's racial inequities, declined. Instead, he attended New York University to study art. While there, he began selling gag cartoons to national magazines such as *Mademoiselle* and *The Saturday Review of Literature*. Brandon returned to Washington, D.C., in 1947 and married Rita Broughton on September 30, 1950. Later that same year he was drafted. He served with the segregated US Army occupation in Germany, and the indignities he experienced in the service, compounded by the humiliations of the Jim Crow laws he faced back home, informed his work for decades to come.

Returning to civilian life in Washington, D.C., Brandon and his wife welcomed their first child, Linda, in 1953, followed by their only son, Brumsic III, in 1957. While cartooning remained Brandon's primary interest, he found it necessary to work as an IBM machine operator, a statistical draftsman, and a technical illustrator to provide for his young family. In 1957 he landed a job in New York City with Bray Studios, a motion-picture animation studio, where he worked until 1970. Their second daughter, Barbara, was born in Brooklyn in 1958. She would follow in her father's footsteps and become a pioneering cartoonist in her own right.

While working full-time as an animator, Brandon began to regularly contribute biting social commentary in the form of cartoons to the

Image courtesy of Barbara Brandon-Croft

journal *Freedomways: A Quarterly Review of the Freedom Movement*, the Black academic, cultural, and political journal founded in 1961 by Louis Burnham, Edward Strong, and W. E. B. Du Bois. The exposure that came from the publication of his cartoon features in *Freedomways* garnered Brandon national notice among the Black intellectual elite, as well as the Black community at large. In 1963, he self-published his first book of cartoons, *Some of My Best Friends*, a scathing critique of race relations in America that received wide acclaim. In 1967, Brandon developed a board game in a similar vein, Cullud: The Game That Tells It Like It Is. The title refers to the more familiar pronunciation of the word "colored" often used in the 1950s and 1960s to identify Black people. It was highlighted in the December 1967 issue of *Jet* magazine with the mention: "Satirical cartoonist Brumsic Brandon, Jr., invented a new parlor game for the holidays called CULLUD; any way you play it, you lose."

In 1968, a long-sought opportunity arose for Brandon to create a comic strip for the mainstream press (a euphemism for the white press). At that time, the very idea of Black cartoon characters being drawn by Black hands with stories written from the Black perspective was non-existent in white newspapers. Brandon created the comic strip *Luther*, which was picked up by Newsday Specials and later distributed nationally by Los Angeles Times Syndicate until 1986.

His acceptance in the mainstream by no means diminished Brandon's commitment to keep the focus of his work on the long-fought struggle for civil rights. On the contrary, in *Luther* Brandon featured a group of predominantly Black kids living in America's inner city, which provided the perfect environment to expose innumerable racial injustices. Brandon deftly brought humanity to his characters and to their condition. Pioneering Black cartoonist Oliver Harrington put it this way in a 1976 issue of *Freedomways*: "The cartoonist is actually violating what has always been an American taboo, and that is to create non-white characters or even poor white characters who are human, sympathetic and even lovable. Brandon employs his irresistible humor to level the walls of racism."

Brandon was one of three Black cartoonists, along with Morrie Turner (*Wee Pals*) and Ted Shearer (*Quincy*), to gain national syndication in mainstream press in the late 1960s, at a time when the nation was reeling from images of racial unrest in the media. The comic strips they created, with their casts of children, presented a nonaggressive, non-threatening way for white newspaper editors to demonstrate that they were not entirely disconnected from communities of color. Indeed, the inclusion of Black characters on the funny pages ostensibly provided a way for the mainstream press to – for the first time – actually reflect the neighborhoods they served.

Brandon's *Luther* ran in more than sixty newspapers nationwide and was collected in six books: *Luther: From Inner City* (1969), *Luther Tells It as It Is!* (1970), *Right On, Luther!* (1971), *Luther Raps* (1971), *Outta Sight Luther!* (1972), and *Luther's Got Class* (1976). The latter included a foreword written by distinguished congresswoman Shirley Chisholm. As a result of Brandon's observations, as articulated in *Luther*, he was invited to be a forum member of the White House Conference on Children in 1970, a series that began in 1910 to bring attention to the needs of the nation's youngest population.

In 1969, Brandon became a part of the groundbreaking all-Black-cast children's show, *Time for Joya* (later renamed *Joya's Fun School*), which aired weekly on WPIX-TV, a New York City–area television station. Prominent jazz vocalist and lyricist Joya Sherrill hosted, legendary maestro Luther Henderson provided music, and Brumsic Brandon supplied artwork for stories and performed as Mr. BB and puppeteer to Seymour the Bookworm until the show ended in 1982. While working on *Joya*, he also wrote and illustrated several "Luther" segments for *Vegetable Soup*, another children's television program produced by the New York State Department of Education, and created "Black Cat's Bebop Fables." These cartoon segments for *Vegetable Soup* were aptly narrated by Dizzy Gillespie. In 1971, Brandon also illustrated *The Six- Button Dragon*, a children's book written by actor, writer, and television producer Matt Robinson, who originated the role of Gordon on *Sesame Street.*

Brandon held court in two worlds for many years, simultaneously producing *Luther* for the mainstream press and penning additional original cartoons for *Freedomways* and Black Media (also known as Black Resources), a consortium of Black newspapers, from 1974 until 1999. His objective remained the same on both fronts – to shed light on the specter of racism so the country could attempt to eradicate it and begin to find ways to heal.

By the mid-1980s, Brandon and his wife (now a retired schoolteacher) craved a different lifestyle than what the Long Island hamlet of New Cassel, where they had raised their children, had to offer. They began traveling the world and started to spend increasing amounts of time in Florida, eventually settling in Cocoa Beach in 1995. While in Florida, Brandon became a regular contributor to *Florida Today*, a Gannett Company newspaper, where he alternately wrote an op-ed column and created political cartoons weekly for ten years. Many of the cartoons published in *Florida Today* were subsequently included in eight editions of Pelican Publishing Company's *Best Editorial Cartoons of the Year* collections.

Brandon began showing symptoms of Parkinson's disease in 2002. He continued to paint, sculpt, draw, write, and exhibit in Florida for as long as he was able. Twelve years after his diagnosis, Brandon succumbed to the disease.

Of all his recognitions, the one Brandon counted among his proudest was being asked to author a tribute to American cartoonist and advocate for racial equality Oliver Harrington for the book *Cartoon America: Comic Art in the Library of Congress*. However, he considered the inclusion of his own work in the Library of Congress Permanent Comics Collection to be his highest honor of all.

# BROADNAX, JAMIE

Jamie Broadnax is the founder and managing editor of Black Girl Nerds, a website providing recent news in comic culture for women of color and other comics fans.

In 2007, Broadnax was heavily involved in the New York independent film scene, blogging and participating in numerous film festivals, including the Hamptons International Film Festival, Tribeca Film Festival, and the Big Apple Film Festival. A few years later, she was searching the internet for information on "Black girl nerds" and realized there was none. To address this critical information gap, Broadnax launched the Black Girl Nerds blog in February of 2012.

**(Apr. 24, 1980– )**
- **Born in Virginia**
- **Norfolk State University, BS in mass communications and journalism, 2002**
- **Regent University, MA in Film Directing, 2005**
- **Managing editor and podcaster at Black Girl Nerds**

Black Girl Nerds (BGN) describes itself as a site for "Black women and women of color to embrace their nerdiness and eccentricities." It offers features such as reporting on the fantasy comic book *Niobe: She Is Life* by actor Amandla Stenberg and artist Ashley A. Woods; providing a platform for Los Angeles–based writers and sisters Shawnée and Shawnelle Gibbs and their brand of comics and animation featuring Black female leads, offering readers comic book reviews and suggested Black comics to read and explore, showcasing the reboot of Marvel Comics' *Black Panther* from writer Ta-Nehisi Coates and illustrator Brian Stelfreeze, and marketing for comic book conventions. The site also includes regular written, audio, and video contributions spotlighting geek and nerd culture.

> "IT'S A SITE FOR BLACK WOMEN AND WOMEN OF COLOR TO EMBRACE THEIR NERDINESS AND ECCENTRICITIES."

From the time of the blog's inception, Broadnax and BGN played a role in comic book culture, discussing topics such as the opening of the first Black female–owned comic bookstore on the East Coast, Amalgam Comics & Coffeehouse in Philadelphia, Pennsylvania. The site also provides commentary on race-bending and gender-bending comic book characters, creating diverse geek and nerd communities, and bringing awareness to Black comic book fandom and exposure to emerging artists, creators, and writers of color.

Over the years, Broadnax has played an active role in bringing national attention to the Black Girl Nerds site and Black nerd comic book culture. She made a guest appearance on the *Melissa Harris-Perry* show in October 2015 and was cited as one of TV mogul Shonda Rhimes's favorite people to follow on Twitter. Broadnax and BGN were also featured in several magazines, including *Geeked* (Spring 2015), *Bitch* (Winter 2015), and *Marie Claire* (September 2014), and were the subject of a podcast feature on the online magazine *Salon* (August 2015). Black Girl Nerds was named one of eleven Black podcasts to follow on the *Huffington Post* (October 2015), and Broadnax was named as a leading figure on TheGrio.com's Top 100 list, for serving as an online community builder and innovator.

Image by Asia Kendrick-Horton, courtesy of Jamie Broadnax

In the Black comic book community, Broadnax assisted with the co-founding of the #BlackComicsChat podcast and was a cofounder of the Blerd Book Club. She has also served on myriad panels on the intersection of race and comic book culture.

Through Black Girl Nerds, Broadnax has created an interactive digital community that explores comic book culture for Blacks and other people of color.

# BROWN, AKINSEYE

Akinseye Brown is a comic artist and graphic designer known for his work with the East Coast Black Age of Comics Convention.

(October 20, 1969– )
- **Born in Philadelphia, PA**
- **The Cooper Union, 1991**
- **Comic artist, writer, and inker**

Akinseye Brown, also known as AKIN, grew up in an artistic household. His parents, a fashion designer and a painter/art teacher, organized local art shows and cultural events in Philadelphia. The family also frequented art exhibits, galleries, museums, and art festivals. As a middle school student, Brown's parents encouraged him to read the work of master cartoonist Morrie Turner, the creator of *Wee Pals*. He also enjoyed Bertram A. Fitzgerald's African American history series, *Golden Legacy*.

After graduating from the Creative & Performing Arts High School in Philadelphia in 1987, Brown went on to attend The Cooper Union for Advancement of Science and Art.

Akinseye Brown has illustrated and written books for youth that combine African culture, science fiction, and fantasy. His works include coloring books like *Vejo Capoeira* and comic books like *Sannkofamaan: Pet the Beast* and *Dara Brown 1996: Unforgivable*. *Sannkofamaan* is the story of a man who travels to Africa to fight an evil multinational corporation fixed on destroying a

Apadamax © 2009 First World Komix, Inc.

Image courtesy of Yumy Odom

small community, while Dara Brown follows a woman who fights both as a political activist and superhero while attempting to keep her small business afloat.

Akinseye Brown is especially active with the East Coast Black Age of Comics Convention, for which he has served as both education chairman and event coordinator. In 2016 and 2017, Brown served as editor of the convention's two publications, Read for Fun Workbook and the ECBACC Program Guide. In 2016, Brown received the Pioneer Award at ECBACC for his books *How to Draw Afrakan Superheroes, Volume* #1 and #2.

In addition to his work in the comics industry, Brown does logo design and branding for corporate clients. He also sells original prints and paintings through his company, Sokoya Productions, LLC. In a 2017 interview, he said, "My artwork and creative skills have supported myself and my family for a long time.… It's a big responsibility but rewarding. I wouldn't change a thing."

# BROWN, BUCK

**(Feb. 3, 1936–July 2, 2007)**
- **Born in Morrison, TN**
- **US Air Force, 1955–58**
- **University of Illinois, BFA, 1966**
- **Freelance cartoonist for *Playboy* magazine**

Buck Brown was a longstanding freelance cartoonist for *Playboy* magazine, which in its early years championed not only an aspirational men's lifestyle, but also countercultural politics and racial equality. His cartoons, including parodies, current events, and the humor feature "Granny," appeared in *Playboy* for forty-five years.

Brown's artistic talent was recognized at an early age. During his US Air Force service, his commanding officers enjoyed his cartoons and encouraged him to sketch in his spare time. After his discharge, he drew the everyday dramas he saw while working as a Chicago Transit Authority bus driver. He also gained some notoriety publishing cartoons in the University of Illinois student newspaper, *The Daily Illini.*

Brown had hoped to work in commercial advertising upon graduation, but there was little work for African American artists in the 1960s. At the age of twenty-five, Brown walked into the Chicago office of *Playboy*, then an up-and-coming gentlemen's magazine, on a whim, and dropped off samples of his work. Hugh Hefner, the magazine's editor

> **"BUCK RENDERED THE MOST INCISIVE COMMENTS ON RACE RELATIONS IN AMERICA IN HIS TOUR-DE-FORCE PAINTERLY STYLE."**
>
> **—MICHELLE URRY, PLAYBOY CARTOON EDITOR**

and publisher, recognized the potential in Brown's work and immediately purchased a few pieces. The first Buck Brown cartoon, a black-and-white drawing of a boy holding a trumpet, appeared in *Playboy* in March of 1962.

Becoming a freelance cartoonist for *Playboy* was a major accomplishment for Brown. In the 1960s, *Playboy* was gaining a reputation for promoting the upscale, carefree lifestyle of its editor and publisher, Hugh Hefner. In every issue, readers could expect articles on fine dining, literature and art, lavish parties, expensive cars, and beautiful women. However, the magazine had a socially conscious agenda as well. Because Hefner unequivocally embraced racial equality, *Playboy* showcased the talents of African American cartoonists/illustrators, short fiction writers, jazz musicians, comedians, and civil rights activists.

At a time when mentioning race was considered political, the gently subversive wit of Brown's visual commentaries on Black and white America suited the countercultural image Hefner had cultivated for the magazine. With his ability to provoke thought and laughter from Black and white audiences alike, Brown claimed fame as a crossover artist.

According to *Playboy* cartoon coordinator Jennifer Thiele, "Buck's cartoons ranged widely in subject matter from the sexual revolution, golfing and westerns to parodies of figures from history and literature." Brown used boldly colored acrylic paint and black charcoal to produce cartoons for *Playboy, Ebony, Jet, Esquire, The New Yorker* and the *Chicago Sun-Times*. His most famous *Playboy* character was "Granny," a naughty little old lady who often appeared in various states of undress. Like most of his sex humor, Granny was not designed for titillation; her wrinkled appearance served as a foil to the airbrushed beauty of the *Playboy* centerfolds.

Brown was not responsible for naming his character Granny; according to Brown's daughter, "She was just an older woman my father drew. But every time he would go into the Playboy offices, the receptionist would laugh and say, 'I love that little granny of yours.' And the name stuck." In 1980, Granny appeared as the centerfold.

Between 1962 and 2007, *Playboy* published more than six hundred pieces of Brown's artwork. His last cartoon appeared posthumously in the August 2007 issue.

# BROWN, GEOFFREY FRANKLIN

**(Oct. 20, 1952– )**
- **Born in Pittsburgh, PA**
- **Bowdoin College, BA in English, 1974**
- **Journalist and editor**
- **Writer for *Jet* and editor at the *Chicago Tribune***

Geoffry Brown's father, George F. Brown, was a journalist who worked for such publications as the *Pittsburgh Courier*, *The Philadelphia Bulletin*, and the *New York Courier*. Brown credits his father with teaching him how to write with style, a lesson Brown kept with him throughout his career.

Brown's career in journalism began when he was hired as a general assignment reporter for *The Pittsburgh Press*. As general assignment reporter, Brown was assigned to local incidents and news conferences where, in between chasing sirens, he would dictate the breaking news over a pay phone to a rewriter, who would interpret and then develop feature stories.

In the 1970s, Brown wrote for the African American culture magazine *Jet*, where his responsibilities included entertainment writer, copy editor, comanaging editor, and features editor. Brown's mentor at *Jet* was associate publisher and executive editor Robert E. Johnson, whom Brown credits as both a positive influence on his journalistic skills and a source of knowledge about America's racial history. At *Jet*, Brown interviewed celebrities from the Chicago area, including singer/songwriter Michael Jackson, actor Gary Coleman, civil rights leader Jesse L. Jackson Sr., and singer/songwriter Curtis Mayfield. Outside Chicago, Brown also interviewed Smokey Robinson, Patti LaBelle, Barry White, the Isley Brothers, Kool and the Gang, and Ron O'Neal, among many others.

In 1980, Brown was hired as a copy editor by the *Chicago Tribune*, the publication where he would find most of his professional success. Brown's positions at the *Tribune* included national/foreign news editor, working with national, foreign, and design editors to create daily reports; north suburban bureau chief, directing news coverage of Chicago's northern suburban areas; and entertainment editor, supervising local entertainment coverage. Brown's mentor at the *Tribune* was then-foreign-editor Howard A. Tyner, who would guide Brown's career until he retired as editor in chief in December 2003.

Brown was promoted to managing editor of entertainment in 1998. He added Aaron McGruder's *The Boondocks* – which shone a stark and humorous light on contemporary African American culture – as a daily feature in 1999, the first African American comic strip to be published in the *Chicago Tribune*. He called *The Boondocks* "edgy social commentary and a fresh style of newspaper artwork, manga-esque and clever." Brown understood that his decision would be controversial, but he felt it was an important addition to make to the *Tribune*. He experienced the most pushback when discussing the strip with editors at different newspapers that had already received backlash over *The Boondocks*, and with others concerned that their readers wouldn't accept the strip at all.

Brown became associate managing editor for lifestyles/features in 2000, then returned to his position as associate managing editor of entertainment in 2009. As the *Tribune*'s developer of entertainment material, Brown oversaw the daily arts and entertainment, dining, movies, and on-the-town sections, as well as their relevant online content. He also supervised the Sunday comics page. In April 2015, Brown was promoted to operations and development editor, and he retired from the *Chicago Tribune* in November 2015.

## BROWN, JABAAR L.

Jabaar Brown is the founder of Underground Comixxx, an independent comic book company that launched in 2008.

After being diagnosed with epilepsy at a young age, concerns about his condition led Jabaar to spend most of his time indoors. He spent his new free time on drawing, re-creating anatomy pictures he found in books, and creating an epileptic comic character. After graduating in 1992, Jabaar sold his first comic, *Da Hounds*, in 1996. From then on, he kept selling his works around the local community, finding a market by putting them in local barbershops.

(Aug. 12, 1972– )
- **Born in Wilmington, DE**
- **Delaware College of Art and Design**
- **Comic artist and publisher**
- **Founder of Underground Comixxx**

In the late 2000s, Brown met creative writer Eric Allen at a local art event. Together, they developed the comic *Soul Rider* and began touring local art shows. In 2009, artist Piaget joined the *Soul Rider* creative team.

Issue one debuted at the 2011 Philadelphia Comic-Con, marking the first self-published work to come out of Underground Comixxx. Since then, the company has released *Soul Riders*, *Hustla*, *Protectors of Sector 5*, *Da Vine*, and *Revolution* magazine. The company serves as a platform for characters and stories that are often ignored or misrepresented in mainstream media, such as urban Black culture.

In 2012, Underground Comixxx launched *The Underground Revolution*, a magazine intended to increase solidarity among independent artists and to create a network of cross-promoting independents.

Once he was introduced to comic book conventions, Jabaar began showcasing his comic books for sale at various events outside of his local community. He held Wizard World Philadelphia's first diversity panel, discussing the creation of ethnically diverse characters. In 2013, Underground Comixxx started its own convention, the Underground Comic-Con, in Wilmington, Delaware, which offered artists a venue outside of local comic book shops, helping them find readers when stores wouldn't carry their titles. It is currently one of very few Black-founded comic conventions.

Jabaar has been teaching art at local organizations for several years. The classes are designed for kids, with a curriculum that covers creative writing, character design, storyboarding, and copyright law. Two of his female students have continued on to develop their artistic skills as undergraduates, one at the University of Nevada in Las Vegas and the other at Penn State in Pennsylvania. Considering that, despite improvements in the last few decades, the percentage of female comic artists, editors, and promoters remains low, Jabaar is particularly proud when his female students succeed. He has also made hiring female creators a priority at his company.

Jabaar L. Brown continues to be proactive in the Delaware community, supporting programs for children and encouraging independent artists and comic book creators.

# BURRELL, CAROL

Carol Burrell is the creator of the popular webcomic *SPQR Blues*, a historical comedy. Her heritage includes African, Italian, and Native American lineages.

Shortly before Burrell began her studies at Cornell University, the school had aggressively recruited a number of Black students for its engineering programs. Burnell initially intended to major in aerospace engineering but was frustrated by the racism she experienced there from academic counselors. More than one advisor told her she

(Aug. 12, 1972– )
- **Born in Riverdale, NY**
- **Cornell University, classics**
- **Webcomic artist and editor of children's graphic novels**
- **Created the webcomic SPQR Blues**

Image from http://spqrblues.com/

was having academic trouble because she must have been "raised in the ghetto." In fact, another advisor had overloaded her with courses – something he was notorious for doing to Black students. Burrell's love of the Latin language, the culture of ancient Rome, and her experience living in the arts-oriented dorm Risley Residential College, led her to change her major to classics.

After an internship in London with the *Evening Standard* newspaper, Burrell was hired as an administrative assistant for children's book publisher Clarion Books, an imprint of Houghton Mifflin Harcourt. She was soon promoted to associate editor, working on books by a number of Caldecott and Newbery award–winning authors between 1990 and 1996.

She left Clarion to work at a software company that was developing a role-playing game set in ancient Rome, then moved to Austin, Texas. After the World Trade Center was demolished in 2001, she felt an urge to return to New York. She worked for the Children's Book Council in New York from 2004 to 2006, doing editorial and marketing work as well as redesigning their website.

In 2005, partly as therapy to recover from a repetitive stress injury, Burrell launched the webcomic *SPQR Blues*. Set in ancient Rome, the comic follows the day-to-day life of ordinary Romans living in the city of Herculaneum. The characters are based on real people, although Burrell added fictional details, including the lineage of the lead character, Felix, whom she portrays as a descendant of a slave of Marc Antony. The title is a play on the television show *NYPD Blues*. In 2015, she ran a successful Kickstarter crowdfunding campaign to print a tenth anniversary *SPQR Blues* graphic novel.

> "THERE'S VERY LITTLE IN IT THAT COULDN'T HAVE HAPPENED. OCCASIONALLY PEOPLE SHOW UP IN PLACES OTHER THAN WHERE THEY'RE BELIEVED TO HAVE BEEN AT THE TIME, BUT IN THE HISTORICAL RECORD THERE'S AN AWFUL LOT OF 'HIS WHEREABOUTS FOR THE NEXT FIVE MONTHS ARE UNCLEAR, BUT HE MUST HAVE BEEN IN ROME IN DECEMBER BECAUSE HE POISONED HIS COUSIN DURING THE SATURNALIA PARTY.'"
>
> - CAROL BURRELL, INTERVIEW WITH HISTMINE.WORDPRESS.COM

In 2007, Burrell joined Lerner Publishing, which had just set up its Graphic Universe imprint. Graphic novels for children were just getting off the ground; Scholastic had launched its Graphix imprint in 2005 with the publication of Jeff Smith's *Bone*, and the independent children's graphic novel publisher Papercutz was founded the same year. First Second Books began publication in 2006.

Burrell worked at Graphic Universe almost from the beginning of the imprint, first as a freelancer on their *Graphic Myths and Legends* and *Twisted Journeys* books, and then coming on staff as editorial director. She was one of the first editors to import French graphic novels for children, starting with *The Elsewhere Chronicles* by Nykko and Bannister, which debuted in January 2009. This children's fantasy series stars a quartet of children who go through a portal into a dangerous alternate world. One of the lead characters was adopted from Rwanda, and the story makes explicit reference to the Rwandan genocide. Burrell both edited and translated the six-volume series. Other French titles she acquired include *A Game for Swallows* by Zeina Abirached, *William and the Lost Spirit* by Gwen de Bonneval and Matthieu Bonhomme, and a series of graphic novels based on Antoine de Saint-Exupéry's *The Little Prince*. She also worked with creators to develop original comics, including Trina Robbins and Tyler Page *(The Chicagoland Detective Agency)* and Colleen AF Venable and Stephanie Yue *(Guinea Pig: Pet Shop Private Eye)*. She left Lerner in December 2012.

In January 2013, Burrell took a job as senior editor at Abrams Publishing, where she worked in the ComicArts division. During her time there she acquired a number of significant books, including *The Imitation Game*, a biography of Alan Turing; *Sing No Evil*, a Finnish graphic novel about a metal band; Chris Schweizer's *The Creeps* and *The Night of the Frankenfrogs;* and Philippe Squarzoni's *Climate Changed*.

In 2009, Carol Burrell was selected by Beacon Press and the estate of Octavia Butler to produce a graphic adaptation of Butler's novel *Kindred*, but she was unable to complete the project due to illness. In 2013, Abrams acquired John Jennings and Damian Duffy's adaptation, for which Burrell served as one of several editors. After she left Abrams in October 2014, another editor saw the project to completion.

In addition to her staff work, Burrell has freelanced for a number of prominent publishers of graphic novels and other types of books, including First Second, Papercutz, and Chronicle Books.

# CAMPBELL, BILL

**(May 1, 1970– )**
- **Born in Pittsburgh, PA**
- **Northwestern University**
- **Author and entrepreneur**
- **Owner of Rosarium Publishing**

Bill Campbell is the owner of Rosarium Publishing, a multicultural publishing house founded in 2013. Based in Washington, D.C., Rosarium offers a wide range of comics and prose fiction.

Rosarium Publishing began as an answer to publishing executives who argued that diversity doesn't sell. After his work was repeatedly turned down at larger publishers for being unmarketable, Campbell decided to create his own company where he could both publish his own work and provide opportunities for other disenfranchised authors.

Having successfully marketed his first three self-published books to college professors and other academics, Campbell opened Rosarium Publishing in 2013 to "introduce the world to itself." Its initial catalog featured several of Campbell's novels, including *Sunshine Patriots* and the antiracism satire *Koontown Killing Kaper*.

The company continues to grow and, as of 2017, was home to more than forty creators, including numerous international authors. Rosarium publishes several comic artists and writers featured in the *Encyclopedia of Black Comics*, including Jennifer Cruté (*Jennifer's Journal: The Life of a SubUrban Girl*), Micheline Hess (*Malice in Ovenland*), Whitney Taylor (*Ghost Stories*, forthcoming), Stacey Robinson (*Kid Code*), and John Jennings (*Blue Hand Mojo*).

> "YES, I AM AN AFRICAN-AMERICAN PUBLISHER, BUT IT'S ALSO IMPORTANT TO ME THAT A NATIVE AMERICAN CREATOR HAS THIS OUTLET, OR A MORMON, OR A LATINO. FOR ME, IT'S IMPERATIVE THAT PEOPLE ARE ABLE TO TELL THEIR OWN STORIES. THEY CAN BUILD THEIR OWN TABLES RATHER THAN ASK FOR A PLACE AT THE TABLE."
>
> *- BILL CAMPBELL,*
> *INTERVIEW WITH PUBLISHERS WEEKLY*

Its other titles include the Afrofuturist anthology *Mothership: Tales from Afrofuturism and Beyond,* coedited by Bill Campbell and Edward Austin Hall, and *DayBlack,* by Keef Cross, an atmospheric tale about a Black vampire who uses his job as a tattoo artist to sustain himself.

In a 2015 interview with *Publishers Weekly,* Campbell said, "There are 100 million brown people in America. That's 20 percent more people than are in Germany. Just get out of our way."

Bill Campbell is the author of *Sunshine Patriots; My Booty Novel; Pop Culture: Politics, Puns, and "Poohbutt" from a Liberal Stay-at-Home Dad;* and *Koontown Killing Kaper.* His editorial credits include *Stories for Chip: A Tribute to Samuel R. Delany* with Nisi Shawl and *APB: Artists against Police Brutality* with Jason Rodriguez and John Jennings.

Image courtesy of Rosarium Publishing

Campbell received a Lifetime/Pioneer Glyph Award for his work on *APB*, a comic book anthology benefiting the Innocence Project.

# CAMPBELL, E. SIMMS

**(Jan. 2, 1906–Jan. 27, 1971)**
- **Born in St. Louis, MO**
- **Art Institute of Chicago**
- **Cartoonist and illustrator**
- **Illustrator for *Esquire* and creator of *Cuties***

E. Simms Campbell was one of the first African American illustrators to work in mainstream, mass-market publications. He is perhaps best known as a key figure in the early establishment of *Esquire*, a magazine geared to a male readership, in the early 1930s.

Campbell's professional career began at the age of eleven, when he produced a sign for a local grocer after negotiating a fee of seventy-five cents. His editorial cartoons for his high school paper brought him heightened attention: In 1923, he won a national high school competition for an Armistice Day cartoon.

Simms studied art at the Lewis Institute in Chicago, briefly attended the University of Chicago, and later attended the Art Institute of Chicago, producing fine watercolors that gained entry into international exhibitions. He held a staff position with *The Phoenix*, a humor magazine produced by University of Chicago students, and cofounded a monthly publication called *College Comics*. When both publications failed, he returned to St. Louis, earning income as a post-office messenger and railroad dining car waiter. He also earned additional income by producing caricatures for train passengers.

In 1927, Campbell secured employment with Triad, one of the Midwest's most prominent art advertising agencies. He worked there until 1929, when he moved to New York City. There, he found work with a smaller advertising firm, Munig Studios, and began taking classes at the Academy of Design, contributing to popular magazines such as *Life*, *Judge*, and *College Humour*. In 1930, *Life* and *Judge* both used his artwork as their Christmas covers.

Campbell was able to secure a steady stream of engagements, although they were not extremely profitable, and he earned additional income by selling ideas to other cartoonists. With the assistance of fellow cartoonists, he began selling black-and-white drawings and watercolors. From 1932 to 1933, Campbell attended the Art Students League, where

Image courtesy of American Art Archives

his professors included the well-known artist George Grosz, who was associated with the Berlin Dada movement and was best known for his biting pen-and-ink caricatures of Weimar Germany.

In 1932, Campbell produced a Night-Club Map of Harlem and had illustrations published in *Southern Road*, a book of poetry by Sterling Brown. He also partnered with Harlem Renaissance writers Arna Bontemps and Langston Hughes on a children's book called *Popo and Fifina: Children of Haiti* (1932), producing an eloquent series of woodblock prints.

In 1933, a major shift occurred in Campbell's career when he was commissioned to produce a full-page color drawing for a proposed magazine called *Esquire*. Campbell's gag cartoons and watercolor illustrations would eventually appear in nearly every issue of the magazine from 1933 through 1958. In 1933, he created the aged, lecherous, and impeccably dressed "Esky," a mascot figure with a drooping white mustache that frequently appeared on the cover and within the pages of the magazine. Encouraged by Russell Patterson, a prominent white American artist known for Art Deco magazine illustrations and attractive, long-legged "good girl" or pinup-style white women in comics and illustrations, Campbell began creating "Harem Girls." These Orientalist-inspired harem scenes included a portly, sultan-like male figure surrounded by a gathering of scantily clad, voluptuous women adorned in vests and pantaloons with exposed midriffs. Campbell's harem scenes quickly became a standard feature at the male-oriented *Esquire*, and their popularity was a significant factor in the artist's prompt promotion to art editor at the magazine.

Campbell's work at *Esquire* brought him increasing attention, and his cover art, cartoons, and illustrations for advertisements soon appeared in other national periodicals such as *Cosmopolitan*, *Collier's*, *Ebony*, *The New Yorker*, *The Saturday Evening Post*, and *Redbook*, as well as in newspapers, on motion picture posters, and as book illustrations. At *Esquire*, he produced several illustrations for each issue while supplying additional ideas for other artists, article texts, and cover art, and he produced ad illustrations for Springmaid, Hart Schaffner, Marx, and Barbasol. When *Esquire* moved away from illustration art, Campbell and several others went to work for *Playboy* and helped to foster its success as well.

Campbell occasionally crafted political cartoons examining racial discrimination for the African American press, sometimes including racially stereotypical material in his satirical work. In 1937, he briefly drew the syndicated comic strip *Hoiman*, which featured an African

American porter depicted in a minstrel-like style. However, Campbell's characters, as a whole, were largely white, and few audiences were aware that the illustrator was African American. Yet Campbell was certainly impacted by discriminatory practices in this period. In 1938, when he attempted to purchase a twelve-acre estate in the fashionable suburb of Mount Pleasant in Westchester County, New York, his offer was rejected and he lost his appeal before the New York State Supreme Court. His attorney, civil rights lawyer Arthur Garfield Hayes, argued that the sale was refused due to Campbell's racial identity.

From 1943 until his death, King Features Syndicate distributed Campbell's single-panel feature *Cuties* to 145 papers throughout the nation. The widely popular gag cartoons were included in numerous anthologies and collected in three volumes: *Cuties in Arms* (1942), *More Cuties in Arms* (1943), and *Chorus of Cuties* (1952).

Image courtesy of Professor W. Foster

Campbell was also a great admirer of jazz and wrote about the musical genre in several magazines. One essay was included in *Jazzmen* (1939), a seminal examination of jazz history. Campbell was also a close friend of the jazz musician and bandleader Cab Calloway, who discussed the pair's bar-hopping escapades in Harlem in his 1976 memoir, *Of Minnie the Moocher and Me*.

Campbell enjoyed a lengthy, prolific, and successful career. He was a member of the Society of Illustrators and won the national Hearst editorial cartoon competition in Chicago in 1936. He received an honorary MFA degree from Lincoln University in 1942 and an honorary doctorate of humane letters from Wilberforce University in 1957.

In 1936, he married his first wife, Constance, who died in 1940. He then married her sister Vivian. In 1956, Campbell and his wife moved to Neerach, Switzerland, and lived there for fourteen years. The couple's life in Europe was documented in a November 1966 *Ebony* magazine article by Charles L. Sanders titled "Escape from the Rat Race: Famous Cartoonist E. Simms Campbell Relishes 'Peace' in Tiny Swiss Village Hermitage." Campbell had one daughter, Elizabeth, a fashion model who was married to the renowned photographer Gordon Parks from 1962 to 1973. Campbell returned to the United States after Vivian's

Image courtesy of American Art Archives

death in 1970 and died at his home in White Plains, New York, in 1971. In 2002, he was inducted posthumously into the Society of Illustrators' Hall of Fame.

## CARPENTER, STANFORD

**(Sept. 16, 1968– )**
- **Born in Glendale, AZ**
- **Oberlin College, BS in archaeology and anthropology**
- **Columbia University, MA in sociocultural anthropology**
- **Rice University, PhD in anthropology, 2003**
- **Cultural anthropologist and comic creator**

Stanford Carpenter, ethnographer, cultural anthropologist, and comic creator, was born at the dawn of the Blaxploitation era. He founded the Institute for Comics Studies, a non-profit furthering the academic study of comics and other visual media. He is also one of the creators of Critical Front, a superhero team developed by Black academics to provide cultural and media analyses through storytelling.

Carpenter was born at Luke Air Force Base in Glendale, Arizona, to Toni Carpenter, a visual artist and an ESL teacher, and Crawford Carpenter, a commissioned officer in the US air force. Carpenter's parents supported their son's interest in comics, recognizing the value of comics as an escape and believing they would help build his literacy skills. To that end, both of his parents willingly purchased comics for him. Carpenter was so fascinated by the medium that he taught himself to read so that he wouldn't have to wait for his parents to read his comics to him. At the same time, his father provided him with nonschool-based experiences that launched the artist's interest in anthropology: on weekends, Stanford often accompanied his father to work at a recycling plant, where he began to understand the relationship between culture, economics, and social outcomes. Stanford and his father would often end their days together with a stop at the local comic book store.

Through connections made at Oberlin College, Carpenter met several comic artists and editors, including Chris Claremont, a longtime writer for Marvel's *Uncanny X-Men*. After college, Carpenter moved to Portland, Oregon, where he wrote and illustrated a comic strip in *The Skanner*, a local African American newsweekly. His strip, *African Tales*, featured African folktales collected by anthropologists and retold in comic form.

Carpenter also worked as a map-maker and illustrator for Portland State University professor Kofi Agorsah's Maroon Heritage Research Project. Carpenter's synthesis of his academic and creative pursuits drew the attention of scholars like Columbia University anthropologist Michael Taussig, who appreciated how *African Tales* presented academic research in an accessible context. With Taussig's encouragement, Carpenter applied to Columbia University and earned an MA in sociocultural anthropology.

Throughout this period, Carpenter continued creating comics whose themes were informed by his interests in anthropology, comics, and race. His growing prominence in all three areas drew the notice of Rice University anthropologists George Marcus, Julie Taylor, and Stephen Tyler. All three were impressed by Carpenter's work combining comic art and anthropology, and Marcus offered Carpenter the opportunity to earn his PhD in anthropology at Rice while continuing to work in comics.

After relocating to Houston, Texas, for his doctoral studies, Carpenter immersed himself in the local artist community. He became involved in Project Row Houses, an African American visual arts organization that selects African American artists to create large-scale installations in a block of shotgun-style houses in Houston's Third Ward. Carpenter's installation, "Imagine the Melanin-Free-Zone," attracted broad attention and eventually traveled to Merritt College in Oakland, California and later to the University of Maryland, College Park.

With the support of a fellowship at the Smithsonian Institution and the Friends Research Institute, Carpenter completed his PhD in 2003. He went on to hold postdoctoral fellowships at the University of Maryland and Johns Hopkins University. Carpenter taught briefly at the Rhode Island School of Design before accepting a position as assistant professor of visual and critical studies at the School of the Art Institute of Chicago.

*"...COMICS, A MEDIUM FILLED WITH VARIOUS IDENTITIES CREATED ON BLANK PAGES THROUGH THE AFFIRMATIVE ACTS OF GROUPS OF PEOPLE, REPRESENTS AN IDEAL SITE TO EXPLORE IDENTITY IN BOTH ITS REAL AND ITS IMAGINED ASPECTS."*

Both Carpenter's comics and his scholarship focus on the relationship between media culture, creative processes, identity, and representation. He conducts ethnographic fieldwork among creators and professionals in various media to create both scholarly and artistic works. He started doing ethnographic fieldwork and interviews at a time when comic scholarship on identity and representation was overwhelmingly focused on interpretations of the images that did not take the creators, creative practices, or productions practices into account. He was also the first American cultural anthropologist to take on comics as primary field of study. In addition to his dissertation, Carpenter's comic scholarship includes "Truth Be Told: Authorship and the Creation of the Black Captain America" and "Black Lightning's Story," which focus on how creators' personal experiences, creative practices, and production processes influence the construction and representation of identity.

These interests are perhaps best exemplified in Critical Front, a superhero team Carpenter developed with a handful of other Black academics, including Columbia University law professor Patricia Williams, University of

Image courtesy of Stanford Carpenter

Pennsylvania Dean and anthropologist John Jackson, University of Maryland College Park American Studies Professor Sheri Parks, and George Washington University Dean and Latin American Historian Ben Vinson. Each member of the group created a superhero alter ego, and they used these figures to offer incisive critiques of contemporary media culture. Carpenter's alter ego, Brother-Story, derived his superpowers from his promise to collect and transmit the stories of Anansi the spider, the famous trickster of

Image courtesy of Stanford Carpenter

African legend. The Critical Front superheroes presented their analyses not in the pages of a comic book but rather in the form of live readings of collaborative stories. In addition, comic creator and illustrator Darick Robinson (*Transmetropolitan* and *The Boys*) created Critical Front action figures based on Carpenter's designs.

Brother-Story also featured prominently in Carpenter's online comic, *My EthnoSurreal Life*. The ethnosurreal is a concept Carpenter developed in conversation with close friend and comic artist John Jennings. In his January 2016 introduction to the comic, Carpenter explained that its title refers, in part, to "my realization that cartoonists (using thought and word balloons) share much in common with surrealists who tried to render the experience of the conscious and the unconscious co-present." Eight installments of the comic appeared on the blog *Michael Davis World*, a website edited and maintained by Davis, an African American comics pioneer and the cofounder of Black comics company *Milestone*

*Media.* Brother-Story also appeared in *The African American Equation,* Carpenter's collaboration with Johns Hopkins University political science professor Lester Spence, a humorous but biting attempt to quantify the wages of systemic racism, racial progress, and nomenclature on Black people and Black communities. The broadside-style one-page comic "Writing on Walls" depicts Brother-Story and ghostly character Headless Man contemplating and opining on Spence and Carpenter's equation, presented as a wheat-paste poster on a city wall.

In 2013, Stanford Carpenter left his position at the School of the Art Institute to help establish the Institute for Comics Studies (ICS), a nonprofit organization dedicated to promoting the study of comics as an academic pursuit. As chair of the ICS Board, Carpenter organized conferences to create and sustain the communities he and the members of Critical Front worked to establish for themselves.

# CHAMBLISS, JULIAN C.

**(December 21, 1971– )**
- **Born in Sylacauga, AL**
- **Jacksonville University, 2004**
- **University of Florida, PhD, 2003**
- **Comic book scholar and academic**

Julian Chambliss, a noted comic book scholar and academic, studies the intersection between comic book narratives, urban history, and societal views of race.

Chambliss obtained both his master's degree and his PhD from the University of Florida. As a graduate student, Chambliss's academic interests did not involve comic books; instead, his dissertation focused on the ideological narratives in city planning and how urban spaces shape community interactions and civic identity. When Chambliss began his career as a visiting professor at Rollins College in 2003, however, he found a connection between America's urban environments and the narratives found in comics.

Using comic book storylines as an example of American urbanization, he gained the attention of undergraduate students taking his course on American history. Soon thereafter, Chambliss teamed up with colleagues to conduct focused research on comic books and to create courses that centralized the study of comic books in the American experience. One of Chambliss's first comic-book-themed courses was titled American Graphic Media: Creating the Comic Book City and the United States since 1945. While recruiting students into these courses was relatively easy, convincing fellow scholars about the usefulness of his courses and research was more difficult. By focusing on the cultural relevancy of comic books and the complex narratives that bridge the divide between fantasy and American history, Chambliss slowly convinced skeptics of the importance of his work.

> "HISTORY IS A LIVING DISCIPLINE. PUBLIC ART, PHOTOGRAPHY, GRAPHIC NOVELS, AND COMIC BOOKS ARE SIMPLY ONE WAY AMERICA'S UNDERSTANDING OF URBAN HISTORY MANIFESTS IN EVERYDAY MEDIUMS."

Chambliss was soon promoted from visiting professor to tenure-track professor. Around the same time, he also began coordinating the African and African American studies program. His commitment to his students earned him recognition from his colleagues, and he received the Presidential Award for Diversity and Inclusion as well as the Cornell Distinguished Service Award.

Some of Chambliss's most important scholarly manuscripts include "Archetype or Token? The Challenge of the Black Panther" (2016); "War Machine: Blackness, Power, and Identity in Iron Man" (2015); and "From Pulp Hero to Superhero: Culture, Race, and Identity in American Popular Culture, 1900–1940" published in 2008. In these and other essays, Chambliss and his coauthors explored how real-world histories regarding America's experiences around race, gender, and nationality manifest in fictitious comic book worlds. As America's urban landscape evolved throughout the twentieth century, so did the visual depictions of these landscapes in popular culture.

As a lifelong fan and comic book collector, some of Chambliss's favorite comic book characters include Iron Man, Teen Titan, and the X-Men. As an academic, Chambliss is particularly interested in the presentation and development of such characters as Black Panther and Black Goliath. Not only does he find the representation of Black comic book characters important, he also has found larger cultural meaning in how these characters have evolved over the years. In essence, the way in which Black characters are depicted at a given moment reflects prevailing views

Image courtesy of Julian Chambliss

Image courtesy of Julian Chambliss

of race in America at that time. By tracking the evolution of Black comic book characters over several decades, a larger narrative emerges about how racial relationships have changed and shifted over a century.

As his work continued, Chambliss found other like-minded scholars and community members interested in community engagement, urban landscapes, and public art. His academic networking allowed him to research and publish through more traditional methods, while his community connections allowed him to explore activism and the arts within various urban environments. By having a hand in both the academic and community art world, Chambliss created projects for his students that encouraged them to conjoin their classroom experiences with local neighborhoods.

For Chambliss, history is a living discipline. Public art, photography, graphic novels, and comic books are simply one way America's understanding of urban history manifests in everyday mediums. By studying the cultural narratives within the pages of comic books, Chambliss believes Americans can gain a more complete understanding of their national, urban, racial, and gendered histories.

# COATES, TA-NEHISI PAUL

Lauded author of *The Beautiful Struggle* and *Between the World and Me*, Ta-Nehisi Coates is also the lead writer for the 2016 reboot of *Black Panther*.

**(September 30, 1975– )**
- **Born in Baltimore, MD**
- **Howard University**
- **Best-selling writer, journalist, and editor**
- **Lead writer for the 2016 reboot of *Black Panther***

Coates grew up in Baltimore in the 1980s during the crack epidemic. While his performance in school was sometimes lacking, his parents – a librarian and a teacher – instilled the value of writing by assigning him essays as discipline. Coates's father, a Vietnam War veteran, was also a Black Panther, and he founded Black Classic Press, which focuses on books pertaining to African American culture. The press celebrated its thirty-fifth anniversary in 2013.

Coates's first book, the memoir *The Beautiful Struggle* (2008) explores his childhood in Baltimore and his relationship with his father. While the book takes the reader through some of the worst times in Coates's life, it also portrays some of his happiest moments, including his time at Howard University, where he met his wife, Kenyatta Matthews.

Coates's second book, *Between the World and Me* (2015), is renowned for prompting dialogue about race. The book, whose title comes from a poem by Richard Wright, directly addresses racial maltreatment in America. Written in the style of a letter to his son, Samori, Coates cautions him about the police, recalling the tragic death of his good friend, Prince Jones, on his way to visit his fiancée. While American discourse on race often highlights how far racial equality has progressed, Coates refuses to sugarcoat things for his son, letting him know he should be prepared for all the obstacles he may face due to his color.

In 2015, Coates was selected to helm the reboot of the *Black Panther* comic. Originally published in 1966, *Black Panther* features the first Black superhero in mainstream American comics. The series follows the king of fictional Wakanda, a technologically advanced African country, as he protects his country from aggressors. The character returned to popular discourse after appearing in the 2016 live-action movie *Captain America: Civil War*.

Ta-Nehisi Coates became involved with the project during a 2015 conference for *The Atlantic*, where Coates held a seminar titled What if Captain America Were Muslim and Female? An onlooker in the audience, Marvel editor Tom Brevoort, asked Coates whether there were any Marvel characters he'd like to write for. Coates sent the studio a list of characters, not including Black Panther. When the *Black Panther* reboot was proposed, however, Coates saw that it was in line with his goal of sparking conversations about race in America.

After the first issue of *Black Panther* sold more than 300,000 copies, Coates brought on writers Roxane Gay and Yona Harvey for 2016's *World of Wakanda*. As of 2017, he was writing a new series with Harvey, called *Black Panther and the Crew*, about an all-Black superhero team.

# COMMODORE, CHESTER

**(Aug. 22, 1914–Apr. 10, 2004)**
- **Born in Racine, WI**
- **Political cartoonist**
- **Editorial cartoonist for the *Chicago Defender***

With a comic career spanning many decades, Chesterfield Commodore was a prolific editorial cartoonist as well as a twelve-time Pulitzer Prize nominee. Encouraged by an uncle, John Prophet, Commodore cultivated an early interest in comic strips and in drawing. In his grandmother's music room, Commodore also encountered well-known African American musicians and other artists who had been denied the use of local white-owned hotels and restaurants.

Commodore moved to Chicago in 1927 and continued drawing at Tilden Technical High School. Upon graduation, he supported himself through a series of jobs – as a mechanic, car washer, chauffeur, and truck driver – in Chicago and Minneapolis.

"LESLIE ROGERS WAS MY KIND OF CARTOONIST. I LIKED THE WAY HE DID HIS FIGURES. HE... DIDN'T MAKE 'EM TRAMPY-LOOKIN'. THEY STILL HAD RESPECT."

In 1938, James Rice, a lawyer, comedic writer, and admirer of Commodore's work, recommended him for a cartoonist position at the *Minneapolis Star* newspaper. Commodore was offered the job based on his work and Rice's referral; however, when he arrived at the newspaper offices, the job offer was rescinded without explanation. The staff had apparently been unaware that Commodore was African American.

During the 1930s, Commodore married Marie (Ruby) Bazel, and had two sons, Chesterfield Jr. and Phillip Joseph. After returning to Chicago in 1940, Commodore became a Pullman porter. While working at Pullman, he was contacted by Charles Browning, a *Chicago Defender* editor and former schoolmate of Commodore's sister Ruth, who offered him an advertising layout position. The paper was in need of additional staff during the 1948 national printers' strike. Commodore was hired in August of that year and soon began producing photo layouts, later making illustrations for ads and articles and then progressing to cartoons.

In 1954, Commodore began drawing the popular, long-running *Bungleton Green* strip, taking over after the unexpected death of the strip's previous artist, Jay Jackson. In the same year, Commodore began a strip that featured a humorous story line focused on a family of four. After a five-month reader contest, Commodore's previously unnamed strip became known as *The Sparks*.

Largely a self-taught artist, Commodore was known for his astute political commentary and for his lifelong efforts to counter stereotypical depictions of African Americans. He was keenly concerned about stereotypical representations of Black people in comic strips, producing figures that represented a pointed departure from the "eight-ball" caricature types prominent in late nineteenth-century to mid-twentieth-century American comics. In an interview in the 1998 documentary titled *The Black Press: Soldiers Without Swords*, Commodore noted that he had been influenced by Leslie Rogers's progressive work at the *Chicago Defender*. "Leslie Rogers was my kind of cartoonist," he said. "I liked the way he did his figures. He... didn't make 'em trampy-lookin'. They still had respect." Commodore also admired the work of cartoonists E. Simms Campbell, Henry Brown, and Ollie Harrington, creator of the nationally recognized *Dark Laughter* comic strip.

Commodore served as primary editorial cartoonist for the *Defender* from 1954 through 1983, producing work that focused on racial discrimination and civil rights. During his tenure at the *Defender*, other newspapers began to reprint Commodore's cartoons on their op-ed pages, resulting in the broadening of his audience and a heightened social status within the larger community of political cartoonists.

After the 1968 assassination of Reverend Martin Luther King Jr., Commodore's work directly addressed social injustices involving African Americans, including poverty, voting rights, striking steel workers, and lynchings. In 1974, the *Defender* began publishing a weekly arts supplement titled *Accent*. Each *Accent* cover featured a full-page Chester Commodore caricature of a contemporary local or national figure, including artists, writers, and others noted in their field. The popular series continued for five years. During his five-decade career at the *Defender*, Commodore worked on several additional strips, including the gag panel *So What?* and the *Ravings of Professor Doodle*.

Also at the *Defender*, Commodore met Mattye Marcia Buchanan Hutchins, who became his second wife in 1955. They remained married until her death in 1990. Commodore retired in 1983 and intermittently produced cartoons until 1992, when he began contributing a weekly political cartoon until his death in Colorado Springs, Colorado.

In addition to his twelve Pulitzer nominations, Commodore received numerous awards throughout his career, including Best Cartoon from the National Newspaper Publishers Association from 1972 through 1978. In 1973, he was named Best Editorial Cartoonist of the Year by *Cartoonist PROfiles* magazine, and he also received awards from the Chicago Newspaper Guild, the National Conference of Christians and Jews (1976), and the Lu Palmer Foundation (1980). In 1985, the Prairie School he had attended in Racine, Wisconsin, established a scholarship and an Achievement Award for Creating and Writing in his honor.

In 2007, the Chicago Public Library acquired the Chester Commodore Papers, a gift from his stepdaughter, Lorin Nails-Smooté, and family.

An exhibition titled *Chester Commodore, 1914–2004: The Work and Life of a Pioneering Cartoonist of Color* was presented at the Carter G. Woodson Regional Library in Chicago in 2008.

# COWAN, DENYS, B.

Denys Cowan is an African American comic book illustrator, creator, animator, and cofounder of the first African American comics company, Milestone Media.

> **(January 30, 1961– )**
> - **Comic creator, illustrator, and animator**
> - **Founder of Milestone Media**
> - **Illustrator and animator for *Static Shock***

Cowan was a student at the High School of Art and Design in New York City when he first began working in the comic book industry. A friend of Cowan's was assisting Rich Buckler (an artist on a number of DC titles) at the time, and happened to invite Cowan to help out as well. Cowan spent some time as a de facto production assistant, drawing backgrounds until he moved on to his next opportunity.

When Cowan was sixteen, he went to work with DC and Marvel artists Ron Wilson and Arvell Jones. He later received an internship at Continuity Comics, the now-defunct company founded by Neal Adams. At Continuity Comics, Cowan became an official production assistant. He worked on backgrounds and colors but mostly performed light janitorial work and ran errands for the other artists in-house. It was during this time that Cowan would do his first solo professional work in earnest.

In 1980, Paul Levitz, an editor at DC Comics, gave Cowan his first work – a three-page story in *Weird War Tales* #93. For the next few years, Cowan did backup work for a number of Marvel and DC properties, including *Spectacular Spider-Man*, *Moon Knight*, and *The Flash*. He eventually went on to do a longer run on Marvel's *Power Man/Iron Fist*.

In the mid 1980s, Cowan began to turn some of his work toward important social issues. He created a story about the oppression of the Black population in South Africa for *Teen Titans* Spotlight #1 and #2. He also created a *Black Panther* miniseries that focused on apartheid, a controversial topic in the 1980s because of the Reagan administration's support for the South African government. The story did not sit well with Jim Shooter, the editor of Marvel. After reading it, he told Cowan, "Looks like all the white people are killing all the black people." Shooter refused to run the Black Panther story, pulling it from publication at the last minute. This encounter frustrated Cowan and drove him to walk away from comics for a short time in the 1980s.

In 1987, Cowan would join writer Dennis O'Neil and inker Rick Magyar on DC Comics' *The Question*, which centered around investigative journalist and martial artist Vic Sage. This would garner Cowan and Magyar the prestigious Eisner Award nomination for Best Art Team for two years in a row, 1988 and 1989.

In the early 1990s, Cowan initiated a partnership consisting of long-time friends Derek T. Dingle and Michael Davis, along with Dwayne McDuffie and Christopher Priest. Creative Partners Ltd. was later re-formed as the groundbreaking comics company Milestone Media Inc.

The Milestone Media team believed that while people of color are active consumers of comics culture, Black characters and creators alike are underrepresented in the industry. Additionally, many stories about Black characters are created by predominantly white creative teams, leading to inauthentic results. The goal of Milestone's founders was to create more inclusive stories by and about people of color.

At Milestone, Cowan and McDuffie created the groundbreaking book *Hardware,* focused on the story of a brilliant Black inventor and his war with his former mentor Edwin Alva. Cowan's work on *Hardware* and other titles, including *Static, Xombi,* and *Blood Syndicate,* garnered both commercial and critical success. However, the comic book market began to flag the same time Milestone was beginning to gain traction. Some chalked up Milestone's failure to the very premise of the company: comics for and about people of color. However, large print runs of special foil, die-cuts, special inserts comics, and an increasing focus on comics as an investment soured the market.

The larger comic companies lost customers, but, because of their size and longevity of their characters, they were able to withstand the falling market. Milestone did not enjoy those same benefits, and the fledgling pioneering comics company folded.

Cowan's work did not close with the closing of Milestone, however. He continued to work in the industry and had success drawing again for DC and Marvel. He also turned his talents to producing animation. He was able to turn the Milestone character Static into the successful series *Static Shock*, which ran for four seasons on the WB Network. Cowan continued working in animation after *Static Shock* ran its course and went on to produce other shows, including the controversial and critically acclaimed *The Boondocks*. As senior vice president of animation at BET, he, along with then-BET president Reginald Hudlin, created the well-received *Black Panther* series for BET.

Cowan, Hudlin, and Dingle announced in 2015 that they intended to revive Milestone Media with a new generation of diverse heroes and creators.

# CRAFT, JERRY

Jerry Craft is the author and illustrator of *Mama's Boyz*, one of relatively few syndicated Black comic strips during the 1990s and 2000s.

After working for more than a decade in advertising, Craft became an assistant to Barbara Slate at Marvel and Harvey Comics, contributing to *Sweet 16* and *New Kids on the Block*. After this brief venture in comics, he returned to advertising, producing sales brochures for world-renowned comics at King Features Syndicate (KFS).

> (Jan. 22, 1963– )
> - **Born in New York, NY**
> - **School of Visual Arts, BFA in advertising**
> - **Author, illustrator, and cartoonist**
> - **Creator of *Mama's Boyz***

While at KFS, Craft had the opportunity to start his own comic strip, *Mama's Boyz.* It told the story of a widow named Pauline Porter raising her two teenage sons, Tyrell and Yusuf, while working full time to run the family's bookstore. The comic ran from 1995 to 2013, making Craft one of the only syndicated African American cartoonists in the nation. The success of *Mama's Boyz* led to several awards and nominations,

Image courtesy of Jerry Craft

Image courtesy of Jerry Craft

including winning five African American Literary Award Show Open Book Awards for best comic strip and a nomination for Outstanding Achievement in Black Comics at the Glyph Awards.

While maintaining a light and humorous storyline, Craft also used *Mama's Boyz* to address several national problems, including leukemia, childhood obesity, and teen pregnancy. Craft teamed up with many foundations over the years for his educational storylines.

During his time at KFS, Craft was hired to work as a web producer at *Sports Illustrated Kids*. During his eight years at the company, Craft was promoted to editorial director, creating an *SI Kids TV* spoof, "Randy Moss Driving School." Craft continued his work with children by hosting an online sports talk show for kids, interviewing athletes such as Derek Jeter.

"IF PUBLISHERS WANT TO PORTRAY KIDS OF COLOR EFFECTIVELY, THEY NEED TO GO OUTSIDE THEIR CONVENTIONAL POOL OF WRITERS AND ARTISTS."

In the fall of 2006, Craft left Sports Illustrated to pursue drawing and illustration full time. He created his own company, Mama's Boyz, Inc., and began illustrating children's books. Craft has since published three books of his original comic: *Mama's Boyz: As American as Sweet Potato Pie!*, *Mama's Boyz: Home Schoolin'*, and *Mama's Boyz: The Big Picture*. The strip has also appeared in two *Chicken Soup for the Soul* books.

After coming to the realization that he could only write the way he wanted without a publisher, in 1997 Craft made the decision to self-publish. By 2007, Craft was able to support his family based solely on his book sales. His newest novel, *The Offenders: Saving the World While Serving Detention!* is a collaboration with his two teenage sons. This adventure story for middle grade readers aims to teach kids the negative effects of bullying.

Craft also created the conference Black Comic Book Days, which takes place in Harlem. This event features artists and writers of color from around the country, drawing audiences of up to 2,500 fans.

In 2015, Craft was honored in a PSA on Cable Vision for Black History Month and was a featured author on *The Brown Bookshelf's* 28 Days Later campaign. He also coaches basketball and teaches cartooning workshops at his sons' schools.

# CRUTÉ, JENNIFER

Jennifer Cruté is an independent comic creator and the author of the autobiographical comic *Jennifer's Journal: The Life of a SubUrban Girl*.

Cruté became involved with drawing and writing comics while working as a freelance commercial illustrator. However, as she described on her personal website, "Some projects were not as enlightened as

(January 22, 1963– )
- **Born in Hackensack, NJ**
- **School of Visual Arts, BFA in illustration, 2003**
- **Art Students League, 2006–2010**
- **Artist, illustrator, and writer**

I had hoped." Besides encountering frequent stereotyping, she was also asked to make her Black characters look more European, with straightened hair and smaller features. As an outlet for her frustration, Cruté would draw and write about her feelings on Post-its or in a sketchbook. "After I had about 250 ideas drawn," she said, "my friends convinced me to write a book." That book became *Jennifer's Journal: The Life of a SubUrban Girl*, an autobiographical comic about her childhood in New Jersey. Volume 1 was published in 2010.

Jennifer Cruté's comics have been featured at comic book shows, in Bitch Media, and in *Ebony*. At the East Coast Black Age of Comics Convention in 2009, Cruté's strips were nominated for "Best Rising Star" in its Glyph Comic Awards category. She was also a finalist in Lambda Legal's Life Without Fair Courts contest.

With a background in illustration and fine arts, Cruté is not only a comic artist but a painter as well. Her interest in comics developed after her love of fine art; the only comics Cruté ever read as a kid were the local newspaper's Sunday funnies.

In a 2012 interview with Bitch Media, Cruté discussed her approach to illustrating painful situations, such as her family's efforts to avoid white violence in the South: "You have to put a jester hat on any oppressor – be that oppressor a person, a group or your own mind." With her rounded, simplified figures, she makes upsetting narratives seem smaller and more approachable.

Cruté credits both the graphic designer Milton Glaser and comic artist Marjane Satrapi, the author of *Persepolis*, as influences on her work.

Image courtesy of Rosarium Publishing

# DAVIS, ANDRÉ LEROY

André LeRoy Davis illustrated the humor column "The Last Word" in the rap publication *The Source* for close to seventeen years. He has also written for *XXL*, *Vibe*, *Rappages*, and *Stress* magazines.

> **(July 8, 1965– )**
> - **Born in Brooklyn, NY**
> - **School of Visual Arts, BFA in cartooning and illustration, 1983**
> - **Artist and writer**
> - **Contributor to "The Last Word" in *The Source***

Although David grew up during the golden period of funk and soul, his true love was hip-hop. He first saw a disc jockey cutting up two copies of Chic's "Good Times" in 1977. This incident, followed by hearing "King Tim III (Personality Jock)" by the Fatback Band and "Rapper's Delight" by the Sugarhill Gang led to Davis's lifetime love of the genre.

After his graduation, Davis did freelance work for publications such as *Emerge, Playgirl,* and *Players.* 1990 would mark the beginning of Davis's lengthy association with the rap music publication *The Source*, with whom Davis would arguably establish his name as an artist. After coming across a copy of the magazine at a newsstand, a cold call meeting with the editor in chief John Schecter led to Davis's first contribution to the column "The Last Word." His subject was N.W.A. member Eazy-E (Eric Wright), who at the time was involved in an altercation with the F.B.I.

While Davis expected his contribution to the column would be a single incident, he would get called back by *The Source* every month for the next sixteen years. He would also contribute music reviews, question-and-answer segments, feature stories, and articles for another column, "Hip-Hop 101." In all, Davis drew 175 installments of "The Last Word" for *The Source*. In tandem with his work on *The Source*, he also contributed to *Smooth* magazine from 2002 to 2004.

Davis found himself drawing hip-hop royalty like Ice Cube, Sean "Diddy" Combs, and LL Cool J repeatedly during his time with the magazine. Drawing on his immersion in the scene, Davis's approach was to take the artist's words as source material for his humorous scenes. Always keen to push the envelope, Davis often found his editors opting for the tamer ideas he presented during meetings. Despite being reined in by his editors, however, Davis still managed to anger many of his subjects, particularly in the early days of the column.

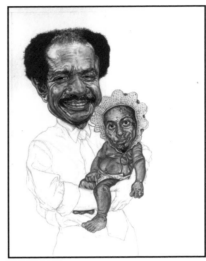
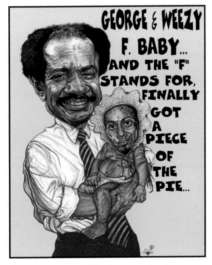
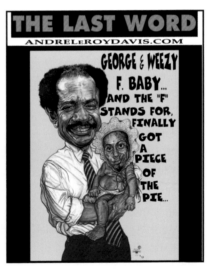

Images courtesy of André Leroy Davis

A complaint from members of X Clan led to Davis arranging a meeting where the two parties could sort out their differences. When Davis's column satirized DJ Quik, the musician warned him against setting foot in California. Only after Doctor Dré of *Yo! MTV Raps* pointed out during an interview that making the column should be considered a badge of honor did Quik's anger subside. Eventually, many artists did come to regard being featured in "The Last Word" as a mark of distinction. Heavy D once claimed that "The Last Word" was the first thing he read in the magazine.

Often, Davis would slip hidden messages into his work. For example, musician Slick Rick's incarceration coincided with the trend of rap artists wearing their jeans lower to expose their designer underwear logos. In the place of a brand name, Davis wrote "Free Slick Rick."

Although some artists wanted to purchase Davis's "Last Word" caricatures of themselves, none wanted to pay his asking price. As a result, he retained ownership of all of his artwork.

Following the final "The Last Word" in 2007, Davis turned his attention to teaching, working with children and the elderly. In 2012, he returned to drawing about hip-hop culture, releasing the first "Last Word" independent of *The Source*.

# DE LA CRUZ, SHARON LEE

Sharon Lee De La Cruz is an artist, entrepreneur, and social justice activist. She has spearheaded numerous projects, ranging from artist collectives that advocate for women's empowerment to multimedia efforts to improve accessibility in STEM education.

- **Born in New York, NY**
- **The Cooper Union, BFA, 2008**
- **New York University, MA in animation and interactive technology, 2015**
- **Graffiti artist and entrepreneur**

Cruz discovered her passion for graffiti art when she moved to Florida at the age of fifteen. As an undergraduate at Cooper Union, she was awarded a Fulbright Fellowship by the Institute of International Education to study experimental filmmaking and mural making in Lima, Peru. In Peru, Cruz refined her mural-making skills and worked with high school students on film and graffiti art projects. She also began to use her artistic ability for social and political purposes, forming Maripussy Crew, a nonprofit, womanist, graffiti collective that works toward social justice for girls and women.

After completing her Fulbright Fellowship in Peru, Cruz returned to the South Bronx in 2009 and served as a community organizer and program director of both ACTION (Activists Coming To Inform Our Neighborhood) and WOMEN (Where Our Minds Empower Needs) at the Point Community Development Corporation in Hunts Point, teaching young women about sexual health issues. In February of 2012,

Project Reach, a youth organizing center, honored her activist work with the Point at a gala dedicated to "Women Warriors." At the ceremony, Cruz was recognized as a change agent whose participation in various art-based, anti-discrimination programs pushed minority youth groups to become civically engaged in their communities.

In addition to her activist work, Cruz's graffiti art has gained international recognition. She appeared in Armory Week 2012 at the Bronx River Arts Center and functioned as a brand ambassador for Calvin Klein's CK One line in 2013. Cruz initiated a global consumer engagement campaign with Calvin Klein using art, music, and fashion; she also designed graffiti-themed packaging for CK One.

Since earning her master's degree from NYU, Cruz has earned residencies at 365 Days of Print, TED Conference, and Wonder Women, all while serving as the practicing artist in residence for her own freelance company, Uno Seis Tres. She also serves as the CEO and creative coder of the Digital Citizens Lab, a design collective with a focus on civic technology. Cruz spearheads a creative team that creates resources for educators to meet the needs of historically underserved students through such project as El Cuco, an interactive digital comic that teaches code logic.

In her roles as acclaimed activist, graffiti artist, and social entrepreneur, Cruz continues to make public art to advocate for underserved populations and inspire change. As of 2017, she was the assistant director of Princeton University's StudioLab, a space for interdisciplinary collaboration spanning technology, music, and the humanities.

# DIXON, DANI

(1982– )
- **Born in New York, NY**
- **Writer, producer, director and comic creator**
- **Creator of comic series 13 and M.I.S.//ing**

Dani Dixon is the author of several independent comics and novels, including *13*, *M.I.S.//ing*, and *Five Nations*. She is also the founder of Tumble Creek Press, an independent publishing company where she writes for a variety of age groups.

Dixon's comic series *13* deals with young teenagers who gain special abilities at the age of thirteen, then lose them within a short span of time. It has since become a web series titled *13: The Interviews*, with Dixon writing and directing each episode. In her comic *M.I.S.//ing*, Dixon combines science fiction and interoffice politics. Having wondered what the people who handle computer needs do during their off time, she imagined a group of IT techs fighting alien threats from the office basement. The comic also functions as a medium to comment on race, gender, and sexuality.

"BEING INDIE TAKES CARE OF MOST OF WHAT PEOPLE THINK OF AS WRITER'S BLOCK. I ONLY WRITE WHEN I HAVE SOMETHING TO SAY. WHEN I'M DONE I SWITCH."

Dixon's series all feature African American characters in both forefront and supporting roles. By focusing on nontraditional superheroes, Dixon shows that people of color have important things to say about society and the human condition. She often works in the manga style, which she sees as particularly empowering for people of color because its open-ended format allows for longer, more complex stories where situations are not always wrapped up in a single issue.

Dixon distributes her comics through Tumble Creek Press, which she founded in 2007, and by owning her own work, she joins a short list of women and an even shorter list of women of color who have maintained the rights to their own stories.

While running a business, establishing collaborations, and maintaining creative control of her stories, Dixon also continually produces new work, including *Five Nations,* a chapter book featuring diverse girls as heroes.

As an African American writer and comic book company proprietor in a predominantly white industry, Dixon is changing the face of comic creators and publishers. She shows that there is room for people of color to be the authors of their own stories.

# EASTON, BRANDON M.

- Born in Baltimore, MD
- Ithaca College, BS in sociology, 1997
- Boston University, MFA in fine arts, 2001
- City University of New York, MA in secondary social studies education, 2005
- Educator, writer, and screenwriter
- Creator of *ShadowLaw*

Brandon Easton is best known for his work on the animated reboot of *ThunderCats*. He wrote episode no. 24 of the television series, which combines aspects of Western and Japanese animation. He also the first writer in the Western world to script a *Vampire Hunter D* comic, based on the Japanese horror franchise.

As a writer of color, Easton often raises the issues of race and discrimination in the comic book industry. His articles regularly address sociological issues, including the problems faced by writers of color. A disciple of Stephen Geller, the Hugo Award–winning screenwriter, Easton also contributes to the panel The Writer's Journey for struggling screenwriters.

Easton's early writing career started with writing for the *Boston Herald* and *Crashpad* magazine. Dreamwave Productions provided his first paid writing job in 2002, where he wrote a supernatural martial arts comic titled *Arkanium*. After spending a few years as a public school teacher in New York City, he moved to Los Angeles for screenwriting, where he has been writing for comics and television ever since.

As an author, he has written many comic books such as *Roboy*, *The Joshua Run*, *Shadowlaw*, and a biographical novel on André the Giant. Out of these, *Shadowlaw*, a graphic novel discussing organized religion through the lens of supernatural creatures, gained widespread popularity. It received coverage in a variety of outlets and publications, including *Ain't It Cool News*, *Wired*, *Forbes*, and *USA Today*.

Easton has provided writing services to Warner Bros. and Studio 4°C. He was also a guest writer for New Paradigm Studios and has worked for the international franchise *Armarauders* from Mecha Workshop. He signed a contract with the St. Louis–based company Lion Forge Comics for a multivolume graphic novel in 2012.

Easton has also written, produced, and directed the documentary *Brave New Souls: Black Sci-Fi and Fantasy Writers of the 21st Century*, which showcases genre publishing, Hollywood, and the comic book industry.

Easton has also conducted a series of interviews with acclaimed writers such as Tony Puryear, Hannibal Tabu, Nnedi Okorafor, Geoffrey Thorne, Erika Alexander, and N. K. Jemisin.

Easton has received many awards and honors. He was a nominee for the Eisner Comic Industry Award for One Shot or Best Single Issue in 2014, and received a Disney-ABC Writing Program grant in 2015. He was also a semifinalist in Project Stargazer, a NASA competition for discovering sci-fi writers of color, during the Hollywood Black Film Festival in 2013. Easton also received three Glyph awards, including Best Writer, Story of the Year, and Fan Award at the 2013 East Coast Black Age of Comics Convention.

# EVANS, ORRIN CROMWELL

Orrin Cromwell Evans made history as the first Black publisher of comic books.

He began his writing career at age seventeen when he began work for a small sports publication, *The Sportsman's Magazine*. Soon thereafter, he moved on to writing for *The Philadelphia Tribune*, which is the oldest African American newspaper in the country.

> **(Sept. 5, 1902–Aug. 6, 1971)**
> - **Born in Steelton, PA**
> - **Journalist and comic publisher**
> - **Founded and published *All-Negro Comics***

In 1929, Evans married Florence E. Baugh, a teacher. By the 1930s, he was hired by *The Philadelphia Record* and joined an otherwise entirely white newspaper staff. At the *Record*, Evans became the first Black reporter to cover general assignments for a large, daily metropolitan newspaper in the United States. Yet his presence as a journalist was not always readily accepted. For example, in 1932, famed aviator Charles Lindbergh once refused to begin a press conference until Evans was removed from the room.

As a journalist in Philadelphia, Evans often wrote about social injustice. In 1944, he wrote a series of articles in the *Record* about segregation in the armed forces, which eventually helped end the practice in the United States. However, Evans's investigative reporting on racial segregation in the US military during wartime also resulted in numerous death threats for Evans and his family.

Shortly after World War II, in addition to his continuous work with *The Philadelphia Record*, Evans's writing began appearing in the *Chicago De-*

Image courtesy of Professor W. Foster

*fender* and the NAACP's *Crisis* magazine, two publications that focused on social issues affecting Blacks across the country. In 1947, the *Record* was hit by a labor strike. Rather than negotiate, its management decided to close the business, leaving Evans, among many others, out of work.

According to *Time* magazine, as he walked the picket line during this strike, Evans thought about a common complaint from Blacks about the comic book industry – that they were often ridiculed and their everyday life was distorted in comics drawn by white men.

Seeing the potential of comic books as a popular medium with which to reach more readers than he did as a journalist, Evans decided to develop a comic to get more accurate, positive portrayals of African Americans in the hands of more people. He was determined that his new comic book should have high moral and educational standards while not including the Black stereotypes common to that era. He joined forces with his former editor at the *Record*, Harry T. Saylor, among several other colleagues, to launch the first issue of *All-Negro Comics*. As a result, in 1947, Evans became the first Black publisher of comic books.

*All-Negro Comics* was the first comic to be drawn and written exclusively by Black artists. It was also the first comic book to focus entirely on Black characters. The cover price was fifteen cents, quite expensive for a comic during that era, when the price of almost all other comic books was ten cents.

The forty-eight-page anthology book contained entirely original content. In an era in which most Black comic book characters were racist caricatures, *All-Negro Comics* contained action-adventure stories with heroic Black characters like Ace Harlem, a skilled police detective, and Lion Man, a scientist dispatched by the United Nations to watch over the African coastline. According to the issue's introduction, Evans intended for Ace Harlem to dramatically point out the "contributions of thousands of fearless, intelligent Negro police officers engaged in a constant fight against crime in the United States." The book issue also contained humorous tales like "The Little Dew Dillies" and "Sugarfoot."

On the inside cover, a photo of Evans appeared along with a letter to the reader describing the publication as "another milestone in the splendid history of Negro journalism." He also noted that he planned to include a monthly historical calendar as a recurring feature in future issues of the comic to highlight and celebrate important people and events in black history.

However, *All-Negro Comics* ceased publication after its first issue. A second issue of *All-Negro Comics* was reportedly prepared, but it was never printed. Newsprint vendors refused to sell to Evans, and the series was abandoned. While no information about the press run or distribution remains, the comic was likely distributed outside of the Philadelphia area. Major publishers were influenced by the independent publication and briefly began publishing titles targeted at Black audiences like Fawcett's *Negro Romance* and Parents Magazine Press's *Negro Heroes*.

Soon after the end of *All-Negro Comics*, Evans returned to the field of journalism. As a reporter for the *Chester (PA) Times*, in 1953 he was the first Black journalist to be named foreign and national wire news editor. He eventually became the city editor for the *Chester Times*, with dozens of white reporters and correspondents working under his leadership. He also worked at the publication's successor, the *Delaware County Daily Times*, before he joined the staff of *The Philadelphia Bulletin* in 1962. At *The Bulletin*, Evans covered the city's government as well as the civil rights movement.

In 1966, Orrin Cromwell Evans received the Inter Urban League of Pennsylvania Achievement Award. *The New York Times* noted that he covered more National Urban League and NAACP annual conventions than any other reporter. When he died in 1971, Temple University established the Orrin C. Evans Memorial Scholarship awarded to minority undergraduates studying journalism.

Evans created a legacy as an award-winning journalist who covered stories and events that many others did not have the courage or perspective to cover. With *All-Negro Comics*, he also broke down a barrier in the comic book industry by challenging the status quo and providing meaningful representation of heroic Black characters. For his outstanding contribution to comics history, Evans was inducted into the Will Eisner Hall of Fame in 2014.

# FIELDER, TIM

**Sept. 2, 1966– )**
- **Born in Clarksdale, MS**
- **Jackson State University, School of Visual Arts, and New York University**
- **Cartoonist, illustrator, animator, concept designer, and instructor**
- **Creator of *Matty's Rocket***

Tim Fielder is among the early practitioners of Afrofuturism in sequential art. His thirty-year career in science fiction imagery includes comics, film storyboarding, animation, and illustration.

Tim Fielder was brought up on a diet of Marvel, DC, and underground comics as well as science fiction and action films. As a young artist, he received unfaltering support from his parents and brothers, and when he relocated to New York City during his teen years, he was encouraged to move away from the all-white cast of characters he had been accustomed to drawing. From that point on, Fielder chose to feature predominately Black characters in his work, heroes and villains alike.

In 1993, Tim Fielder created the comic book series *Matty's Rocket*. When the initial incarnation of *Matty's Rocket* hit a roadblock at DC Comics, Fielder found work as a freelance artist for Marvel Music, a division of Marvel Comics. Before the division folded, Fielder completed his graphic novel *Dr. Dre: Man With a Cold, Cold Heart*. He also created the concept design for the aborted Parliament Funkadelic sci-fi film *The Mothership Connection*. These three projects cemented Fielder's position as one of the nation's pioneers of Afrofuturism.

Fielder's next push was into animation, game design, and instruction. Revisiting concepts from earlier parts of his career, Fielder resurrected *Matty's Rocket* and transformed it into an animated web series and comic book series for Dieselfunk Studios. Additionally, his work was extended into a platform called The Dieselfunk Show, which he founded with his twin brother, Jim. This venue showcases a new form of digital journalism with graphics referred to as "glogging."

Ever prolific, Fielder remains busy. While teaching classes at institutions such as New York University and the New York Film Academy, his additional activities include touring the country as a public speaker and teacher of comic art and creating new content for Dieselfunk Studios. He was also the first plein-air artist to capture the White House via tablet.

Fielder lives in New York City with his three children and his wife Melanie Maria Goodreaux-Fielder, an actor, writer, and playwright.

## FITZGERALD, BERTRAM A.

As a young man growing up in Harlem in the 1940s, Bertram Fitzgerald's love for reading grew out of his interest in comic books. One particularly influential series was *Classics Illustrated*, which introduced young readers to canonical works in literature such as *Moby Dick* and *The Last of the Mohicans* through the comic book format.

(Nov. 6, 1932– )
- **Born in Harlem, NY**
- **Brooklyn College, accounting, 1953**
- **Publisher of *Golden Legacy* educational comics**

While the books were easy to read and filled with exciting adventures, they were not without problems. When reading *Uncle Tom's Cabin*, Fitzgerald was bothered by the images of African Americans in the comic book, particularly the men. He found the happy-go-lucky servant character of Uncle Tom to be an unfair representation of Black manhood, completely uncharacteristic of the Black men he knew growing up in Harlem.

The negative portrayals of African Americans presented in *Uncle Tom's Cabin* and other *Classics Illustrated* books led Fitzgerald to turn away from comic books. Now a teen in late-1940s New York, he turned his attention to reading historical biographies. When reading biographies of people of color such as Alexandre Pushkin and Alexander Dumas, he noticed that, while their contributions to the literary world were well established, there was very little information on their racial identity. This led Fitzgerald to start thinking about writing and publishing his own comic book devoted to an accurate and truthful account of the lives of African American historical figures.

The idea stayed in the back of Bertram's mind as he entered the air force in the 1950s and attained a degree in accounting. While working as an accountant for the New York State Department of Taxation and Finance, Fitzgerald decided to act on the idea by becoming a comic book publisher. In 1966, he created the Fitzgerald Publishing Company and began to publish the *Classics Illustrated*–influenced series he named *Golden Legacy*.

The first *Golden Legacy* book Fitzgerald published was on Toussaint L'Ouverture and the birth of Haiti. Later editions included *The Saga of Harriet Tubman: The Moses of Her People, Crispus Attucks and the Minutemen, The Life of Benjamin Banneker,* and *The Life of Matthew Henson.*

With *Golden Legacy*, Bertram Fitzgerald intended to educate young African American readers about their history and culture. By using the comic book format, he captured the reader's interest with colorful illustrations and compelling artwork.

Publishing *Golden Legacy* created two major challenges for Fitzgerald: printing and distribution. Initially, Fitzgerald used account executives to sell ads for the series, hoping to cover the cost of production that way. However, these commission men frequently kept the money they received from the businesses and made no mention of their "mistake" to Fitzgerald, putting the publication of the book in jeopardy.

Image courtesy of Professor W. Foster

Fitzgerald soon turned away from commission men and toward corporate sponsorship. By the 1970s, Bertram had brokered a deal with the Coca-Cola Company: in return for a full-page ad on the back cover of the comic book, Coca-Cola would print and distribute *Golden Legacy* to local schools, libraries, and African American organizations without charge.

As *Golden Legacy* gained increasing attention in the Black community, Bertram was able to broker advertising deals with companies such as Exxon, McDonald's, A&P, and Woolworth. Subsequent titles included *Black Cowboys*, *Joseph Cinqué and the Amistad Mutiny*, *The Life of Martin Luther King Jr.*, and *Ancient African Kingdoms*. In total, Bertram Fitzgerald published sixteen issues of *Golden Legacy*.

Bertram Fitzgerald and his *Golden Legacy* series hold an important place in the history of Black comics. By featuring dignified images of important men and women, the comic subverted racial stereotypes and educated young readers about Black contributions to history. It also helped lay a foundation for the educational comic format that would flourish in later decades.

# FOSTER, WILLIAM, H., III.

(Apr. 1953– )
- **Born in Philadelphia, PA**
- **University of Massachusetts, BA in journalism and mass communications, 1975**
- **Wesleyan University, MA, 1986**
- **Writer, educator, researcher, and comics historian**
- **Author of *Looking for a Face Like Mine***

William H. Foster is the author of fifteen books and ten plays, including *Looking for a Face Like Mine*, a collection of essays and interviews about racial stereotyping in American comics. Published in 2005, it is the culmination of decades of research on African American representation in comics.

Both of Foster's parents encouraged his writing from an early age. His first published work, a witty poem about what kids do when they get out of school for the summer, appeared in *Judge* magazine when he was eleven years old.

After his graduate studies, William Foster took an English professorship at Naugatuck Valley Community College while continuing to pub-

## DID YOU KNOW?

Professor William H. Foster III created, with his friend, artist David Quintana, the first African American/Native American superhero team in the comic book, *ANUBIS*. It was also the first comic book created by an African American and a Native American.

lish poems, plays, essays, and editorials. In the 1980s, Foster became interested in comics once more, but this time his interest was scholarly: he began collecting and studying comics, looking for Black characters. This took his career in a new direction, as he began writing articles and giving talks on the evolution of African American representation in comics. He put together a traveling exhibit titled *The Changing Image of Blacks in Comics*, which was displayed at the 1998 Comic Arts Conference at Comic-Con International and the Museum of Comic and Cartoon Art in New York.

In Foster's seminal work *Looking for a Face Like Mine*, he notes the evolution of depictions of people of color from clownish caricatures to real people, providing examples both well known and obscure, dating from the 1920s to the 2000s. His second book on comics, *Dreaming of a Face Like Ours*, was published in 2010.

In addition to his research on the depiction of African American characters, Foster has also published about the underground comix movement that began in the 1960s and is known for its satirical treatment of controversial topics including sex, race, drugs, and violence.

William H. Foster has presented at numerous international conferences on books and media analysis. In 2006, he was an invited panelist for both the Harlem Book Fair and the Studio Museum of Harlem. He was also appointed to the editorial board of *The International Journal of Comic Art* in 2008.

In 2014, he served on the six-member judge panel for the Eisner Awards, the most prestigious in the industry. The same year, he accepted the Hall of Fame Award for Orrin C. Evans *(see Evans, Orrin Cromwell)*, who published the first and only issue of *All-Negro Comics* in 1947. His body of work serves to preserve the legacies of many comics creators whose names would otherwise have been forgotten.

Image courtesy of Professor W. Foster

# GIBBS, SHAWNEÉ AND SHAWNELLE (THE GIBBS SISTERS)

Shawneé and Shawnelle Gibbs are the creators of several films and animated series, as well as the coauthors of webcomic *Fashion Forward*.

**(Born c. 1982– )**
- **Raised in Oakland, CA**
- **University of Southern California, film**
- **Writers, directors, television producers, and animators**
- **Creators of the webcomics *Fashion Forward* and *The Invention of E.J. Whitaker***

Self-professed geeks, the Gibbs sisters always had an interest in cartooning and writing. Heavily influenced by both 1990s culture depicting strong female characters and the pro-Black movements of the 1960s and 1970s, they sought out opportunities to perfect their skills and spent much of their childhood and high school years drawing and creating stories.

While in college, they began writing and creating their own webtoons and animated shorts. Perhaps the most well-known animated series, *Adopted by Aliens* and *Old Ladies Driving*, gained traction and a dedicated following in the early 2000s. Also during this time, the sisters were garnering accolades for their screenplay *A Star Is Reborn*, earning the University of Southern California Guy Hanks and Marvin Miller Screenwriters Fellowship, a fifteen-week screenwriting workshop designed to deepen participants' understanding of and appreciation for Black history and culture.

In 2010, the Gibbs sisters took their first step in becoming comic writers with their webcomic, *Fashion Forward*. The idea was birthed during a road trip in 2005, when Shawnelle had the idea about a fashionista who could travel through time, garnering inspiration from clothing

> "PART OF OUR MISSION WAS TO TELL STORIES ABOUT YOUNG GIRLS OF COLOR GOING ON ADVENTURES BECAUSE THAT'S SOMETHING THAT WE DIDN'T REALLY SEE GROWING UP. THERE WAS EVERYTHING YOU COULD IMAGINE [ON TV AND IN MOVIES], BUT WE WERE WATCHING SORT OF AS OUTSIDERS. WHAT WE REALLY WANTED TO CREATE WERE MAGICAL AND ADVENTURE-BASED STORIES FOR GIRLS LIKE US."

throughout history to create her own fashion designs. The sisters created the script and reached out to Linda Chung and JM Tolman to illustrate the graphic novel. *Fashion Forward* received an Honorable Mention at the 2013 Hollywood Book Festival.

In addition to comics, the Gibbs sisters have also made films and worked on television productions. They created the short film *Ravishing Raspberry*, which won the Best of Festival Award at the Berkeley Video and Film Festival in 2003. In 2010, they made their directorial debut with *Sule and the Case of the Tiny Sparks*, which won the 2011 Best Animated Short Film Award at the Montreal International Black Film Festival and has since received both national and international acclaim.

In 2014, their screenplay *PrePuptial Agreement* was a finalist at the Lady Filmmakers Festival. They hold producing credits for *X Factor*, *Food Network Star*, *The Ultimate Fighter*, National Geographic's *Wicked Tuna*, and the Emmy Award–winning series *Project Runway* and *Top Chef*. In addition, the sisters have made contributions to Disney's *Wizards of Waverly Place*. The Gibbs sisters are also members of the Writers Guild of America West, the Academy of Television Arts and Sciences, and the Organization of Black Screenwriters.

Image courtesy of Shawneé and Shawnelle Gibbs

In 2016, the sisters set up a successful Kickstarter crowdfunding campaign to finance their second comic series, *The Invention of E.J. Whitaker*. Set in 1901, the indie steampunk comic details the adventures of a young woman who invents a flying machine but has to contend with the sexism of the time.

The Gibbs sisters have been featured in articles in the *Oakland Tribune*, *BET J*, *Graffiti Verité*, *G4*, the *Los Angeles Wave*, and *Essence* magazine.

# GILL, JOEL CHRISTIAN

Artist and writer Joel Christian Gill specializes in graphic novels about little-known Black historical figures. His two graphic nonfiction series, *Strange Fruit* and *Tales of the Talented Tenth*, feature pioneering figures such as Bass Reeves, a Black man who was at one time the most successful federal marshal in US history, and Bessie Stringfield, a female motorcyclist who traversed the country eight times and worked as a civilian courier for the US military during World War II.

**(January 15, 1975– )**
- **Born in Roanoke, VA**
- **Roanoke University, B.A. in fine arts; Boston University, MFA in fine arts**
- **Artist, author, historian, and professor**
- **Creator of *Strange Fruit* and *Tales of the Talented Tenth***

Joel Christian Gill is also an advocate for better incorporation of Black history into mainstream American history. In 2014, Gill founded a popular social media hashtag, #28DaysAreNotEnough, to draw attention to the relegation of Black history to a single month. In an article in the *Huffington Post*, he wrote, "Black people epitomize the rags to riches, bootstrap mentality that is the American mythos. In a few generations, black people went from property to politicians, professors, doctors and lawyers. So, why, as Americans, as patriots, would we celebrate this group of people for a mere 28 (or sometimes 29) days a year?"

*"THIS IS NOT JUST THE HISTORY OF BLACK PEOPLE. THIS IS OUR HISTORY. IT'S AMERICAN HISTORY."*

With their focus on shared American values like freedom from oppression and triumph in the face of adversity, Gill's critically acclaimed graphic novels demonstrate the universality of their individual dramas. His work serves as a rallying cry for younger generations of historians, encouraging current and future scholars to continue his efforts in expanding the historical narrative.

Image courtesy of Joel Christian Gill

Joel Christian Gill has received numerous awards for his work, including Kirkus Reviews's Best Books of 2016 *(Bessie Springfield)*, the Young Adult Library Service Association's Best Book for Teens *(Strange Fruit, Volume 1)* and a 2015 Glyph Award for Best Male Character *(Bass Reeves)*. In 2016, he was featured in *New Hampshire Magazine's* It List and received the Boston University College of Fine Arts Alumni Award. In 2017, Gill spoke at the Black Heritage Trail of New Hampshire's Juneteenth celebration in a panel discussion of art as activism. He currently serves as the chair of visual arts at the New Hampshire Institute for Arts in New Boston, New Hampshire.

Image courtesy of Joel Christian Gill

## GRAHAM, BILLY

Artist Billy Graham is best known for his work on the pioneering series *Black Panther* and *Luke Cage: Hero for Hire*, Marvel's first two forays into stand-alone series featuring Black protagonists.

**(July 1, 1935–1999)**
- **Born in New York, NY**
- **Artist and illustrator**
- **Illustrated the original runs of *Black Panther* and *Luke Cage: Hero for Hire***

As a young comics reader, Graham was particularly fond of early Marvel Comics work produced by Jack Kirby and Stan Lee. While Graham respected their artistry and storytelling, he was troubled by the lack of Black representation in Marvel and other mainstream comics. He resolved then to create his own heroic Black characters and see them distributed on a national scale.

Billy Graham's career as a comic book artist started at Warren Publishing in the 1960s. Not long after Graham was hired, publisher James Warren promoted him to art director, a pioneering move at the time. In Graham, Warren saw both immense potential as an artist and a way to reach out to Black audiences. Under Warren's tutelage, Graham excelled in his new position. His art was featured in two Warren projects: a single issue of the *Creepy* anthology series and the first twelve issues of *Vampirella*.

While Graham's work proved popular with Warren readers, his artistic ambitions remained unfulfilled. In the 1970s, Graham left Warren to work as an artist for Marvel Comics.

While Marvel had introduced Black supporting characters from the early 1960s forward, such as Ororo Munroe (Storm) in Stan Lee's *X-Men*, in the 1970s there were still no African American title characters. Billy Graham worked to usher Marvel toward development of titular series built around Black protagonists.

Graham contributed artwork to all sixteen initial issues of *Luke Cage: Hero for Hire.* As one of Marvel's first Black protagonists, Cage appeared on a recurring basis in a number of ensuing Marvel series. Graham also contributed his artistic talent to the early incarnation of Black Panther, who received his own series in the mid-1970s as a response to *Hero for Hire* readership.

Working on groundbreaking Black protagonists at Marvel Comics afforded the artist an opportunity to fulfill his lifelong ambition. Unlike DC Comics' short-lived *Black Lightning* (1976–77), Black Panther and Luke Cage proved immensely popular with reading audiences. Long after their original runs concluded, the characters continue to fuel contemporary projects like Amazon's live-action series *Luke Cage* and Marvel's upcoming *Black Panther and the Crew*.

The success of Graham's artwork helped incorporate Black voices into mainstream comics and increased the demand for Black title characters from major publishers.

# GRANT, SHAUNA J.

(January 16, 1989– )
- **Born in New York, NY**
- **School of Visual Arts, BFA, 2011**
- **Creator of the webcomic *Princess Love Pon***

Shauna Grant's best-known work is the critically acclaimed biweekly webcomic *Princess Love Pon.* A self-professed "cute expert," Grant specializes in comics and illustrations she describes as soft, cute, round, and colorful. Attracted to manga by the diversity of the art and stories, Grant strives to merge Japanese and American styles in her work.

In the tradition of *shoujo* (girls') manga, *Princess Love Pon* is a magical girl story about a high school student, Lia Sagamore, who becomes the envoy of love. She has to figure out her future and navigate her personal relationships all while protecting the emotional well-being of others from the Dark Queen, a villain who seeks to steal others' hearts.

By combining a predominantly Black cast with the magical girl genre, Grant weds images of traditional femininity, strength, and diversity. As she has pointed out in interviews, media portrayals of women rarely combine strength and femininity, and Black female characters in particular are more often portrayed as cool or intense than cute. In Lia Sagamore, Shauna Grant created the type of Black female character she wants to see more of: a happy, girly person with inner strength.

Image courtesy of Shauna Grant

Image courtesy of Shauna Grant

Magical girls such as Card-captor Sakura or Sailor Moon demonstrate strength, determination, and love for others while facing their problems. By embracing the virtues of femininity, *Princess Love Pon* inspires readers to embrace their gender expression as well as their racial identity.

Beyond *Princess Love Pon*, Grant has created several shorter webcomics in a variety of genres. Her first webcomic was *O'Panda*, which played with the tropes of the superhero genre and with the treatment of female characters in comics. Another webcomic, *Cry Baby*, addressed her struggles with anxiety and depression. In 2016, she planned to do more comics and illustrations dealing with mental illness – a topic that touched her life in several ways and one that she believed was not adequately addressed in the Black community.

In addition to appearing at such venues as the Women in Comics Con, Anime Boston, Katsucon, Youmacon, and Otakon, in 2016 she was also named one of 20 Black Comic Book Creators on the Rise by Comics Alliance. Her work has been featured in the *Comfort Food* zine curated by Lauren Jordan, Glitter Milk Gallery's 2015 *NSFW: A Burlesque Exhibit*, anthologies from Dirty Diamonds, and on variant covers for *Adventure Time* comics and *Cash + Carrie*.

Grant has celebrated the opportunities afforded to emerging artists in digital and self-publishing venues, especially as avenues that made it easier for people of color to get involved in the comics industry, but she has also argued that companies need to hire more diverse creators and not just create more diverse characters. She wants to see more "dark-skinned cuties" in games and more strong and cute Black female leads in comics.

# GRANT, VERNON ETHELBERT

Vernon Grant is remembered both for writing the first English-language manga analysis and for being the first American comic artist to incorporate Japanese illustration techniques into his work. Grant's cartooning life can be divided into two periods: pre-1972, marked prominently by his creation of military cartoons, and post-1973, notable for his philosophical science-fiction series *The Love Rangers*. After spending eight years in Japan, Grant's work was heavily influenced by Japanese manga, particularly the work of Goseki Kojima and Kazuo Koike's *Lone Wolf and Cub* and Mikiya Mochizuki's *The Wild Seven*.

> (Feb. 14, 1935–July 23, 2006)
> - **Born in Cambridge, MA**
> - **US Army, 1958–1967**
> - **Sophia University, BA in Asian studies, 1970**
> - **Writer and cartoonist**
> - **Creator of *The Love Rangers***

As a child, Grant read and was inspired by a range of comics, from *Donald Duck* and *Archie* to *Daredevil, Blackhawk,* and *Bulletman.* He also wrote comic books, which he sold out of a suitcase as a child and out of his locker as a teenager for two cents each. As an adult, he studied the art of *TinTin, The Fabulous Furry Freak Brothers,* Vaughn Bode in *Cavalier* magazine, Robert Crumb, and other underground comix.

Grant served in the U.S. Army as both an enlisted infantryman and commissioned officer. He received basic training at Fort Dix in New Jersey and then trained in Europe as a supply sergeant and studied Japanese and French. He was assigned to the Tokyo Olympics in 1964 as part of the Defense Department's tri-team charged with broadcasting the games worldwide for Armed Forces Radio and Television Service. In 1966, he was awarded the Army Commendation Medal for meritorious service in Japan as deputy information officer and command information officer. He served two tours of duty in Vietnam where, in 1967, he took command of the First Signal Brigade in Saigon, providing security for twenty-three communication sites.

*"I HAD THE TALENT TO SEE THINGS OTHERS DID NOT."*

He was mostly too busy in the army for his comics art, other than creating cartoons for his 1962 class book and some art for a division

Image courtesy of Betsy Grant

banquet. After being discharged in January 1967, Grant became a regular cartoonist for the *Stars and Stripes* newspaper, which featured *Grant's Grunts*. Grant's book of cartoons lampooning battle and life in the Vietnam War, *Stand-By One!* (1969 and 2015), was distributed to the armed forces in the early 1970s. Grant's two-volume graphic novel *The Adventures of Point-Man Palmer and His Girlfriend "Invisible Peppermint": Vietnam to Tokyo R&R* (1970), also distributed to the armed forces in the early 1970s, was a satirical fantasy about military responsibility, which Grant sent to his commanding general to argue for more radios.

While serving in Vietnam, Grant traveled throughout the region on assignment, including his stint with the Tokyo Olympics. He returned to Tokyo in 1968 and stayed through 1973 to attend Sophia University, where he studied contemporary Chinese and Japanese economic history and met his future wife, Betsy Reese. During this time, he wrote a three-part article on *Lone Wolf and Cub* for the *Mainichi Daily News* as part of a potential graduate thesis on manga. This is believed to be not only the first but also a seminal academic consideration of manga to appear in English. He also wrote illustrative and editorial cartoons as well as book and movie reviews for the *Mainichi Daily News*. He later wrote about manga and the elements of tone, setting, culture, and relationships for *The Comics Journal*.

Grant is credited with introducing the manga artistic style to Western comics, using composition angles he saw used by Japanese illustrators but not by American cartoonists. In 1984, he was described as possibly the only American artist who was currently incorporating the Japanese sensibility of style, structure, design, story, and length throughout his work. The influence of manga and contemporary Japanese folk culture came together in Grant's *A Monster is Loose!—in Tokyo* (1972). The premise of the story grew from Grant's understanding of Japanese culture at the time: an affinity for monsters and a curious animosity toward foreigners. He is credited as the first American cartoonist to bring *kaiju* (Japanese monsters or "strange beasts/creatures") to the American market in an English-language book, and he did so at a time when Japanese products and productions were an object of ridicule.

Science fiction was also a major source of inspiration for Grant's work. He read a lot of pulp fiction, especially *Buck Rogers* and *Andy Gump and the Lost City of Gold*. His own science-fiction creation, *The Love Rangers*, was shaped by his experiences in Japan; his exposure to sci-fi, including the *Star Trek* television show; and his knowledge of military technology. *The Love Rangers* were a racially mixed spaceship crew of robots and genetically engineered men and women whose mission was to bring peace to crises through the use of love. The interplanetary stories occasionally featured devices that were developed for military use ten to fifteen years after their appearance in the comic. Although the self-published series was critically acclaimed by the *Boston Phoenix*, *The Comics Journal*, and the *Comic Buyers' Guide*, it lasted only seven of a planned twenty issues between 1977 and 1988.

Grant never supported himself completely from comics work. He worked cautiously with Japanese and military presses while in Asia and frequently self-published his work, creating, copying, stapling, selling, and shipping his comics directly to consumers. Grant thought that if his work was good enough, becoming a full-time cartoonist would happen naturally, but he learned that good self-promotion was key. *The Love Rangers* gained its audience mostly through word of mouth. Grant would exhibit illustrations at the New England Science Fiction Convention (now Boskone), where lauded speculative fiction writer Harlan Ellison purchased one of his drawings.

A lifelong athlete, Grant attributed much of his creativity to running. He was a marathoner who ran over 3,500 miles per year for more than twenty-five years. Grant got a lot of his story ideas when he was running, which he would put on paper later. He ran hundreds of road races and thirty-three marathons. He died in Cambridge, Massachusetts, of complications following a heart attack during a daily run.

In 2014, Grant's wife, Betsy, began republishing some of his work, especially his Vietnam War comics and cartoons, first in a memoir of Grant's life and then with a rerelease of his army cartoon book *Stand-By One!*, which have been the focus of exhibits, talks, and news features in Massachusetts, North Carolina, and Wisconsin. Bhob Stewart, writer, editor, filmmaker, and cartoonist for EC Comics, was a friend and a fan of Grant and his biggest supporter inside the comics industry. Stewart was instrumental in Betsy Reese Grant's efforts to market her late husband's work and to publish his biography.

Works by Vernon Grant are housed in the Comic Art Collection of Michigan State University and were exhibited at the Cambridge Public Library in 2007 and 2008. The governor of Massachusetts and the mayor of Cambridge, in conjunction with the Cambridge African American Heritage Alliance, declared July 28, 2016, "Vernon E. Grant Day" in recognition of Grant's contributions to the world of cartooning.

# GREASON, WALTER DAVID

Historian Walter Greason studies the intersection of race and the American economy. His published work includes both academic texts *The Path to Freedom* and *Suburban Erasure* and Afrocentric fiction such as *Communion*, "Forced Passage," and "We Play Evil Games."

> **(1973– )**
> - **Born in Freehold Borough, NJ**
> - **Villanova University, BA in history, 1995**
> - **Temple University, PhD in history, 2004**
> - **Historian and professor**
> - **Author of *The Path to Freedom* and *Suburban Erasure***

Greason's educational path was largely determined from his first day of primary school, when he and his mother planned his future pursuit of a PhD. His role as a teacher began even before graduating high school; while earning a diploma in humanities at Ranney School in New Jersey, Greason helped prepare lesson plans and conduct research for John Yale, the chair of the History Department.

While attending Villanova University as an undergraduate, Greason was certified to teach Africana studies, peace and justice studies, English, and philosophy. He also co-instructed politics and philosophy of hip-hop with Dr. Maghan Keita.

An active voice in historiographical literature, Greason published *The Path to Freedom: Black Families in New Jersey* in 2010, which details the defeat of Jim Crow segregation through the eyes of influential African American families. In 2014, Greason published his second monograph, *Suburban Erasure: How the Suburbs Ended the Civil Rights Movement in New Jersey*, which tracks the ways that global suburbs undermined racial justice activists after 1965, highlighting the stories of prominent individuals such as Lenora Walker McKay and Reverend Caleb Oates.

Greason has also published two historical fiction stories, "Forced Passage" and "We Play Evil Games." The first former follows a young man named Miguel as he takes a train into town. By showing Miguel in a variety of interactions – his passive engagement with a politicized classmate, in confrontation with another passenger, having lunch with a female friend – Greason highlights the difficulty of creating identity in an environment that demands constant code-switching. Published two years later, Greason's "We Play Evil Games" challenges the prison-industrial complex through an Afrofuturist lens. In this piece, prisons have transitioned from places of proposed rehabilitation to institutions profiting from gladiator-style games between inmates.

*Communion*, first published in 1997, marks another Greason foray into sci-fi Afrocentric literature. It was influenced by his correspondence with Christopher Priest, writer for the graphic novel *Black Panther*, as well as with Dwayne McDuffie, best known for creating the superhero Static Shock.

Greason most recently published *The American Economy*, an anthology of works that argues for a shift in conventions for understanding economic change between 1750 and 2010. In this capacity, much of Greason's work follows a similar line of thought, encouraging academics, professionals, and interested citizens to challenge their existing knowledge of race and the economy.

Walter Greason has taught at numerous colleges and institutions over the course of his career, including Drexel University and Ursinus College. At the time of this writing, Greason serves as a lecturer in Monmouth University's Department of History and Anthropology, where he instructs courses on industrialization, suburbanization, and the economic analysis of slavery.

# GREENE, SANFORD

**(Jan. 1, 1972– )**
- **Born in Greeleyville, SC**
- **Benedict College**
- **Artist, graphic designer, and illustrator**
- **Illustrated *Power Man and Iron Fist: Heroes for Hire***

An artist and graphic designer, Sanford Greene is known for his contributions to superhero comics such as *Superman*, *Spider-Man*, and the 2016 reboots of *Luke Cage* and *Iron Fist*. As one of the most successful and prolific Black artists of the twenty-first century, Greene's success stands as a testament to the powerful influence that preceding Black artists offered Greene from an early age.

Like many of the authors featured in this volume, Sanford Greene grew up as a devoted fan of comic books during one of the medium's creative peaks. Throughout the 1970s and 1980s, Greene grew up on the Black protagonists offered by pioneering artists like Marvel Comics' Billy Graham (*Black Panther*, *Luke Cage: Hero for Hire*), and DC Comics' Tony

Isabella (*Black Lightning*). Exposure to comic book art provided Greene access to a variety of different art styles and influences at an early age.

After his undergraduate studies, Greene quickly gained success as a graphic designer with an eye for culturally authentic Black representation. His projects included popular advertising campaigns for subsidiaries of Disney, Fox, MTV, Nickelodeon, Nintendo, and Sega as well as box art for an assortment of video game publishers. Greene also designed an array of iconic LP covers for Black musicians such as David Banner, MF Doom, and multiple members of the Wu-Tang Clan.

Greene left advertising to pursue a career as a comic book artist for the major comic publishers, starting at Dark Horse Comics with a film adaptation of Tim Burton's *Planet of the Apes* (2006). Later, he was one of the first Black artists to work on established franchises with white protagonists such as *Spider-Man* and *Superman*.

As of 2016, one of Greene's most recognizable projects was the reconceptualization of Marvel Comics' successful *Power Man* and *Iron Fist* series of the 1980s. Titled *Power Man and Iron Fist: Heroes for Hire* (2016–), Greene's recent work with Marvel Comics imbues warmth into the comparatively somber and stoic aesthetic that characterized the initial run of *Luke Cage: Hero for Hire* (1973–74). His illustrations downplay the original series' reliance on violence and urban decay with a lush color palette and an increased degree of humor. With a more accessible tone than the intentionally edgy, predictably explicit content of preceding efforts such as *CAGE* (1993–95) and *Cage MAX* (2000), Greene's revitalization of *Luke Cage* distances the franchise from harmful stereotypes.

Greene is currently collaborating with Viacom Media to produce a series of digital graphic novels, along with a semi-autobiographical digital graphic novel through MTV. He is also collaborating with Marvel Comics to illustrate a series of children's books to be published in 2017.

Greene's artwork is routinely displayed in a touring exhibit sponsored by Benedict College. The exhibit features a thorough overview of Greene's work, from advertisements and album covers to box art and comics illustration. He presently resides in Columbia, South Carolina, and interacts regularly with art students at Benedict College.

In June of 2017, Sanford Greene announced his first creator-owned series, *1000*, which he described as a Final Fantasy–style world with contemporary tensions and politics. Cowritten with Chuck Brown, the comic premiered on LINE Webtoon, a vertically scrolling webcomic platform, the same year.

# GREVIOUX, KEVIN

**(Sept. 9, 1962– )**
- **Born in Chicago, IL**
- **Howard University, BS in microbiology, 1987**
- **Comics writer, screenwriter, and actor**
- **Author of *I, Frankenstein* and *ZMD: Zombies of Mass Destruction***

Kevin Grevioux is a comics writer with numerous credits at Marvel Comics. He has also written or cowritten several original comics, including *Underworld, ZMD: Zombies of Mass Destruction,* and *I, Frankenstein.*

Kevin Grevioux was born in Chicago and grew up in Bloomington, Minnesota, also spending time in New Jersey, Oklahoma, Alaska, and Massachusetts. When he was about five years old, Grevioux became interested in science. Although he was too young to read, he was fascinated by an encyclopedia that had pictures of dinosaurs and outer space, and that in turn led him to become a fan of science fiction, particularly movies such as *Godzilla* and television shows such as *Lost in Space* and *Ultraman.*

He also read comics, starting with *Superman* as a young boy and then moving on to Marvel comics; he particularly liked *The Fantastic Four* and *The Hulk* because their main characters were scientists. As an adult, Grevioux described himself as a "Marvel zombie" (an obsessive Marvel Comics fan) and amassed a collection of more than 10,000 Marvel Comics.

As an undergraduate at Howard University, Grevioux studied microbiology, chemistry, and psychology. He then entered a master's program in genetic engineering, also doing a stint as a research assistant at the National Cancer Institute at the National Institutes of Health in

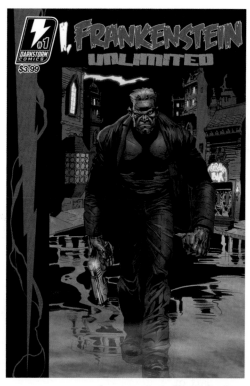

Image courtesy of Kevin Grevioux

Bethesda, Maryland. At the same time, he was taking classes in screen-writing and cinematography, and he decided that his prospects would be better in the film industry than in research. Before his first year of graduate school was over, he moved to Los Angeles to start a career as a writer.

About a month after Grevioux moved to Los Angeles, a friend got him a small role as a palace guard in Michael Jackson's music video *Remember the Time*. His first credited work as an actor was as the "Bulky Robber" in the 1993 video game *Sim City*. Throughout the 1990s he is credited for a number of small parts as thugs and police officers in a variety of movies and television series. He also had some larger roles such as Leon Spinks in the television movie *Don King: Only in America*.

In 1994, while working as a prop assistant on the film *Stargate*, Grevioux met Len Wiseman, who was an extra in the film. They became friends and collaborators, and together they came up with the concept for the 2003 film *Underworld*, a story about a human and a vampire caught up in a war between vampires and werewolves. The concept of lovers caught between two warring clans was based not only on Shakespeare's *Romeo and Juliet* but also on Grevioux's own experiences with interracial dating. He and Wiseman shared the writing credits for the film with two other writers; Wiseman directed it, and Grevioux played the character of Raze.

The success of *Underworld* led to several more films in the franchise, including two that Grevioux coproduced, *Underworld: Evolution* (2006) and *Underworld: Rise of the Lycans* (2009), as well as other short and full-length films and a video game. It also led Grevioux to comics: his first comics credit is as one of the writers of IDW's *Underworld* comic, published in 2003.

Grevioux credits Paul Levitz, the former president of DC Comics, with giving him valuable advice about becoming a comics writer; the two met at Comic-Con International in San Diego one year and had a conversation that helped Grevioux plan his next steps.

In 2006, he launched Astounding Studios, which focused on all-ages comics, and DarkStorm Studios, a mature line, both published by Alias Enterprises. Alias was founded in 2005 by Brett Burner and Mike Miller as a publisher of all-ages and Christian comics. Grevioux met Miller on an internet comics message board, and several years later, when Miller was starting up Alias, Miller introduced Grevioux to Burner and invited him to publish there. Although all-ages comics were not a big part of the industry at the time, Grevioux was inspired by two well-known creators, Scott Christian Sava (*The Dreamland Chronicles*) and Mike Kunkel (*Herobear and the Kid*), who showed him some properties they were developing for animation. Grevioux also felt that the comics industry was moving away from children and wanted to create stories that were accessible to them. In 2006, Alias published *The Hammer Kid* #0, *Valkyries* #1 and #2, *Guardian Heroes* #1, and *Toy Box* #1, and under the DarkStorm imprint, *Alivs Rex* #1 and *Astounding Heroes Starring The Vindicators* #0. No other issues of these comics ever appeared; Alias transitioned to a Christian publishing company in late 2006 and most of its comics went to other publishers.

Most of Grevioux's comics writing from 2007 to 2009 was for Marvel, including *New Warriors* (2007–09), *Adam: Legend of the Blue Marvel* (2009), and stories in *Spider-Man Family* #5 (2007) and #8 (2008), *The Phantom Annual* #2 (2008), *What If? Civil War* #1 (2008), and *Young Avengers Presents* #5 (2008). During that time he also wrote *Sista Samurai* #0 (2008, Ape Entertainment) and *ZMD: Zombies of Mass Destruction*, a six-issue series created by DarkStorm and published by Red 5 Comics from 2008 to 2010. He continued his acting and screenwriting career, and he wrote the two-part *Underworld: Rise of the Lycans* (2008, IDW Publishing), which was based on the movie. In May 2009, Grevioux was included in *Ebony* magazine's Ebony Power list of the 150 most influential Black Americans as a result of his work on *Underworld*.

From 2010 to 2017, most of Grevioux's comics writing was short stories for anthologies or multistory issues. He contributed stories to *JSA 80-Page Giant* #1 (2010), *Batman 80-Page Giant* #1 (2010), *Wetworks: Mutations* #1, and *DCU Holiday Special 2010* (2011), all at DC; *What If? Secret Invasion* #1 (2010), *Age of Heroes* #3 (2010), *Breaking into Comics the Marvel Way* (2010), *Fear Itself: The Home Front* #4 (2011), and *The Amazing Spider-Man* #700.5 for Marvel; and *Grunts: War Stories* (2010), published by Arcana Comics and IDW's 2012 and 2015 *Zombies vs. Robots* omnibuses. His one continuing story for Marvel during this time was *Spider-Man vs. Vampires*, a three-part digital series published in 2010.

In 2013, Grevioux also published a graphic novel, *I, Frankenstein*, through his own DarkStorm Comics. The book was adapted into the 2014 film of the same name by Lakeshore Entertainment, the producer of the *Underworld* films. Grevioux played the role of Dekar in the film.

In 2017, Grevioux launched a new DarkStorm series with *Underworld: Blood Wars* #1 and began writing *The Odyssey of the Amazons* for DC Comics.

Image courtesy of Kevin Grevioux

# Guillory, Rob

(June 2, 1982– )
- **Born in Lafayette, LA**
- **University of Louisiana**
- **Artist**
- **Cocreator of *Chew***

Rob Guillory is a comic artist best known for illustrating the independent comic *Chew* (Image Comics), which ran from 2009 to 2016. Cowritten with writer John Laymon, the series follows a Food and Drug Administration agent who receives psychic impressions from the food he ingests. A *New York Times* best seller, it was both a critical and popular success; *Chew* was nominated for two Harvey Awards and two Eagle Awards, and won an Eisner Award for Best New Series in 2010. In an interview with *My Spilt Milk*, Guillory recalls the development of his signature illustration style. In college, he gave a friend two work samples, one in the mainstream superhero genre and the other more sketchy and expressive.

"I really wanted him to respond to the superhero thing, which was really self-important and taking itself too seriously. He didn't care about that and talked about the goofy, cartoony thing. I didn't understand that at all. That thing was way too easy to do and was just me goofing around."

> **"MY CHARACTERS TEND TO BE VERY EXPRESSIVE AND OVER THE TOP, WHICH HELPS CONVEY STORY WITHOUT WORDS."**

Having learned where his strengths lie, Guillory now focuses on storytelling and characterization. "My characters tend to be very expressive and over the top, which helps convey story without words." He also often includes visual jokes, sometimes slipping them into the background of employers' comics to see if they make it to the final product.

A prolific artist, Rob Guillory's other works include *Conan the Cimmerian* (Dark Horse Comics), *Dynamo 5 Holiday Special 2010* (Image Comics), *The Li'l Depressed Boy* (Image Comics), *Teenage Mutant Ninja Turtles* (2011) #6 (IDW Publishing), *Skullkickers* (2010) *TPB* vol. 04 (Image Comics), *The Walking Dead 100 Project* (Hero Initiative – Image Comics), *Peter Panzerfaust* (2012) #11 (variant) (Shadowline – Image Comics), *Burn the Orphanage: Born to Lose* (2013) #1 (cover B) (Image Comics), *Mars Attacks the Real Ghostbusters* (2013) One-Shot (IDW Publishing), *Adventure Time* (2012) – 2013 Summer Special (cover C)

*KaBOOM!* (BOOM! Studios | BOOM! Entertainment, Inc.), *Quantum & Woody* (2013) #4 (Rob Guillory variant) (Valiant Entertainment), and *Samurai Jack* (2013) #1 "Samurai Jack and the Threads of Time" (IDW Publishing). As an undergraduate, he also contributed to the independent comic anthologies *Teddy Scares* and *PopGun*.

## CREATIVE TIPS

As a newcomer to the creative industry, it can be hard to know when to persevere and when to throw in the towel. Rob Guillory advocates creating a predetermined timeline for success.

"When I began my career, my wife and I made a deal. She had a good 'real' job that could potentially keep us afloat, so she agreed to be the primary breadwinner for five years while I pursued comics full time. And if, at the end of that five years, I hadn't made any progress, I would get a real job, we'd begin our family, and I would still do comics on a more part-time basis. That way, if I wasn't right for comics, I wouldn't put life on hold forever while trying to break into comics. And thank God, it all worked out."

# HARRINGTON, OLLIE

Ollie Harrington was a highly respected and prolific editorial cartoonist during the 1930s to the early 1990s.

When Harrington was in grade school, his family moved to the South Bronx. They lived on a block-long African American enclave surrounded by families of first-generation European immigrants. This multiethnic community exposed him to people of varying backgrounds: some with respect for Black culture, others less so. While still a child, Harrington turned to cartooning to cope with the racial bias he experienced from white adults. He found catharsis by illustrating his bigoted grade school teacher, Ms. McCoy, and a brutal white neighborhood policeman suffering a series of terrible fates.

(Feb. 14, 1912–Nov. 2, 1995)
- **Born in Valhalla, NY**
- **Yale University, BFA, 1940**
- **Editorial and humor cartoonist, painter, journalist, educator, and activist**
- **Creator of *Dark Laughter***

Discovering that he had natural talent, the practice of cartooning neighborhood characters became a habit. By high school, Harrington had created his own newspaper with his drawings and articles. Once, when the paper made reference to "Jewtown," Ms. Linksy, a supportive white teacher, pointed out the derogatory term. This prompted Harrington to make associations with hateful language against his own race, as well as with his mother's Jewish background.

Harrington graduated from DeWitt Clinton High School in 1929 and soon after moved to Harlem, the heart of the Black cultural renaissance. While doing odd jobs and searching for employment opportunities, Harrington took classes in drawing and painting after earning a scholarship to attend the National Academy of Design. The field of cartooning was still young, particularly in the Black press, and careers for Black cartoonists were rare. He sold his first editorial cartoons to the *New York State Contender* and the *New York National News* in 1932. They called for the recognition of Black voting power in the impending presidential election and the community's power to resist white aggression. Harrington also sold short-lived humor comic strips called *Boop and Scoop* to the *Pittsburgh Courier* that year.

In May 1935, Harrington was hired as a regular contributor by the *New York Amsterdam News* with his strip *Dark Laughter*, and later *Pages from Negro History*, a series of illustrated vignettes. On his first day, a full-page advertisement boasted of Harrington along with a group of talented writers and cartoonists. Included among them were E. Simms Campbell, a well-known cartoonist and illustrator of beautiful women in both the Black and white press, and Jay Jackson, an established and unforgiving editorial cartoonist, versatile comic strip creator, and illustrator.

Harrington's *Dark Laughter* became popular among the Black working class and cultural elite alike and was published for nearly thirty years. The strip ran in a number of Black newspapers, including the *Pittsburgh Courier*, the *Baltimore Afro-American*, the *People's Voice*, and the *Chicago Defender*.

Brother Bootsie, a recurring character, was particularly popular among readers. To Harrington's surprise, he would see clippings of his series in windows and shops throughout Harlem. In 1958, a collection titled *Bootsie and Others: A Selection of Cartoons* was published by Dodd Mead. In the introduction, Langston Hughes described Harrington as "Negro America's favorite cartoonist."

Using melancholy, irony, and a resigned, matter-of-fact tone, Harrington was eloquent in tackling his mainstay subjects of racial segregation and inequality. When focusing on social disparities, Harrington often depicted children in order to make his point. In one such cartoon, two Black children trudge through the newly fallen snow. The caption reads, "Man, do you realize that if we was in Alabama it would be against the law for us cullud kids to walk on this stuff?"

Each *Dark Laughter* cartoon was a luscious single-panel graphite illustration that used captions rather than word bubbles. Harrington often employed a variety of styles and textures within one cartoon – foreground characters were drawn in more detail, with nonessential characters in a looser, sketchier style. Harrington's use of rich pencil shading gave the comic a lush atmosphere and provided gravity to each cartoon.

In February 1942, Harrington was recruited as a full-time art director for the newly founded *People's Voice*, a weekly newspaper cofounded by soon-to-be Democratic congressman Adam Clayton Powell Jr. and Charles Buchanan. The paper took radical stances on racial issues in the United States and abroad. In addition to employing artists, Harrington contributed his own *Dark Laughter* strip, editorial cartoons, the first iteration of an adventure cartoon strip called *Jive Gray*, "Star Reporter," and illustrations for a serialized reprinting of Richard Wright's *Native Son*. Harrington continued at the paper until July 1943, when he took on assignments as a traveling journalist and war correspondent for the *Pittsburgh Courier*.

Assignments for the *Courier* sent Harrington to several military bases in the United States in 1943, where he drew and sketched portraits of Black soldiers and military scenes. He submitted editorial cartoons with the theme of the "Double V" campaign: victory for Black Americans fighting abroad and those in the United States. Harrington visited the 332nd Fighter Group in Michigan and submitted a full-page feature that included his observations, drawings, and interviews. Also for the *Courier* that year, Harrington revised the *Jive Gray* comic strip, and the adventurer returned as a member of the Tuskegee Airmen.

As World War II continued, Harrington was part of the only contingent of African American journalists to be employed as war correspondents by the US State Department. He traveled to North Africa and Europe and visited the front lines of Italy with NAACP executive secretary Walter White.

World War II drew to a close, and while there was victory abroad for America, there was not victory at home for African American citizens. Harrington's cartoons reflected the glaring racial injustice in the United States. In one cartoon, a wheelchair-bound Black veteran with no legs holds a picket sign reading "NOW" while confronting a policeman with a raised nightstick. The caption reads, "Officer, what Alabama bar was you holed up in back in '44 when I was in Normandy protectin' your civil rights?" Harrington joined the NAACP in 1946 as public relations director, a position that required him to work both publicly and behind the scenes. Among Harrington's concerns was the lack of federal action against brutality and lynchings directed toward Black veterans. In the case of veteran Isaac Woodward, beaten and blinded by white police officers while wearing his uniform, no investigation was made. Harrington shortly lobbied the support of writer Orson Welles. Welles, calling for transparency and justice, garnered public support after hosting a series of five fifteen-minute national broadcasts on ABC. An investigation took place, and the perpetrators of the crime were finally identified, though found not guilty at trial. Harrington was also vocal in challenging US attorney general Tom Clark, and by the late 1940s was under the scrutiny of the House Un-American Activities Committee for communist affiliations.

During this time, Harrington produced cartoons and drawings, taught art classes, and became art editor for *Freedom*. In 1951, his second children's book with writer Ellen F. Tarry, *The Runaway Elephant,* was selected by the American Institute of Graphic Arts for their competition, Fifty Best American Books. He was the first Black artist to be recognized.

That same year, Harrington received a quiet tip from a friend employed by army intelligence advising him to leave the country. He moved to Paris, where he joined an enclave of African American expatriates and continued to earn a living with the American Black press. Among Harrington's closest friends were noir writer Chester Himes (1909–84) and acclaimed novelist Richard Wright (1908–60). In a foreword to Harrington's collected essays *Why I Left America*, Julia Wright, Wright's daughter, recalled Harrington as her father's best friend in his last years of life, a fact she observed was missing or obscured in Wright's most prominent biographies. Harrington found Wright's untimely death deeply suspicious, which he wrote about in "The Last Days of Richard Wright" for *Ebony* magazine in February 1961.

Harrington moved to East Berlin in the fall of 1961 for a job illustrating a series of books, but he ultimately became stranded due to East Germany's political conflicts. Stuck without the proper exit visa, Harrington found work regularly selling material to a humor magazine called *Eulenspiegel* and a general-interest periodical called *Das Magazine*. While in East Germany he met Helga Richter, a broadcast journalist. They eventually married and had a son, Oliver Jr. During this time he continued to send cartoons to the United States. In 1968, Harrington was invited to contribute to the *New York Daily World* by his friend, editor John Pittman, which he did regularly thereafter.

Harrington's disdain for racist, classist, and imperialist policies perpetrated by the American government and his allegiance with the working class were never more apparent. His style changed dramatically as he incorporated color and ink into his work with fraught crosshatching that replaced his previous graphite shading. Although never a member of any Communist Party, he continued to ally himself with party members and sympathizers. His work frequently condemned Ronald Reagan's presidency for promoting domestic class warfare, record rates of homelessness, cuts in social programs, and rises in drug use. Through cartoons, Harrington remained vocally opposed to apartheid and the rise of white supremacist ideas internationally.

A true expatriate, Harrington returned to the United States on occasion but only to visit. In 1992, Harrington was a guest speaker at the Festival of Cartoon Art hosted by Ohio State University. He was fittingly billed as "the dean of African American cartoonists." In 1994, he returned to the United States as a visiting artist-in-residence at Michigan State University's School of Journalism, where he taught a course on political cartoons and journalism.

For sixty years – more than forty of those as an expatriate – Harrington used his skills to speak passionately and eloquently about racial and class inequality, daily life, and American social hypocrisy. At the time of his death in Berlin, Harrington was survived by his wife, Helga; their son, Oliver, of Berlin; and a sister, Earthaline Williamson.

# HARRIS, N. STEVEN

Steven Harris has provided illustrations for a number of comics publishers, including DC Comics, Image Comics and Dark Horse Comics. His most critically acclaimed effort to date is *Ajala: A Series of Adventures,* which won two Glyph Awards for best female main character.

(May 3, 1963– )
- **Born in NJ**
- **School of Visual Arts, BFA in illustration**
- **Illustrator, penciler, and storyboard artist**
- **Cocreator of *Ajala: A Series of Adventures***

Ajala: A Series of Adventures is copyrighted© 2017 Robert Garrett and N. Steven Harris
Illustration by N Steven Harris and Walt Msonza Barna

Image courtesy of N. Steven Harris

As a child Harris watched shows such as *Star Blazers*, *Battle Star Galactica*, and *Battle Bots*, going on to draw fan art featuring his own original characters. While studying at the School of Visual Arts, he was a student of Denys Cowan, cocreator of *Static Shock* and one of the founders of Milestone Media. He later went on to be an assistant of another Milestone founder, Michael Davis.

Steven Harris got his first job as an illustrator at Personality Comics. He then worked for DC Comics in 1993 on penciling *Showcase '93 Volume 1 #8*. In 1994, he was a penciler for Dark Horse's *X: One Shot to the Head*, while also working on Triumphant's *Chromium Man* comic series. In 1995, he was recruited to work on a five-book miniseries called *The Crush*, copublished by Image Comics and Motown Records.

In 1996, he once again started working with DC. Together with Grant Morrison and Mark Millar, he created a character called Aztek. They worked together for ten issues of *Aztek: The Ultimate Man*. In 1997, while working at Marvel on *Generation X,* he cocreated a character who was a merging of M and her brother Emplate. In 2000 he returned to DC to do issue #73 of the 1993 *Robin* comic book.

In 2010, he came out with *Brotherhood of (The Fringe)*, based on characters that he had created in the early 1990s. In 2011, he was asked by the late author L. A. Banks to work on a comic book adaptation of her best-selling series *The Vampire Huntress*. That year he also worked on a Jimmy Hendrix motion comic and on an arc of Dynamite's *Voltron* comic, issues #7 through #11.

In 2014, Harris won five Glyph Awards, one for his cocreated comic *Ajala: A Series of Adventures*, which won best female main character. He received four Glyph Awards and an Eisner nomination for *Watson and Holmes #6*. In 2015, *Ajala* once again received a Glyph Award for best female main character.

As of 2017, Harris lived in New York with his wife. He continues to draw and create original comics, and he is currently working on the revived *Solar Man* produced by Scout Comics. He is also working as an illustrator at Xmoor Studios. He does work as a freelance storyboarder and illustrator for a variety of companies, such as Samsung, Berlin-Cameron, BBH, Vitamin Water, and Rock Star Games. When he isn't volunteering with charity organizations with young artists, he can often be spotted in the artist alley of different comic book conventions such as MECCAcon and New York Comic Con.

Ajala: A Series of Adventures is copyrighted © 2017 Robert Garrett and N. Steven Harris.
Illustration by N. Steven Harris

Image courtesy of N. Steven Harris

# HENDRICKS, PAUL

- **Comics editor at King Features Syndicate**

Paul Hendricks was the first and only Black editor at King Features Syndicate. During his time there, he served as a role model and mentor to young artists and was a champion for African American–created comics like Jerry Craft's *Mama's Boyz* and Ray Billingsley's *Curtis*.

Paul Hendricks was originally an editor at North American Syndicate, which was purchased and merged with King Features in 1990. Little is know about his personal life outside of the fact that he took his role as the only African American comics editor at a major comics syndicate seriously. Always well-dressed, he was one of the first to arrive at work every morning. According to coworkers, he was even-tempered and professional, the kind of man who always kept his composure even when angered.

At a time when many comics publishers had a sometimes tense divide between comic creators and "the suits," Craft recalled that Paul Hendricks had a good relationship with all the cartoonists he worked with. Many of the artists who came in to drop off their work would end up going to lunch with Hendricks. He offered not only friendship but also editorial and creative advice. "I learned a lot about editing from him," Jerry Craft said. "So many other comics editors at the time were so concerned with making sure the grammar was proper. He really showed me the ropes on how to create natural sounding dialogue."

Hendricks had an eye for upcoming talent, and he saw promise in comics that others overlooked, like *Mama's Boyz* and *Curtis*. Another editor at King Features, Dave Astor, wrote of him, "Interestingly, the King person who first saw [the comic's] potential was Paul Hendricks, one of the very few black syndicate editors back then.... Lo and behold, comics by cartoonists of color started entering syndication."

In 1997, King Features sent all of the editors down to Florida, and that is where Craft and Hendricks parted ways. They would speak now and again until they completely lost touch.

# HERRIMAN, GEORGE

George Herriman was the creator of *Krazy Kat*, an influential surrealist comic strip that ran from 1913 to 1944.

(Aug. 22, 1880–Apr. 25, 1944)
- **Born in New Orleans, LA**
- **Newspaper cartoonist**
- **Creator of *Krazy Kat***

While as an adult Herriman described his parents as either French or Greek – he was nicknamed "The Greek" by his colleague Tad Dorgan – census and birth records indicate that his parents were French-speaking Creoles of color. Herriman's family lived in New Orleans' Tremé neighborhood, where they attended Saint Augustine's Catholic Church. Records are incomplete, but he had at least three siblings – two sisters and a brother.

When the young Herriman was ten, the family moved to Los Angeles, California. There, Herriman attended St. Vincent's Academy, a Roman Catholic boys' school. Stories of his youth are peppered with contradictory anecdotes, with Herriman himself as the likely source. These stories portray him as either a prankster, colorful sad sack, or both. One consistent detail is that his father disapproved of Herriman's interest in art, encouraging his son to pursue a practical career. Herriman did work as a barber and at his father's bakery while still in school. Soon after his departure from St. Vincent's in 1897, Herriman sold a sketch of the Hotel Petrolia to the *Los Angeles Times*; he parlayed the sale into a two-dollar-a-week job as either an office boy or an assistant in the engraving department.

Accounts of Herriman's early adulthood are also peppered with inconsistencies. The most romantic version of his career is that he illegally boarded a freight train around 1900 to look for artistic work in New York City, sometimes working as a sign or house painter or as a Coney Island carnival barker. His first break came in 1901 when the New York–based political-humor magazine *Judge* bought and published eleven of his cartoons, which they published between June 15 and October 26, 1901. Starting on September 29 of that same year, the Pulitzer newspaper chain published several of Herriman's one-shot half-page or full-page comics. That same day, September 29, marked Herriman's first cartoon contribution to the Philadelphia North American Syndicate; October 20, 1901, marked the publication of his first color comic, in the Sunday supplement for the T. C. McClure Syndicate. This early success encouraged Herriman, and thereafter he focused on newspaper work.

Herriman's first continuing comic strip was *Musical Mose*, three strips running from February 16, 1902, to March 9, 1902, in the Pulitzer newspapers. Mose was the first of a string of obsessive characters featured in Herriman's strips, but as Herriman's first Black creation, he also occupies a unique place in the cartoonist's history. The *Musical Mose* strips are, on their face, offensive – using caricatures from racist minstrel shows popular at the turn of the twentieth century. However, the plot repeated in *Musical Mose* strips is the story of a talented Black musician who believes in his own talents. When Mose tries to pass as various white ethnicities, he is badly beaten for his trouble.

*Musical Mose* represents only a small portion of Herriman's artistic legacy, but it depicts an important part of his personal and professional life. Following his family's move to Los Angeles, the Herrimans all worked to pass as white. Herriman always wore hats and cut his hair short to disguise its texture, and he allowed a rumor that he was Greek or "black Irish" to stand for most of his life. Given these facts, it's hard not to see an artist both mocking the society that would have persecuted him for his race and secretly giving voice to his own fears.

*Musical Mose* was followed by *Professor Otto and His Auto*, a strip about a destructive driver running from March 30, 1902, to December 28,

1902, and Herriman's first "kid strip," *Acrobatic Archie*, running from April 13, 1902, to January 25, 1902.

Herriman married his childhood sweetheart, Mabel Lillian Bridge, on July 7, 1902, in Los Angeles, California, traveling back from New York for the wedding and returning immediately afterward. The couple had two daughters, Mabel "Toots" Herriman (May 10, 1903–November 13, 1962) and Barbara "Bobbie" Herriman (ca. 1909–November 14, 1939).

The year 1903 proved eventful for the Herrimans. On January 11, Herriman continued his run as a cartoonist for the Pulitzer newspapers, who published his sailor misadventure strip *Two Jollie Jackies* in their color supplement for much of the rest of the year. On May 10, Herriman's first daughter, Mabel, was born, and in June Herriman began his first position on staff at a newspaper, Joseph Pulitzer's *New York World*. Here he provided illustrations for humorist Roy McCardell's columns in the Sunday metropolitan section of the paper. While working in New York, he continued to create and submit other strips for syndication, and in September 1903, Herriman's cowboy comedy *Lariat Pete* began running in the *San Francisco Chronicle*. Another short-lived strip, it ran until November of that year.

Image courtesy of Comic Strip Library

The period from 1904 to 1906 saw a flurry of activity in Herriman's career. He worked in turn for the *New York World*, the *New York Daily News*, the *New York American* (where he met longtime friend, sports writer/cartoonist Tad Dorgan), the World Color Printing Company, and the *Los Angeles Times*. During this time, Herriman illustrated newspaper columns, created sports and political cartoons, and launched an extraordinary six comic strips, with *Major Ozone's Fresh Air Crusade* proving the most popular. In August 1906, Herriman attracted Hearst's comics editor Rudolph Block's attention; Block hired him as the *Los Angeles Examiner*'s staff cartoonist. Herriman was publishing syndicated strips throughout this period, but in December 1906 Herriman stopped working on strips and focused on his work as the *Examiner's* cartoonist for several years.

In the summer of 1910, Herriman was called back to New York to cover for Tad Dorgan by doing sports cartoons for Hearst's *New York Evening Journal*. Within a few days, Herriman began a new comic, *The Dingbat Family*, featuring the hapless E. Pluribus Dingbat and his family. After only a month, the title was changed to *The Family Upstairs*, which lasted a little over a year before being reverted to the original *Dingbat Family*.

While the strip ran for almost six years, its most significant contribution to comics history occurred exactly one year into the strip's run. On July 26, 1911, an unnamed mouse threw a brick at the Dingbats' cat, who was named Kat. Herriman began drawing the cat and mouse as filler underneath *The Dingbat Family*, and the pair proved unexpectedly popular. New details emerged in this filler strip – surreal shifting backgrounds, a dog named Bull Pupp, and forgotten characters from Herriman's earlier *Gooseberry Sprigg*. In July 1912, the Dingbats went on vacation, and the cat and mouse took over the strip for a week, even retitling the strip *Krazy Kat and I. Mouse*. Herriman had set a juggernaut in motion, and while *The Dingbat Family* would continue until 1916, *Krazy Kat* debuted on October 28, 1913. It would grow into one of the most respected and influential works in comics history and would run almost uninterrupted until after Herriman's death, thirty-one years later.

*Krazy Kat* was unique from its inception, and it only grew in scope, size, and influence over time. The strip was given a full page on Sundays in 1916, and Herriman made use of every inch. The strip is characterized by an incredibly simple plot – Ignatz Mouse throws a brick at Krazy Kat, Krazy mistakes this for a token of love, and Offissa Pupp arrests Ignatz and pines for Krazy – a large supporting cast of animals, and surreal backgrounds that shift magically while the characters remain static and unaware of the chaos behind them. In these brief stories, Krazy is an eternal romantic and Ignatz is a cruel cynic, both characters self-defeating but philosophical in turns. Once he was given the space, Herriman incorporated his fascination with the extraordinary rock formations of New Mexico's Enchanted Mesa into the strip's distinctive look. He placed the strip in a landscape called the Magic Mesa, set in a fictional version of Arizona's Coconino County.

Herriman continued writing other strips during his work on *Krazy Kat*. *The Dingbat Family* ran until 1916, when it was replaced by the Dickens- and Chaplin-inspired *Baron Bean*, which ran through 1919.

He would continue to create other strips until late 1932, although they never garnered the influence of *Krazy Kat*'s masterful whimsy.

At its height, *Krazy Kat* enjoyed tremendous popularity with the intelligentsia and the arts community alike. E. B. White, Gilbert Seldes, and President Woodrow Wilson were all fans. In 1916, the first *Krazy Kat* animated films were produced by Hearst's International Film Service. In 1921, John Alden Carpenter approached Herriman about writing a *Krazy Kat* ballet, which was produced in 1922. Also in 1922, Hearst granted Herriman a lifetime contract of $750 a week with King Features Syndicate, granting Herriman security and freedom in his work. Herriman moved to North Sierra Bonita in Hollywood, frequently indulging in walks in the Arizona desert. During this time, Herriman developed a love for Navajo culture and made frequent trips into Navajo country, sometimes incorporating their traditional designs into his work. In 1927, Herriman illustrated a collection of Don Marquis's poetry titled *archy and mehitabel*, a series that began as columns in the *Evening Sun* newspaper. The poems were written in the voices of a cockroach poet, who hurls himself around on a typewriter to generate verse, and his best friend, an alley cat.

In 1930, Herriman sold his Sierra Bonita home and purchased a Spanish-style mansion on Maravilla Drive. Its decor reflected Herriman's love of southwestern and Navajo art, with an extensive Mexican flagstone garden.

On May 22, 1932, his daughter Barbara married screenwriter Ernest Pascal, and in 1934 she gave birth to Herriman's only granddaughter, Dinah. This could have been an idyllic time for the Herrimans, but on November 14, 1934, his wife, Mabel, died in a car crash. He continued to live in his mansion with his daughter, alongside five dogs and thirteen cats. By 1935 it was evident that *Krazy Kat* had lost much of its popularity; it was running in fewer than fifty newspapers across the country. Herriman offered to have his King Features salary reduced, but Hearst refused his offer and made sure that Herriman understood that both he and *Krazy Kat* would always be welcome. From 1935 on, the strip was printed in color, allowing Herriman to further prove his mastery of the medium.

In 1938, *Krazy Kat* suffered its only interruption as Herriman underwent kidney surgery. The syndicate ran reruns for Herriman's ten weeks of recovery, and he resumed his work as soon as he was able. In 1939, the Herriman family suffered another unexpected loss as his youngest daughter Barbara died of complications in surgery.

Herriman continued his work on *Krazy Kat* until his death at his home in 1944 following an extended illness. His cause of death was listed as "nonalcoholic cirrhosis of the liver." He was survived by his oldest daughter, Mabel, and his granddaughter, Dinah. On his death certificate Mabel inaccurately identified her father as "Caucasian" and stated that his father was from Paris and his mother from Alsace-Lorraine. Comics running in Hearst newspapers usually were handed off to new artists following the death or dismissal of a creator, but Hearst allowed *Krazy Kat* to die with its creator. Hearst understood that Herriman was irreplaceable.

Still widely regarded as the greatest master of the newspaper comics medium, Herriman's

Image courtesy of Comic Strip Library

influence on comics is immense. He influenced artists as diverse as Will Eisner, Charles Schulz, Walt Kelly, Patrick McDonnell, Chris Ware, Bill Watterson, Dr. Seuss, and R. Crumb. Herriman was the first comics creator to be taken seriously by the literary community; Gilbert Seldes's 1922 *Vanity Fair* article "Golla, Golla, the Comics Strip's Art" was the first to talk about comics in literary terms. In 1997, the Small Press Expo instituted the annual Ignatz Awards, named after Krazy's paramour/nemesis Ignatz Mouse, which celebrate achievements in independent comics.

# HESS, MICHELINE

**(1971– )**
- **Born in New York, NY**
- **Artist and writer**
- **Sarah Lawrence College, BFA 1993**
- **Parsons School of Design, MA in design and technology, 2004**
- **Creator of Malice in Ovenland**

Micheline Hess is the creator of *Malice in Ovenland*, a middle-grade adventure comic with a young woman of color as the protagonist.

Hess spent her formative years in the Roosevelt Island section of New York, later moving to the Flatbush section of Brooklyn. She gained a love of comics from the ones her father brought home from business trips, including *Lucky Luke*, *TinTin*, and *Pif et Hercule*.

After college, Hess worked in retail to make ends meet until she discovered Milestone Comics, the African American owned Imprint of DC Comics started by Dwayne McDuffie, Denys Cowan, Michael Davis, and Derek T. Dingle. On a leap of faith, Hess quit her retail job and focused her energies on creating a portfolio to present to the company. She was soon hired as a colorist under the guidance of another Milestone member, Jason Scott Jones.

At Milestone Comics, Micheline Hess worked on *Static*, *Icon*, *Rocket*, and *Shadow Cabinet*. A year later, however, she and many other staffers were laid off. Not seeing any other opportunities for Black female comic book artists, she went back to working in retail. It wasn't until she took a language immersion trip to Japan that she recognized her potential to create her own professional path.

*"I WANTED A YOUNG WOMAN OF COLOR TO BE THE STAR BECAUSE AS A LITTLE GIRL, I FELT COMICS WERE SORELY LACKING THAT KIND OF CHARACTER."*

After downloading a trial version of Flash 2, Hess taught herself how to draw digitally and create simple interactive elements. Next, she taught herself Photoshop, which eventually landed her a graphic design position at About.com. From there, Cartoon Network hired her to design animation for online games featuring characters like Bugs Bunny, SD Gundam, and Courage the Cowardly Dog.

Image courtesy of Rosarium Publishing

Hess started creating her own comics in 2006, when she was hired as senior designer for the marketing division of Nick Online. Her early works include *The Anansi Kids Club in The All Saints' Day Adventure* as well as series of short comic strips titled *Punchclock Princess.*

Her most popular series to date is the middle-grade comic *Malice in Ovenland.* With homages to *Alice in Wonderland* and other works of children's literature, it tells the story of Lily Brown, who falls into a bizarre world of grease-eating monsters while cleaning her mother's oven.

Publishing the first issue of *Malice In Ovenland* led Hess to meet other African-American creators and publishers, such as Bill Campbell of Rosarium Publishing. After Campbell convinced her to sign with the fledgling company, Hess published three subsequent volumes of *Malice* while working as a senior designer at Publicis North America, a New York-based advertising agency.

Micheline Hess credits Nilah Magruder, Junji Ito, Moebius, and Juanjo Guarnido as inspirations for her comic and writing work.

# HOLLINGSWORTH, ALVIN CARL

(Feb. 25, 1928–Jul. 14, 2000)
- **Born in New York, NY**
- **City University of New York, BA, 1956; MA, 1959**
- **Comic artist, illustrator, professor, and fine artist**
- **Creator of *Kandy* and illustrator of numerous Golden Age comics**

Alvin Hollingsworth was, along with Matt Baker, part of a small number of prominent African American cartoonists working in mainstream comic book publishing during the Golden Age of comics. He also worked on syndicated comic strips that were published in both mainstream and African American newspapers.

Hollingsworth was best known as a fine artist, as a member of the art collective Spiral, and for his Golden Age–era work on crime and horror comic books for Fawcett, Fiction House, Avon, Lev Gleason, and others. He sometimes signed his work as A. C. Hollingsworth, Alvin C. Hollingsworth, or Alvin Holly.

Hollingsworth graduated from the High School of Music and Art in New York City, which he attended at the suggestion of Joe Kubert. Kubert, who would later gain fame as an editor and artist for DC Comics, was then a student at the famed high school, two years ahead of the younger artist. After high school, Hollingsworth attended the City University of New York, where he attained both his bachelor's and master's degrees. From 1950 to 1952, he continued his studies at the Art Students League of New York, where his instructors included Ralph Fabri, Dr. Bernard Myers, and the esteemed Yasuo Kuniyoshi, best known for complex still lifes and female circus performers inspired by American folk art, Japanese design, and Cubism and other European modernist styles.

Around 1941, Hollingsworth began illustrating crime-focused comic books at several publishing houses. His earliest work has been difficult to identify, due to the era's common omission of comic book credits. Hollingsworth's earliest confirmed work is a signed, four-page war comic called "Robot Plane" in Aviation Press's *Contact Comics* #5 (1945), for which he completed both penciling and inking. Throughout the late 1940s, he drew for Holyoke's *Captain Aero Comics* (under the name Al Hollingsworth) and Fiction House's *Wings Comics*, where he produced "Suicide Smith" intermittently from 1946 to 1950. In 1945, he is credited as "A. H." on the story "Captain Power" in Novack Publishing's *Great Comics.*

Hollingsworth's work was featured at the center of a 2011 PBS *History Detectives* episode in which historian Shaun Clancy, citing Fawcett Comics writer-editor Roy Ald, identified Hollingsworth as the illustrator of racially sensitive representations in Fawcett's *Negro Romance* #2 (August 1950). As noted in the episode, Hollingsworth was the first African American artist hired by Fawcett Comics.

In the 1950s, as Alvin or A. C. Hollingsworth, he worked on a variety of series for several publishers, including Superior Publishers Limited's *The Mask of Dr. Fu Manchu*, Premier Magazines' *Police Against Crime*, Ribage's *Youthful Romances*, and horror comics like Master Comics' *Dark Mysteries* and Trojan Magazine's *Beware*. As Al Hollingsworth, he provided artwork for Avon's *Witchcraft* and Premier's *Mysterious Stories*, and romance comics such as Lev Gleason's *Boy Loves Girl*. He has also been credited for work on Fox Comics' "Numa" in *Rulah, Jungle Goddess* and "Bronze Man" in *Blue Beetle.*

In 1955, Hollingsworth created *Kandy*, an action-packed romance centered on an independent young female engineer in the world of competitive auto racing, published in the African American newspaper the *Pittsburgh Courier.* Hollingsworth also produced the *Scorchy Smith* strip and, with George Shedd, *Marlin Keel.*

Around 1955, Hollingsworth shifted from comics and began focusing solely on fine arts, producing representational and abstract paintings and collages. His paintings dealt with themes involving the civil rights movement, women's rights, spirituality, jazz, urban life, and dance. Hollingsworth also produced numerous painting series, including Cry City (1963–65), the Prophet series (c. 1970), and the Subconscious series. During the 1960s, he began to experiment with fluorescent light, later collaborating with electronic music pioneer Edgard Varèse to create a large-scale multimedia installation.

In addition to a 1965 solo exhibition at the Terry Dintenfass Gallery, Hollingsworth's work appeared in group exhibitions at The Metropolitan Museum of Art, the Whitney Museum of American Art, the Rhode Island School of Design, the Boston Museum of Fine Arts, and the Museum of Modern Art in New York.

Alvin Hollingsworth was a founding member of the influential African American art collective Spiral, which sought to address civil rights concerns through visual art. Established in 1963, its members included Charles Alston, Emma Amos, Reginald Gammon, Norman Lewis, Richard Mayhew, and Hale Woodruff.

In 1966, Hollingsworth married Stephanie Ann Knoepler, with whom he later had four children. In 1970, the artist hosted the NBC television series *You're Part of Art*, produced in cooperation with the Art Students League of New York. Hollingsworth toured the East Coast while filming the ten-part series, lecturing and conducting painting demonstrations, In the same year, he published two books, *I'd Like the Goo-Gen-Heim*, about a child's visit to the Guggenheim Museum in New York, and *Black Out Loud: An Anthology of Modern Poems by Black Americans*.

Additional book projects included *Art of Acrylic Painting* (1969, co-author) and, as illustrator, *The Sniper* (1969) and *Journey* (1970). During the 1960s and 1970s, Hollingsworth completed murals for the Don Quixote Apartment Buildings in the Bronx, New York, and produced a series of six Don Quixote–themed lithographs. In the spring of 1970, he completed a mural for the Paul Robeson Lounge at Rutgers University.

Throughout the latter part of his career, Hollingsworth taught at academic institutions including the Art Students League and the City University of New York, where he worked as a visual and performing arts professor until his retirement in 1998.

Alvin Hollingsworth's many awards include the 1963 Emily Lowe Art Competition Award and the 1964 Whitney Foundation Award. His work is included in the collections of the Brooklyn Museum of Art and the Smithsonian Museum of African Art in Washington, D.C.

# HOLLOWAY, WILBERT LOUIE

Wilbert Holloway was best known for creating the long-running *Pittsburgh Courier* comic strip *Sunny Boy Sam*. Originally published in 1928, the gag-based strip ran for forty-one years. The strip was the *Courier's* second-longest-running series, second only to the popular *Bungleton Green*

**(Aug. 11, 1899–Apr. 1969)**
- **Born in Jeffersonville, IN**
- **John Herron Art Institute**
- **Cartoonist**
- **Creator of *Sunny Boy Sam***

strip, created by Leslie Rogers in 1920 and executed by numerous artists over a forty-three-year period. Wilbert Holloway also the created of the "Double V" campaign logo as well as many editorial cartoons.

Holloway attended the John Herron Art Institute in Indianapolis, the first Indiana school devoted to professional art instruction. Other notable Herron Institute alumni included the African American artists John Wesley Hardrick (1891–1968) and William Edouard Scott (1884–1964). During this period, Holloway shared a studio apartment with Hale Woodruff (1900–80), a fellow Herron student who would later become well known for his Harlem Renaissance murals, paintings, and prints.

> "ONE DAY HE SAID, 'MAN, THIS FINE ART IS TOO MUCH FOR ME. I'M GOING TO GET INTO SOMETHING WHERE I CAN DEAL WITH THE PEOPLE.' SO HE WROTE TO MR. ROBERT L. VANN, WHO WAS EDITOR OF THE COURIER IN PITTSBURGH, AND GOT A JOB THAT PAID HIM $50 A WEEK AS CARTOONIST."
>
> - HALE WOODRUFF, 1968 INTERVIEW

Holloway began working at the *Courier* as a staff artist in 1928. Holloway created *Sunny Boy Sam* in that same year, initially producing the strip in black and white. From 1950 through 1955, the strip ran in color as part of the *Courier's* color magazine section. After the demise of the newspaper's color section, Holloway returned *Sunny Boy Sam* to its earlier black-and-white format, producing the strip until his death in 1969. It continued after his death with thematic and stylistic variations by Bill Murray and other artists.

*Sunny Boy* characters, largely male, were initially rendered with stereotypical physiognomic features, spoke in dialect, and were engaged in the numbers racket. Later, as pointed out by John D. Stevens (1976), Sheena C. Howard (2013), and Tim Jackson (2016), Holloway dramatically departed from physiognomic stereotypes. In addition, by 1947, as Stevens noted, Sunny Boy had begun to speak in a more refined fashion, more like a college graduate.

Holloway wrote editorial cartoons as well as gag strips, winning numerous awards for his editorial cartooning. His editorials in the *Courier* addressed the Ku Klux Klan, immigration, labor issues, the 1935 invasion of Ethiopia, and the dictatorship of Benito Mussolini. In May 1927, Holloway's political cartoon titled "Senator Lynch of Mississippi," a satirical critique of hypocritical, racist legislators, was published in *The Messenger* (1917–28), a Harlem Renaissance–era, African American monthly periodical. The comic depicts a white senator with two mixed-race children seated on his lap. Below, the caption reads "Senator Lynch of Mississippi whiles away an hour or so with his children after a strenuous fight in the legislature for the passage of his racial integrity bill."

Holloway also produced the logo for the *Pittsburgh Courier's* extremely popular 1942 "Double V" campaign. Arising from a letter to the editor, it linked victory over racial discrimination in America to victory over Axis fascism abroad. As *Courier* editors noted in an editorial statement regarding the popular campaign, "We, as Colored Americans, are determined to protect our country, our form of government and our freedoms ... therefore, we have adapted the Double 'V' war cry – victory over our enemies on the battlefields abroad. Thus in our fight for freedom we wage a two-pronged attack against our enslavers at home and those abroad who would enslave us. WE HAVE A STAKE IN THIS FIGHT ... WE ARE AMERICANS TOO!"

Other African American newspapers soon joined the Double V campaign, with several printing reproductions of Holloway's logo. In *Sunny Boy Sam*, Hollway made the Double V campaign an overarching theme of the strip for several months. In one strip, Holloway incorporated a cartoon image of boxer Joe Louis to provide African American service members with words of support and encouragement.

After his death, the National Newspaper Association, a trade association of Black community newspapers, established the Wilbert L. Holloway Award for Best Editorial Cartoonist. He is remembered as a pioneering newspaper artist of color.

# HOWARD, SHEENA CHERI

Dr. Sheena C. Howard is the author of several scholarly texts, including *Black Comics: Politics of Race and Representation* and *Black Queer Identity Matrix: Towards An Integrated Queer of Color Framework*. The *Encyclopedia of Black Comics* is her fourth book.

**(Aug. 23, 1983– )**
- **Born in Philadelphia, PA**
- **New York Institute of Technology, MA, 2007**
- **Howard University, intercultural and rhetorical communication, 2010**
- **Comics scholar and writer**
- **Author of *Black Comics* and *Black Queer Identity Matrix***

As a child, Howard was not an avid comics fan. Her interest in comics began when she was in graduate school, when she discovered *The Boondocks*. This began her interest in the political impact, imagery, and iconography of comics as a form of protest art.

While Howard was writing her dissertation on Black comic strips, she was dismayed that there were very few books in the library on the history of Black comic artists and their contributions to the field of comics. This void in literature prompted Howard to write her first book, *Black Comics: Politics of Race and Representation*. The book was coedited with Dr. Ronald Jackson in 2013. It documents the history of Black

Images courtesy of Sheena C. Howard

comic strips and addresses cultural gatekeeping in the comics industry and Black female representation in comics, among other topics. It also featured prominent comic scholars and practitioners, including Professor William Foster, Jeet Heer, and David Deluliis.

*Black Comics* was reviewed by several journals, including *Studies in American Humor*, the *Journal of Graphic Novels and Comics* and *Image-TexT*. In 2014, Howard and Jackson went on to win an Eisner Award for Best Scholarly/Academic Work, making Howard the first Black woman ever to win an Eisner – considered the Oscars of comics.

Howard has since published two more books: *Black Queer Identity Matrix: Towards An Integrated Queer of Color Framework, Critical Articulations of Race, Gender and Sexual Orientation*, and the *Encyclopedia of Black Comics*. Howard's books are known for their creative covers, which are symbolic and eye-catching. Howard worked closely with the Eisner Award–winning writer and artist John Jennings on the cover design for all four.

In 2016, Howard wrote, produced and directed the film *Remixing Colorblind*, which examines how the educational system shapes public perspectives of race and "others." In late 2016, Lion Forge Media announced that Howard would be a cowriter with David Walker on its new comics universe, *Catalyst Prime*. She also headlined the 2017 comic book *Superb*, the first comic about a superhero with Down syndrome. This moved Howard from a cultural critic of comics to a comics writer.

Howard continued to expand her writing repertoire, focusing on social justice and community impact. She wrote for the *Huffington Post, Curve Magazine*, the *Philadelphia Inquirer*, and others on topics ranging from sexual identity negotiation to media representation to police brutality.

In 2016, Howard became a tenured faculty member at Rider University, where she is an associate professor of communication studies. The same year, Howard set out on a national tour for her film, *Remixing Colorblind*. It screened at the Roxbury International Film Festival, the Long Beach Indie International Film Festival, the National Communication Association, Social Justice Unit, and the Boston Museum of Fine Arts.

In 2015, Howard was named an HBCU (Historically Black College/University) Alumna of the Year finalist by *HBCU Digest*. In 2016, Howard received recognition for her social justice work and literary achievements from both the City Council of Philadelphia and the Pennsylvania State Senate. In 2016, Howard married Wafiyyah Packer, who was also the creative director and editor of *Remixing Colorblind*.

# HUDLIN, REGINALD

Reginald Hudlin's career has spanned film, television, and comics writing. His work as a writer for the Marvel universe is most noteworthy for reframing the *Black Panther* franchise through a lens of colonial critique and Black nationalism, and for elevating the Black Panther to a fully developed, headlining character.

> (Dec. 15, 1961– )
> - **Born in St. Louis, MO**
> - **Harvard University**
> - **Writer, director, and producer**
> - **Writer for *Black Panther***

Hudlin grew up in the city of East St. Louis, down the street from such cultural icons as Tina Turner and Katherine Dunham. He is descended from early Black activists who protested the representations of African Americans in *Birth of a Nation*. In the late 1970s, Reginald's brother, Warrington Hudlin, founded the Black Filmmaker Foundation in New York around the same time that Reginald was studying at Harvard University.

As an undergraduate, Hudlin produced a senior thesis film that won first place at the Black American Cinema Awards. This short would eventually become *House Party* (1990), his first feature-length film. *House Party* was a part of the early Sundance school of indies, which introduced a generation of diverse filmmaking voices into Hollywood. The film grossed $26 million for New Line Cinema after being produced for much less and remains a cult classic (HE).

Hudlin would go on to write, direct, and produce several sequels as well other classic nineties Hollywood hits, such as *Boomerang* (1992), starring Eddie Murphy and Robin Givens, and *The Great White Hype* (1996), starring Samuel Jackson, Jeff Goldblum, and Damon Wayans. He also produced the first African American animated feature film, *BeBe's Kids*, in 1992.

As his film career progressed, Hudlin continued to write and direct for television and in 2005 came to head up Black Entertainment Television (BET). He later worked with Quentin Tarantino as a producer to make *Django Unchained* (2012), for which he received an Academy Award nomination for Best Picture, and developed a pilot for the acclaimed television series *The Boondocks*.

Hudlin's first venture into comics writing was a comic graphic novel titled *Birth of a Nation* with Aaron McGruder. This independently developed comic novel quickly graduated to an offer from Marvel Comics to reintroduce *The Black Panther* in 2005.

Christopher Priest, the Black Panther's previous writer, was under tremendous editorial pressure toward the end of the run, even including a white American government agent, Everett K. Ross, as a sidekick to interpolate T'Challa and his African kingdom. This trope was in part a response to the company's fears that a primarily white readership could not relate to the African king.

Hudlin's Black Panther, on the other hand, embraces an identity that refuses to accommodate these types of racialized market fears. He begins the series with *Who Is the Black Panther?* (2007), which depicts Wakanda's extraordinary ability to defend itself in its first, beautifully illustrated pages (John Romita Jr., Klaus Janson, lettered by Dean White). Embedded in the narrative is both a utopian Black nationalism and a proto-Afrofuturism. Hudlin establishes the world of Wakanda as one of superheroes and advanced technology, while also introducing us to the greed and brutality of colonizers who attempt to attack the small, hidden nation for its riches. The African warrior and his kingdom represented in this run of *The Black Panther* allows readers to imagine what the African continent might have become without five hundred years of colonialism, slavery, and foreign interference.

Despite its popularity, Hudlin's *Black Panther* had its detractors in a white male readership that objected to its explicit Afrocentrism. Gauging from both Hudlin's discussion board disclaimers and from fans reporting online, his experience is consistent with that of Christopher Priest and other Black comics artists targeted by a subset of the fan base for depicting Black characters with the same heroic tropes found in white characters, or even with heroic tropes consistent with African or the African American experience.

After his time writing *Black Panther* ended in 2008, Hudlin wrote a yearlong run of *Spider-Man*, which included the crossover *Spider-Man: The Other* (2009). Hudlin also wrote and produced a spin-off graphic novel of *Django Unchained* for Dynamite Entertainment called *Django Meets Zorro*.

Hudlin's career spans platforms and genres, from film and literature to the entertainment business, all shaped by an explicitly political framework. He the husband of Chrisette Suter, whom he married in 2002.

# IGLE, JAMAL YASSEEM

Artist Jamal Igle is the author of the independent comic series *Molly Danger*. A 25-year veteran of comics publishing, he has also worked on high-profile properties for DC Comics and Marvel Comics as well as Image Comics' *Venture*. He is a strong advocate for creator-owned comics.

> **(July 19, 1972– )**
> - **Born in Harlem, NY**
> - **School of Visual Arts**
> - **Illustrator and comic creator**
> - **Creator of *Molly Danger***

Jamal Igle obtained his first job at DC Comics as an intern while attending the High School of Art and Design in Manhattan; his second job as a comic book artist was at Majestic Entertainment, shortly after attaining his bachelor's degree. In 1999, Igle left the comic world to work for Sony Animation. While there, he worked as a storyboard artist for several CGI series, including *Max Steel* and *Roughnecks: Starship Troopers Chronicles*.

In 2000, he returned to comics to illustrate Marvel's *New Warriors* with Jay Faerber. The duo later completed an *Iron Fist/Wolverine* miniseries for Marvel and the creator-owned *Venture* for Image Comics. Igle then transferred to DC Comics, with whom he signed an exclusive contract in 2005. His work for DC includes *Firestorm* (2004–07), *Nightwing* (2007), and *Supergirl* (2008–10). He also did fill-in stints for *Green Lantern*, *G.I. Joe*, and *Martian Manhunter* and worked on titles based outside the United States, including *Army of Angels* and *Perry Rhodan*. In 2011, he received the Inkpot Award for Achievement in Comic Art.

In 2012, Igle ended his contract with DC to crowdfund his creator-owned series *Molly Danger*, a superhero story about a young girl with fantastic powers. After the crowdfunding effort exceeded its goal, *Molly Danger: Book One* was published in 2013 by Action Lab Entertainment.

Jamal Igle has recently informed his fans that he would no longer carry merchandise that was not his own work, allowing him to focus solely on promoting his own intellectual property. In a 2015 post on 13th Dimension called "Why I'm Walking Away From Characters I Don't Own," he explained, "Much like a stage father, I have to groom and mold my creation to be everything I need her to be. I can't do that, however, If I'm trying to sell prints of Batman."

"MY DAUGHTER CATHERINE INSPIRED ME TO REWORK THE CONCEPT FOR MOLLY. WHEN SHE WAS OLD ENOUGH TO READ, I WANTED HER TO ENJOY A STORY THAT WAS POSITIVE, GROUNDED AND HAD A STRONG YOUNG FEMALE HERO. A ROLE MODEL WHO, IN SPITE OF ALL THE SLINGS AND ARROWS THROWN AT HER, WOULD REMAIN A GOOD PERSON."

In 2016, Igle contributed art to the independent series *Black* by Kwanza Osajyefo. Positing a world in which only Black people have superpowers, this politically engaged comic explores oppression, police brutality, and black resilience.

As of 2017, Jamal Igle lived and worked in Brooklyn, New York.

# ILLIDGE, JOSEPH PHILLIP

**(Oct. 23, 1969– )**
- **School of Visual Arts, BFA, 1990**
- **Writer, editor, columnist, and public speaker**
- **Cowrote *Solarman***

Joseph Illidge is a comic writer and editor who has worked with Milestone Media, DC Comics, Lion Forge Comics, and Archaia. He is the cofounder of Verge Entertainment and the cowriter with Brendan Deneen of *Solarman,* an independent superhero comic.

After attending the High School of Art and Design and the School of Visual Arts, Illidge's first editorial position was at Milestone Media, Inc. This Black comic book company founded by Denys Cowan was the first to have a publishing deal with industry giant DC Comics. Illidge worked on Milestone's various superhero titles, including *Static,* which featured a teenage superhero who later appeared in the award-winning *Static Shock* animated series.

In 1998, Illidge became an editor for DC Comics, serving as the first person of color on the Batman editorial team. He worked on *Batman:*

*No Man's Land*, *Batgirl*, *Birds of Prey*, and *Batman Beyond*, which was adapted from the Warner Brothers animated series. During his two-year editorial tenure, Joseph worked on characters that would later appear in television and film, including Detective Crispus Allen from the FOX series *Gotham* and the heroes Black Canary and Huntress from the CW Network's *Arrow*.

In 2000, Illidge cofounded Verge Entertainment with partners Shawn Martinbrough and Milo Stone. This production company offered a library of original ideas for film, television, and the internet.

From 2007 to 2008, Illidge worked as a comics editor for Archaia, a critically acclaimed independent publisher of creator-owned comics, including the top-selling *Mouse Guard* series. While there, he acquired *The Many Adventures of Miranda Mercury*, an adventures series starring a Black female protagonist, by Brandon Thomas and Lee Ferguson. He also was the editor of *The Bond of St. Marcel*, by Jennifer Quintenz and Christian Gossett; the zombie graphic novel *Awakening*, by Nick Tapalansky and Alex Eckman-Lawn; and *The Sisterhood*, by Christopher Golden and Tom Sniegoski.

In 2014, Illidge began writing a weekly column, "The Mission," for pop culture site CBR (formerly Comic Book Resources). The series was dedicated to examining cultural and gender diversity in comic books, television, and film. Illidge also wrote a monthly column for the sports industry website The Shadow League. He became a senior editor for Lion Forge Comics in 2016.

In addition to his editorial work, Illidge has written several original comics. He and fellow writer Brendan Deneen cowrote the comic book miniseries *Solarman* for Scout Comics. Solarman was a preexisting character owned by his creators, David Oliphant and Deborah Kalman. He had previously appeared in a two-issue miniseries written by Stan Lee and published by Marvel Comics in 1989. For the rebooted comic, the character was redesigned as a Black teenage computer hacker living in Brooklyn. Illidge has also worked on a historical graphic novel, *The Ren*, a romance set during the Harlem Renaissance.

## DID YOU KNOW?

**Joseph Illidge was the first person of color to become a member of the Batman Editorial Group at DC Comics.**

# JACKSON, JAY

**(Sept. 10, 1905–1954)**
- **Born in Oberlin, OH**
- **Cartoonist, illustrator, and designer**
- **Creator of As Others See Us and illustrator of Bungleton Green**

Jay Jackson is best known for his two long-standing newspaper comics, *(Seeing Ourselves) As Others See Us* and *Bungleton Green*. Eventually becoming the operator of a national art service, Jackson also created work for *Ebony* and the *Pittsburgh Courier,* winning two Guild Awards for his newspaper cartoons.

In 1925, Jay Jackson married Adeline C. Smith and began attending Wesleyan University. His schooling only lasted a year, however, as his career had already begun to take flight. In 1926, he was hired to the *Pittsburgh Courier*, where he published *As Others See Us* and *The Jingle Belles*. In 1928, he started designing posters for Warner Brothers theaters and taking classes at the Chicago Art Institute. The same year, he met Robert S. Abbot, the owner and publisher of *Abbott's Monthly*, a short-lived publication, and the *Chicago Defender*.

The *Chicago Defender* was a voice for Abbott's vision for the Black community, featuring a unique blend of conservatism and progressivism that touted racial solidarity and focused on self-help. It was here that Jackson created *As Others See Us*, a serial strip that examined the idea that dominant groups contributed to the construction of both the Negro and New Negro images. Aimed at Northern-bound migrants from the South, this nuanced comic criticized manners, education, and social mores. With strips dealing with social ills such as gambling, colorism, and financial irresponsibility, it aimed to inspire self-reflection and self-improvement.

After the death in 1928 of his first wife, Adeline Smith, in 1935, he married Eleanor K. Poston, a secretary and writer at the *Chicago Defender*. This was also his most prolific period. In the 1930s, he wrote and illustrated *The Adventures of Bill* (1934), *Bungleton Green* (1934), *Fan Tan Anne* (1935), *Society Sue* (1935), *Bibsy* (1935), *Between Us* (1936), *Memphis Blue* (1936), *Cream Puff* (1936), *Tish Mingo* (1937), *Ben Franklin* (1938), *So What?* (1939), and *Billy Ken* (1939).

Jay Jackson was the third artist to draw *Bungleton Green* during its forty-three-year tenure in the *Chicago Defender*. Originally illustrated by Leslie Rogers in 1920, *Bungleton Green* featured a perpetually down-on-his-luck fellow, the sort whose strips often ended with a kick in the pants. Like Wilbert Holloway's *Sunny Boy Sam*, the gag strip was popular with audiences who enjoyed its wry take on city life.

The early 1940s saw the entry of the United States into World War II. As a result, Jackson soon started producing cartoons for the Office of War Information. He also created the strip *The Sergeant* for the Office of Price Administration in 1945. His best-known works during the time, however, were his many pinup illustrations. Being a socially conscious pragmatist, Jackson drew to sell, but he flavored his art with social commentary. Drawing white glamour girls in risqué poses and positions that commented on integration and segregation was a controversial choice, the likely reason why most are not listed in Colourpicture Publishers, the cards' publishing company.

At some point in the 1940s, Jackson moved to Los Angeles. It was during this time that he illustrated the strips *Exposition Follies* (1940), *Speed Jaxon* (1942–47), *Ravings of Professor Doodle* (1947), and *Glamour Town* (1948). In 1947, he also worked on Pepsi's groundbreaking "Leaders in Their Fields" ad campaign, which featured dignified and successful Black Americans such as university students, well-to-do families, and the future Nobel Laureate Dr. Ralph Bunche.

In 1949, Jackson began studying with renowned artist Norman Rockwell. He passed away unexpectedly in 1954, at age forty-eight.

# JACKSON, TIM

Tim Jackson is both an editorial cartoonist and the author of a major work of comics scholarship, the 2016 book *Pioneering Cartoonists of Color*. Encompassing decades of research, it offers an overview of African American cartoonists from the mid-1880s to 1968, when Black cartoonists gained greater syndication in the wake of Martin Luther King Jr.'s assassination.

> (Jan. 16, 1958– )
> - **Born in Dayton, OH**
> - **School of the Art Institute of Chicago, BFA in visual arts**
> - **Cartoonist, writer, and historian**
> - **Author of *Pioneering Cartoonists of Color***

Jackson began drawing comics early on, with his first cartoon feature published in his hometown newspaper, the *Dayton Journal-Herald*, at age fourteen. After an ignorant viewer exclaimed "I never knew black people drew comics!" Jackson was determined to keep developing his work and to help ensure that the rich history of other Black cartoonists in the United States be recorded and remembered.

After attending the School of the Art Institute in Chicago, Jackson self-published a series of educational comic books throughout the 1980s, including *Friends Are for Signing: A Story about Sign Language*; *AIDS: Just the Facts Jack*; and *The Case of the Great Graffiti*. During this time, Jackson also began to produce political cartoons for distribution in newspapers, including the *Chicago Tribune* and *The Cincinnati Herald*.

In 1999, Jackson joined the staff of the *Chicago Defender,* one of the nation's most renowned African American newspapers. Working as a contributing editorial cartoonist under the wing of pioneer Black cartoonist Chester Commodore, Jackson remained at the paper for fourteen years. While there, he had access to decades of archives of cartoons written and drawn by Black cartoonists, which further ignited his interest in preserving the history of unsung cartoonists of color.

In 1997, Jackson developed a website, A Salute to the Pioneering Cartoonists of Color, which cataloged the information Jackson had collected throughout the years on African American cartoonists. His goal was to make information about Black cartoonists searchable online so that their contributions would not be overlooked during the nation's 100th anniversary celebration of American cartoon art. It attracted the attention of the University of Michigan Press, which suggested he develop a book from the website.

In preparation for his forthcoming book, Jackson dismantled the website and worked on the book exclusively. It would take years for everything to fall into place, and ultimately the University Press of Mississippi would publish *Pioneering Cartoonists of Color* in 2016. The book includes biographies of more than seventy African American cartoonists, placing them in historical context and sharing samples of their work.

Tim Jackson continues to call Chicago home, where he has amassed a large assemblage of young admirers whom he considers family. Many of the budding artists and comic art appreciators he met early in his career are now adults with children of their own who refer to him as "Grandpa Tim." Jackson is proud to have inspired so many during his decades of comics creation and scholarship.

# JENNINGS, JOHN IRA

John Jennings has played many roles in the world of visual and comic arts. After creating his first graphic novel, *The Hole*, in 2008, he has gone on to adapt Octavia Butler's *Kindred* to graphic novel form, produce socially critical visual art with Stacey Robinson under the pseudonym Black Kirby, found multiple comic book conventions, and produce a range of books, including the 2010 anthology *Black Comix: African American Independent Comics Art and Culture*.

**(Nov. 5, 1970– )**
- **Born in Brookhaven, MI**
- **Jackson State University, BA in art, 1993**
- **University of Illinois at Urbana Champaign, MEd, 1995; MFA, 1997**
- **Visual artist, curator, and scholar**
- **Illustrator of *Kindred* graphic novel**
- **Co-editor of *Black Comix* and *The Blacker the Ink***

John Jennings was first introduced to comics when his mother gave him a copy of Marvel's *Mighty Thor*. Growing up in a relatively remote, rural area of Mississippi, he had both time and space to imagine and explore the world through stories. As he continued his education, he came to appreciate comics' uniquely democratic potential: for him, anyone with an idea could make a comic. All you needed was a story, some art, and a copy shop.

While he was initially inspired by the superhero genre, reading Scott McCloud's graphic treatise *Understanding Comics* was a revelation. McCloud's explanation of the fundamental elements of sequential art revealed the inner workings of the comics medium to him in entirely new ways.

Image courtesy of Rosarium Publishing

Jennings produced his first graphic novel, *The Hole: Consumer Culture, Volume 1*, in collaboration with Damian Duffy in 2008. The first graphic novel to be distributed by the University of Chicago Press, it is an exploration into the ways in which Black culture is consumed as a commodity in neoliberal America.

In 2016, Jennings's nonfiction work *The Blacker the Ink: Constructions of Black Identity in Comics and Sequential Art* won the Eisner Award for Best Scholarly Work in Comics.

In 2017, Jennings once again teamed up with Damian Duffy to adapt acclaimed science fiction novelist Octavia Butler's *Kindred* to the graphic novel format. Debuting at number one on the *New York Times* Best-Seller list for hardcover graphic novels, *Kindred*, a neo-slave narrative, features a twentieth-century protagonist who is forced to travel back into the time of the transatlantic slave trade to ensure her own existence. This major milestone occurred almost simultaneously with his promotion to full professor and his acceptance of the Nasir ("Nas") Jones Hiphop Fellowship at Harvard University.

After years of mentoring and collaborating with fellow artist Stacey Robinson, he and Robinson teamed up under the pseudonym Black Kirby to produce a series of prints, essays, and lectures on race in American comics. Beginning in 2012, Black Kirby paid homage to the pioneering work of comic artist Jack Kirby, while adding their own Afrofuturistic flare grounded in the remix ethos of hip-hop culture (see *Robinson, Stacey*).

Jennings is the cofounder of three independent comic book conventions: The Schomburg Black Comic Book Festival, The Black Comix Arts Festival, and SŌL-CON: The Brown and Black Comix Expo. He is a leader in creating platforms for creators of color to present their work, also publishing the work of aspiring comics artists and writers in his coedited anthology *Black Comix: African American Independent Comics Art and Culture*.

As a graphic design and visual arts professor, John Jennings has taught at numerous institutions, including Jackson State University; the University of Illinois; the State University of New York, Buffalo; and the University of California, Riverside. He has curated or exhibited more than fifty shows and installations nationwide, and written, drawn, edited, or coedited more than a dozen books.

He is also well known in professional circles as an exemplary book cover artist, having designed book covers for numerous projects, including

Image courtesy of John Jennings

Daniel José Older's *Shadowshaper* and the special anniversary edition of Joan Morgan's *When Chickenheads Come Home to Roost*. He has, in short, left his professional mark on a range of fields, institutions, scholarly work, and curative platforms. Jennings is currently a professor in the Department of Media and Cultural Studies at the University of California, Riverside.

# JETTER, AVY

**(Dec. 11, 1968– )**
- **Born in Minneapolis, MN**
- **California College of Art, BFA in painting, 1994**
- **Comic writer and artist**
- **Author of *Nuthin' Good Ever Happens at 4 A.M.***

Avy Jetter is the author and illustrator of the independent horror comic *Nuthin' Good Ever Happens at 4 A.M.*

Avy Jetter began her postsecondary education at the California College of Arts, which at the time, like most US visual arts programs, had few students and faculty of color. After a short time at the Oakland-based institution, Jetter transferred to the historically Black Fisk University in Nashville, Tennessee. Ultimately, though, the Black-centered environment on this historic campus could not offset the overt racism she experienced off campus, and she returned to CCA to complete her degree in 1994.

After attaining her BFA, Jetter settled in Oakland, California, and began building an art practice centered on her interest in portraiture. Jetter's work emphasizes drawings in pen on paper, using detailed line work and rich texture. For some portraits and illustrations, she also makes use of color washes, most often in watercolor.

In August of 2012, Jetter debuted *Nuthin' Good Ever Happens at 4 A.M.* at the San Francisco Zine Fest, where the comic was well received. The first four issues were released annually, with subsequent issues appearing more frequently. *Nuthin' Good Ever Happens at 4 A.M.* explores the impact of apocalyptic devastation on working-class and poor communities of color. Set in downtown Oakland, *Nuthin' Good* writes Black people and other people of color into a horror subgenre whose protagonists are more often white and middle-class.

Influenced by a range of horror writers and directors—from George Romero, writer and director of the classic zombie films *Night of the Liv-*

Image courtesy of Avy Jetter

*ing Dead, Dawn of the Dead,* and *Day of the Dead,* to more recent innovators like Kevin Grevioux, African American actor and writer of the films *Underworld* and *I, Frankenstein*—Jetter embraces many conventions of the genre, while simultaneously challenging others. Her choice to include only people of color among her characters constitutes a rejection of the marginalization of people of color throughout the genre.

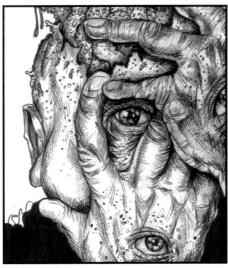

Jetter's interest in portraiture informs the aesthetic of *Nuthin' Good,* which incorporates richly detailed and expressive drawings of both the living and the undead. For Jetter, the zombie tale is a vehicle for exploring family relationships, transformation, and cultural adaptation through the lens of communities of color.

Image courtesy of Avy Jetter

# JOHNSON, ARIELL

(Jan. 8, 1983– )
- **Born in Baltimore, MD**
- **Temple University, accounting, 2005**
- **Comic shop owner**

Ariell Johnson is the owner of Amalgam Comics & Coffeehouse, a bookstore and community gathering place for comic fans of all ages. When Johnson opened her doors in December of 2015, it made her the only Black woman to own a comic book store on the East Coast. As of 2017, Amalgam Comics and Coffeehouse was one of only five Black-owned comic stores in the United States.

Growing up, Ariell Johnson aspired to become a dancer and even auditioned for Philadanco, a Philadelphia dance company. She also loved comics, crediting the X-Men character Storm as the character that kept her interested in the world of comics. In a 2016 interview with *Essence,* she said, "When you are a person of color, you're scraping the bottom of the barrel to find someone you can identify with. I always felt like I was watching other people's adventures. Being introduced to Storm was a pivotal moment for me because had I not come across her, I might have grown out of my love for [comics]."

In 2017 she added, "Storm is the first superhero that I ever saw that looked like me. Before "meeting" Storm I always felt like I was watching from the sidelines while watching cartoons and such, but Storm made me feel like I could be a part of the action."

The idea for Amalgam Comics & Coffeehouse came while Johnson was in college. The loss of her favorite coffee shop, where she had spent many Friday afternoons reading the week's newest comics, inspired her to one day open her own community space centered around geek culture.

**"IN MY STORE, HAVING BROWN PEOPLE, WOMEN, AND QUEER PEOPLE ON THE SHELVES IS NOT AN AFTERTHOUGHT, IT'S INTENTIONAL."**

Opening Amalgam Comics catapulted Johnson onto the national and international stage, as book industry outlets from Shelf Awareness to Publishers Weekly covered the opening. The store quickly became a critical space for diverse comics and comic creators. In a 2017 interview with author Sheena Howard, Johnson said, "I did not know how important my opening the store would be to the larger geek community. I didn't know until we went viral that first time. But I think the reason people connect with my story and my mission and why it has become so important on a larger scale all comes back to representation and ownership. In my store, having brown people, women, and queer people on the shelves is not an afterthought, it's intentional."

In 2016, Ariell Johnson appeared alongside Marvel hero Riri Williams, the first Black woman to put on the Iron Man armor, on a variant cover of Invincible Iron Man #1. The illustration shows the two trailblazing women in Johnson's coffee shop, chatting and enjoying a meal.

In 2017, Johnson received a $50,000 grant from the Knight Foundation to add a programming space, called Amalgam University, to the store. As Johnson told the *Philadelphia Inquirer,* offering classes on writing, drawing, production and design for aspiring comic book creators will help elevate the level of self-published work available. The expansion, which is due to be completed in 2018, will double the size of the store and provide opportunities for a range of creators from diverse communities.

# JOHNSON, MAT

**(August 19, 1970– )**
- **Born in Germantown, PA**
- **Quaker Earlham College**
- **Columbia University, MFA**
- **Comic creator, professor, and novelist**
- **Author of *Incognegro*, *Right State*, and *Dark Rain: A New Orleans Story***

Mat Johnson is the writer of acclaimed novels, comics, and nonfiction prose. His comics writing credits include *Hellblazer Special: Papa Midnite*, the historical fiction comic *Incognegro*, the satirical *Dark Rain: A New Orleans Story*, and *Right State*, a thriller about an assassination attempt on the second Black president of the United States.

Johnson was born to an African American mother and Irish American father. Growing up, Johnson knew he was Black, but due to his straight hair and light skin, most people didn't realize it. Thus his Blackness became a statement, something he had to confirm aloud even as he worked to equally honor his white side.

> "GERMANTOWN WAS A PHYSICAL REPRESENTATION OF MY ETHNIC IDENTITY: THIS CONTRAST BETWEEN EUROPEAN CULTURE AND AFRICAN CULTURE, THIS CONTRAST BETWEEN WEALTH AND POVERTY, AND THIS OVERWHELMING WEIGHT OF HISTORY."
>
> *- MAT JOHNSON*
> *INTERVIEW WITH NPR, JUNE 29, 2015*

At the age of sixteen, Johnson learned he could buy an entire novel for the same price as an issue of a comic book. He began to read science fiction, satire, and Black American fiction. This new inspiration fueled him through high school and college, during which Johnson received the Thomas J. Watson Fellowship for future leaders, a one-year grant awarded for study outside of the United States. With the grant, Johnson traveled throughout West Africa and Europe to interview Black expatriates.

In 2000, Barnes & Noble selected Johnson's novel *Drop* for its Discover Great New Writers series. He followed up with *Hunting in Harlem* (2003), a satire on the intersection of gentrification and idealism, for which he won the Zora Neale Hurston/ Richard Wright Legacy Award in 2004.

Novels would lead Johnson back to comics in the mid-2000s. He had become a fan of Vertigo Comics via series like *The Sandman* (1989) and *Hellblazer* (1988). After a friend introduced him to Karen Berger, the original executive editor of Vertigo, a DC Comics imprint, he approached her with several comic ideas. They ultimately decided to apply the setting of his nonfiction book on eighteenth-century slave revolts, *The Great Negro Plot,* to a Hellblazer miniseries.

In 2005, *Hellblazer Special: Papa Midnite* went to press. With art by Tony Akins and Dan Green, this series saw the Papa Midnite character blossom from a mystical savage stereotype into a Vertigo icon, one possessing a complex, often nefarious history. Johnson placed Midnite in 1700s Manhattan, where the character embroiled himself in two historic slave revolts, the New York Slave Revolt of 1712 and the New York Slave Conspiracy of 1741. The series established Johnson as a comic book creator of note and cemented Vertigo as the home of his comics work.

In 2007, Johnson published *The Great Negro Plot* and was named the first USA James Baldwin Fellow for literature before returning to comics. His second Vertigo project, *Incognegro,* originated from his childhood and his ability to pass for white. It rose from the memory of young Johnson and a cousin who imagined they were secret agents for the Underground Railroad, posing as white people to help others escape from slavery. Johnson was also inspired by the story of Walter White, a 1930s journalist who passed as white in order to unmask lynching in the South. Johnson blended these influences into *Incognegro,* the story of a man who must pass for white and travel to Mississippi to save his brother who was accused of murdering a white woman. It was illustrated by Warren Pleece with cover art by Stephen John Phillips.

Johnson's next project, *Dark Rain: A New Orleans Story,* pitches a pair of penny ante ex-convicts into a bank heist set during the Hurricane Katrina flood. This darkly humorous graphic novel was illustrated by Simon Gane.

Johnson released his fourth novel, the acclaimed satire *Pym,* in 2011 and was awarded the John Dos Passos Prize for Literature the same year. In *Pym,* the lead character goes on a quest to search for a rumored all-Black island in Antarctica. In an interview with NPR, Johnson remarked, "I didn't even realize that the book, in part, was about my own biracial identity until the end."

Johnson published his most explosive graphic novel, *Right State,* in 2012, coinciding with President Barack Obama's reelection bid. In it, the Secret Service discovers an extremist plot to assassinate the second Black president of the United States. Much like *Incognegro,* the ex-commando hero of *Right State* must infiltrate the group to avert a sociopolitical disaster. The influence of the taut political climate surrounding the forty-fourth president's tenure resonates throughout the book.

*Loving Day* (2015) is a return to Johnson's largely autobiographical prose. The novel tells the story of a man who returns to Philadelphia to meet the daughter he's never known, who in turn never knew she was Black. In August 2015, Showtime signed on to adapt the work into a comedy series with Johnson set to serve as executive producer.

Mat Johnson is a faculty member of the University of Houston's creative writing program, where he has worked since 2007. His wife, Meera Bowman-Johnson, joined him there as director of communications in September 2016.

# JONES, ARVELL

**(Sept. 5 1952– )**
- **Born in Detroit, MI**
- **Comic artist, illustrator and entrepreneur**
- **Founder of Encode Media Group and Comic Art Workshop**

Artist and entrepreneur Arvell Jones has worked as a penciler with Marvel Comics, DC Comics, and Milestone Media. He also founded several media startups and education centers, including Encode Media Group and the Detroit-based Comic Art Workshop.

In the early 1970s, Jones was well known in Detroit's fan scene, where he worked to bring one of the earliest comic fan conventions in the country, Detroit Triple Fan Fare, to life. He also gained attention for his work in *Fan Informer,* a local fanzine. His involvement in Triple Fan Fare allowed Jones to meet local talent destined to become industry professionals, including Rich Buckler, Tom Orzechowski, Jim Starlin, and Keith Pollard.

As the skills of this group matured, Rich Buckler broke in as a penciler at Marvel, allowing Jones to also begin his professional career by assisting Buckler with his work. His first professional credit was for penciling assists on *Thor* #228, dated October 1974. His break came in 1972 with the publication of *Marvel Premiere* #20, starring Iron Fist. Jones continued to work on Iron Fist stories and, along with Tony Isabella, created the Black superheroine Misty Knight as a supporting character.

After the end of his Iron Man run, Jones left to pursue work at rival DC comics. Starting with *Super-Team Family*, Jones went on to illustrate a Supergirl/Doom Patrol team-up published in *The Superman Family* #191–#193 and 1985's *All-Star Squadron*. He then took take a hiatus from comics to focus on work in television at Detroit's CBS affiliate WJBK Channel 2.

Returning to comics in 1993, Jones became a part of Denys Cowan and Dwayne McDuffie's ambitious Milestone Media imprint with DC Comics. He went on to pencil several issues of *Blood Syndicate*, *Hardware*, and *Kobalt*. He returned to Marvel that same year to pencil *Captain America Annual* #13 and do breakdown assists on *Daredevil* #343.

Arvell Jones's entrepreneurial work spans several decades. In 1991, he started the Comic Art Workshop to help launch a new generation of Detroit comics creators. In 1995, Jones founded the internet startup Fantasticon.net, where he and his team were early adopters of web series and interactive webcomics. Finally, in 2004 he founded Encode Media Group, becoming the executive producer and director of Encode Entertainment LLC, its subsidiary, in 2008.

# KNIGHT, KEITH EDGAR

Keith Knight is the author and illustrator of *The K Chronicles*, *th(ink)*, and *The Knight Life*. *The K Chronicles* and *The Knight Life* are semiautobiographical depictions of daily and family life, with an eye to political commentary. His more overtly political comic, *(th)ink*, is a weekly single-panel cartoon addressing current events and social issues.

(Aug. 24, 1966– )
- **Born in Malden, MA**
- **Salem State College, graphic design, 1990**
- **Cartoonist, screenwriter, and public speaker**
- **Creator of The K Chronicles, th(ink), and The Knight Life**

While Knight had been drawing cartoons for much of his life, his first professional work was in 1993, when he began the multipanel weekly strip *The K Chronicles* for the *San Francisco Examiner*. Semiautobiographical in nature, the strip is now well known for its satirical take on American politics and current events, and its frank discussion of racial tension in America. The strip spread to the progressive news website Salon.com after the site's founding in 1995, and has since been published in twenty-eight websites and local and national print publications. As of this writing, *The K Chronicles* was being distributed weekly by the liberal political website Daily Kos.

Besides his work in comics, Keith Knight has also worked as a screenwriter and musician. In 1996, he turned three episodes of *The K Chronicles* into a script for a seven-minute episode of the German cartoon series *Jetzt kommt ein Karton!* (Now Comes a Cartoon!). During this period also helped found the independent comedy punk/hip-hop group The Marginal Prophets alongside Jeff Kramer under the name K-Squared. In 1997, the Prophets' first album, *Twist the Knob*, sold 20,000 copies. Knight created cover art for both *Twist the Knob* and the group's two successive albums. That same year marked the release of the first of many *K Chronicles* collections, *Dances with Sheep*.

Starting in the early 2000s, Knight began public speaking, narrating slideshows based on his comics. In 2002, the Marginal Prophets' first live album, *Dead Hippie Bootleg*, was released. This album was closely followed by the Prophets' final and most lauded album, *Bohemian Rap CD*, which won the 2004 California Music Award for Outstanding Rap Album. He also married Kerstin Konietzka, who changed her name to Konietzka-Knight.

In January of 2002, Keith began his second comic strip, the single-panel self-distributed weekly satire *(th)ink*. Less autobiographical than *The K Chronicles*, *(th)ink* is a political commentary strip that draws largely from current events, especially events that affect communities of color. Already no stranger to controversy, *(th)ink* cemented Knight's reputation as a humorist who is willing to shine a light on uncomfortable American truths.

In 2006, Knight was awarded the Glyph Award for Best Comic Strip, the first of a string of major comics awards that marked wider recognition of his work. He won additional Glyph Awards in 2007, 2009, and 2010. In 2007, *The K Chronicles* was awarded the highest honor in syndicated comics, the Harvey Award for Best Syndicated Strip, beating out industry luminaries like Gary Trudeau (*Doonesbury*) and Patrick McDonnell (*Mutts*).

While living in San Francisco, Knight also worked closely with writer Dave Eggers and served on the board of Eggers's nonprofit writing center, 826 Valencia. Knight also taught at and worked with San Francisco's Charles Schulz–founded Cartoon Art Museum.

The late 2000s brought some of Knight's most significant life events. In February of 2007, he and Kerstin moved from San Francisco to Los

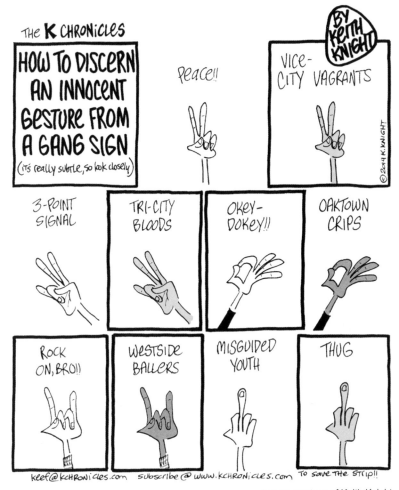

Image courtesy of Keith Knight

Angeles. That July, he starred in *Independents,* a documentary about independent comics creators. In May of 2008, Knight started his next big endeavor, an autobiographical comic called *The Knight Life.* Distributed by United Features Syndicate, the black-and-white strip featured a quieter version of Knight's razor-sharp eye for social satire. Increasing his work output considerably, Knight also started contributing to *MAD* magazine, with features titled "Father Flannity's Hot Tub Confessions" and "Bully Baby," and to *ESPN,* with the sports editorial "SportsKnight."

Also in 2008, Kerstin gave birth to the Knights' first son, Jasper. Keith Knight has spoken extensively about the joys of parenting and how being a father forced him to take the final step into adulthood. Knight's children (his second son, Julian, was born in 2013) are also a significant part of his artistic work, and are featured regularly in *The Knight Life*.

In 2010, Salon.com, one of Knight's original publishers and distributors, elected to stop carrying *The K Chronicles*, marking the end of an era. However, 2010 also brought Knight yet another major award: the Comic-Con Inkpot Award, which he was awarded along with other major independent and mainstream comics creators, including Peter Bagge (*Hate*), Berkeley Breathed (*Bloom County*), and prolific comic book creators like Phil Jimenez and Kurt Busiek.

Image courtesy of Keith Knight

Noted for some time as a public speaker, in 2015 Knight began performing his best-known slideshow "They Shoot Black People, Don't They?" a cartoon history of police violence in the United States. The show has been performed across the United States and in Germany; Knight's stated goal is to take the show to every state in the country.

In 2015, Keith Knight was named an NAACP History Maker. The same year, the Knight family moved to the college town of Chapel Hill, North Carolina, where Knight is a frequent attendant and speaker at local comic conventions and other public events.

To date, Knight has published fourteen collections of his comics and has written two how-to books – one on community-based art, the other on launching a successful Kickstarter. His titles continue to play an important role in contemporary comic culture and in the discussion of race relations in America.

# LOUIS, MILDRED

- **Born in Boston, MA**
- **Sheridan College, animation**
- **Comic creator and illustrator**
- **Author of *Agents of the Realm***

Mildred Louis is the author of the fantasy webcomic *Agents of the Realm*. Inspired by the *mahou shoujo* (magical girl) subgenre of manga and anime, it tells the story of a group of college-age women of diverse backgrounds who take on the role of magical protectors.

Originally published in 2014, the series has been featured in a variety of publications, including A.V. Club, Comics Alliance, Autostraddle, and Black Girl Nerds. The first print volume was published in 2016 by Sapphire Shard Press.

In an interview with Autostraddle, Louis noted a desire to see more people like herself in her favorite genres, noting, "Oftentimes when you see people of color in stories, they get reduced to stereotypes and/or very, very, very basic roles. I just wanted to use this as my chance to unapologetically put them at the forefront and show that we, too, can be heroes.

"Growing up, I didn't really come across much representation of women of color in queer romances. This ended up really messing up how I saw myself and that aspect of my identity. As much as it's important to show queer content, it's also just as important to diversify how that content is presented."

Louis also spoke with Black Girl Nerds about being an African American woman in the comic industry: "I know that for me, getting into comics really opened my eyes to how many women of color illustrators and storytellers there actually are out there. I think the fact that there aren't currently a lot in mainstream companies, though, makes it seem like there really aren't that many, if any at all. I think a lot of us are gravitating towards the independent route because we have more control here. We don't have to worry about being rejected by companies, we don't have to worry about another person actively telling us how we should be or what we should be selling. So we're definitely out there! It's just a lot of us are working on building a name on our own, so it may take a little more searching to find us."

> "I LOVED MAGICAL GIRL STORIES WHEN I WAS GROWING UP.... THE KIND OF INFLUENCE [SAILOR MOON] AND OTHER SHOWS HAVE HAD ON ME HAS IMPACTED ME THROUGH MY ENTIRE LIFE, SO IT WAS KIND OF INEVITABLE THAT I'D END UP DOING A MAGICAL GIRL STORY AT SOME POINT."
>
> - MILDRED LOUIS
> INTERVIEW WITH COMICS ALLIANCE

# MAGRUDER, NILAH

**(March 1982– )**
- **Born in Pasadena, MD**
- **Fredrick's Hood College, BA in communication arts**
- **Ringling College of Art and Design, BFA in computer animation**
- **Writer, artist, and comic creator**
- **Author of M.F.K.**

Nilah Magruder is the creator of *M.F.K.*, a fantasy adventure webcomic. In 2016, she also became the first Black woman to write for Marvel Comics with a crossover story in *A Year of Marvels: September Infinite Comic* #1.

Magruder began drawing at a young age, influenced by her parents' art that was displayed throughout her childhood home. After working inconsistently on an original comic series throughout college, she started the webcomic *M.F.K.* in 2012.

*M.F.K.* follows a young girl, Abbie, as she journeys across a wide desert to return her mother's ashes to her homeland. Written for young audiences, it features evocative artwork and engaging characters, including a deaf protagonist. In 2016, Insight Comics licensed *M.F.K.* for print distribution, with its first volume scheduled for September of 2017.

The webcomic was inspired in part by a lack of representation in Magruder's favorite comic and manga series. They featured few people of color, and female characters were often portrayed as less than their male counterparts. In response, Magruder's work is peopled with characters of many ages, ethnicities, and abilities. She represents people of color not as oddities or caricatures, but as fully rounded human beings with rich internal lives.

In September 2016, Magruder became the first Black woman to write for Marvel Comics. First appearing in *A Year of Marvels: September Infinite Comic* #1, her crossover comic features the characters Tippy-Toe, Squirrel Girl's animal sidekick, and Rocket Raccoon, from *Guardians of the Galaxy*. Its publication predates Roxane Gay and Yona Harvey's Black Panther spinoff series, *World of Wakanda*, by only a few weeks.

Nilah Magruder received the inaugural Dwayne McDuffie Award for Diversity in Comics in 2015. Her work has been reviewed in publications ranging from the *Washington Post* to Comics Alliance, 13th Dimension, and Comics Beat.

Image courtesy of Nilah Magruder

# MANCE, AJUAN

(September 19, 1966– )
- **Brown University, BA in English**
- **University of Michigan, MA and PhD in English**
- **Scholar and artist**
- **Creator of** *1001 Black Men*

Ajuan Mance is the creator of *1001 Black Men*, a portrait series dedicated to representing Black men in all their complexity and diversity. She is also an academic and the author of numerous scholarly articles, presentations, and books.

Her inspiration for *1001 Black Men* came from an issue of a Black women's publication designed to celebrate Black men and masculinity. Despite its good intentions, Mance noted that it focused exclusively on physically attractive, expensively dressed, successful men. Modeling her project after Elisha Lim's *300 Butches*, she set out to present Black men as they are, rich and poor alike. Mance published the series online over seven years, beginning in June of 2010 and ending in January of 2017 with a portrait of her father, Alphonzo Mance, Sr.

Image courtesy of Ajuan Mance

Reaction to the project was largely positive, with male viewers responding that Mance's work marked the first time an artist actually saw them. The few dissenting opinions came from older Black women who felt her illustration style was too cartoonish and looked too much like street art. Although Mance understood their critiques, she wished the women had recognized that her work seeks to celebrate Black masculinity and dismantle negative stereotypes.

Her work employs the thick lines and geometric shapes found in stained glass windows. Featuring flat panes of color and varying shades of the same hue, her illustrations resemble both Cubist portraits and contemporary design. She typically begins with the nose and lips of her subjects, noting that while they are the features for which Blacks are most maligned, to her they are the most beautiful.

Outside of her illustration work, Mance is the author of numerous scholarly articles and two books, *Black Women: African American Women Poets and Self-Representation, 1877–2000* (University of Tennessee Press, 2008) and *Proud Legacy: The Colored Schools of Malvern, Arkansas and the Community that Made Them* (Henson-Benson Foundation, 2013). She is currently an associate professor of English at Mills University, having previously taught at the University of Oregon.

Image courtesy of Ajuan Mance

Mance views her scholarly position as political, voicing frustration with those who act as if she and other African Americans in academia are invisible. She is the recipient of numerous awards and accolades, including the Outstanding Academic Title award from the American Library Association *Choice* magazine in 2009.

In 2000, she spoke at the Carnegie Foundation's National Leadership Conference on Service Learning in Higher Education. From 2005 to 2008, she occupied the post of Wert Chair in American Literature at Mills College, and the Aurelia Henry Reinhardt Chair thereafter. She was also one of thirty-five scholars to serve in a one-day workshop at the Social Sciences Research Council in 2008.

# MARTINBROUGH, SHAWN C.

(April 1971– )
- **School of Visual Arts, BFA in illustration, 1993**
- **Born in Harlem, NY**
- **Illustrator of *Luke Cage Noir* and *Thief of Thieves***

Since his professional debut in 1993, Shawn Martinbrough has worked on numerous titles for Milestone, Marvel, DC, and Image Comics, including *Luke Cage Noir* and *Black Panther: The Most Dangerous Man Alive*. He is also the author of *How to Draw Noir Comics: The Art and Technique of Visual Storytelling*.

After attending the arts-focused LaGuardia High School and the School of Visual Arts, Martinbrough worked with Marvel Comics as a featured artist for Clive Barker's *Hellraiser* series. Later that year he joined Milestone Comics, where he was an inker for *The Shadow Academy* and *Static*.

As a creator and illustrator at DC Comics, Martinbrough cocreated characters that were featured in the *Batman: Gotham Knights* and *GOTHAM* animated series. For two years, Martinbrough was the artist on *Detective Comics*, the flagship Batman title for DC Comics with author Greg Rucka. His distinctive use of light and shadow were an ideal fit for capturing Batman's Gotham City, and noir became his signature style and technique. In 2007, Martinbrough authored *How to Draw Noir Comics: The Art and Technique of Visual Storytelling*, published by Random House.

In 2011, he contributed to a limited edition issue of *Captain America* for the US Army & Air Force Exchange Service. As a tribute for their service, one million copies were distributed to military service personnel, timed to coincide with the debut of the *Captain America* film.

Martinbrough's graphic novel projects for Marvel include *Luke Cage Noir* and *Black Panther: The Most Dangerous Man Alive*, which debuted in 2010. With the success of the 2016 debut of the Netflix *Luke Cage* series, the character has resurfaced as a popular topic of interest. Reviewers listed *Luke Cage Noir* as one of the superior Marvel Noir texts, due in large part to Martinbrough's illustrations.

Since 2012, Martinbrough has illustrated the graphic novel *Thief of Thieves*, authored by *The Walking Dead* creator Robert Kirkman. Published by Image Comics, it tells the story of an elite art thief whose efforts to retire are made more difficult by the opposition of his business associates and pursuit by the law. Martinbrough also cocreated and cowrote *The Ren*, a noir graphic novel set during the Harlem Renaissance and published by First Second Books. In 2016, the feature film *Deadpool* introduced characters Martinbrough cocreated with DC Comics president Geoff Johns.

In addition to comics and film, Martinbrough is also active in marketing and advertising. He continues to introduce new ideas for television, film, and print publications.

# MARTINEZ, ALITHA EVELYN

Alitha Martinez is a veteran of the American superhero comic industry. Her talents are diverse; she has experience as a penciler, colorist, inker, cover artist, and writer. She is also the creator of an original comic, *Yume and Ever*.

- **Born in New York, NY**
- **Artist and comic creator**
- **Illustrated *Black Panther* and *New Crusaders***
- **Author of *Yume and Ever***

Martinez began her professional career as Joe Quesada's assistant on the 1997 Azreal/Ash crossover between DC and Event Comics. While working on that project, she was also co-inker on *Aquaman* and assisted with JG Jones's *Black Widow*. After those early uncredited projects, her first credited work was on Marvel Knights' 1998 *Black Panther*. She worked with Mark Texeira doing pencil, ink, and gray-tone wash.

*"I CAN'T BELIEVE THAT A COVER I'VE DRAWN WAS WRAPPED AROUND AN ADAM HUGHES BOOK! I'VE LOVED HIS WORK SINCE I WAS A KID!"*

In addition to her work on *Black Panther*, in 1998 she also contributed to various *Battlebook* series for Marvel characters such as Spider-Girl, Thor, Ironman, Gambit, Rogue, Shi, and Captain America. She also started producing cover art, beginning with *Iron Man* #37 and #39. Her first independent work was in the 1999 issue of *Cable Annual*. Also in 1999 came the opportunity to participate in *Iron Man ½*, where she replaced Sean Chen and published as A. Martinez. Further projects included *Voltron: Defender of the Universe*, NBC's *Heroes*, and *New 52: Batgirl*.

In 2008, Martinez began working as an illustrator for Lerner Publishing, providing art for the Choose Your Own Adventure books *Kung Fu Masters* and the *Quest for Dragon Mountain*. She also partnered with author Dan Jolley on the title *My Boyfriend Bites* for the young adult graphic novel series *My Boyfriend Is a Monster*.

*The New Crusaders* for Archie Comics was a shift from her previous projects, featuring a markedly different art style from that of DC and Marvel. During this time, she illustrated covers for *The New Crusaders* as well as *Betty and Veronica* and *Josie and the Pussycats*. About her work on Archie, Martinez stated, "I can't believe that a cover I've drawn was wrapped around an Adam Hughes book! I've loved his work since I was a kid!"

Alitha Martinez is the author of two original stories, the 2006 comic *Yume and Ever* and the illustrated novella *Foreign*. Published by her own imprint, Ariotstorm Productions, they present universal themes, such as love, conflict, and coming-of-age.

# McGRUDER, AARON

**(May 29, 1974– )**
- **Born in Chicago, IL**
- **University of Maryland, College Park**
- **Writer, producer, and cartoonist**
- **Creator of *The Boondocks***

Aaron McGruder is the author of *The Boondocks*, a syndicated comic strip that ran from 1996 to 2006. Originally created for the University of Maryland's student newspaper, the strip would later become a household name, with a popular but controversial animated series and widespread audience familiarity with its main characters – the wry, rebellious Huey and Riley Freeman.

When he was a child, McGruder's family moved from a primarily Black neighborhood of Chicago to a majority-white suburb of Baltimore. This firsthand experience with life as a racial minority had a defining impact on him, going on to inspire his later work in comics.

As a student at the University of Maryland, McGruder developed a comic strip for the school newspaper that combined his interests in music, culture, and current events. After a period of being published exclusively in the *Diamondback*, McGruder began posting his strips online. Attaining increasing popularity, in 1998 *The Boondocks* was featured nationally in the rap magazine *The Source*.

In 1999, McGruder negotiated a contract with Universal Press Syndicate. Its debut, appearing in 160 newspapers nationwide, was the largest debut to date for a syndicated comic strip. Almost immediately, the comic's satirical take on racial issues and public events mired it in controversy. Both Black and white audiences accused it of derogatory portrayals of its subjects. Others saw the strip as a refreshing change, conveying a once-silenced voice of the Black community. A few years later, in the wake of the September 11 attacks, several newspapers pulled the comic from publication entirely when the characters were shown making fun of the media and its praise of President George W. Bush.

While controversy continues to surround the work, its lasting success is undeniable. In 2000, McGruder joined Adult Swim as the executive producer of the animated *Boondocks* series. It ended after four seasons when McGruder had a falling out with some of the show's contributors. He maintained an amicable relationship with Adult Swim, however, and is now working on a live-action comedy, *Black Jesus*, about a modern-day Jesus living in the hood. He also cowrote George Lucas's *Red Tails*, based on the Tuskegee Airmen from World War II, which aired in 2012.

Never afraid of speaking his mind through his creations, McGruder continues to spark national conversations about race and stereotyping.

## MILLS, SHAWNA

Shawna Mills is the creator of *Violator Union*, an independent graphic novel cowritten with Josephine Basch. She has also directed music videos, created character designs, developed video games, and worked on myriad other artistic projects.

> **(December 16, 1986– )**
> - **Born in Harlem, NY**
> - **Bradley Academy for the Visual Arts, 2005–2007**
> - **Artist and animator**
> - **Creator of *Violator Union***

Shawna Mills's first major project was a planned HBO series called *Jungle Crook*. She was still a student at the High School of Art and Design when she joined the developer team. After two years of study at the Bradley Academy for the Visual Arts, she worked as an intern, directed music videos, and contributed to various other projects.

Her vivid art style, which was heavily influenced by graffiti and early hip-hop, caught the attention of editors Damian Duffy and John Jennings, who featured her work in their 2010 anthology, *Black Comix: African American Independent Comics Art and Culture.*

In 2011, Mills worked as a 2-D art director for Marroni Electronic Entertainment. Later that year, she released a sketchbook, *N.A.P.* (Not A Pro). In 2012, she collaborated with rapper Ja Rule for the animated music video *Parachute.* This was also the year Mills joined Marvel and Disney XD, working on projects such as *Hulk: Agents of S.M.A.S.H.,* *Guardians of the Galaxy,* and *Ultimate Spider-Man.*

As she gained more exposure, Mills started contributing character designs to DMC Comics, an imprint launched in 2013 by hip-hop legend Darryl McDaniels of Run-DMC. She also created storyboards for the popular Cartoon Network/Adult Swim animation series *Black Dynamite.*

In 2014, Mills debuted a futuristic graphic novel, *Violator Union,* publishing two volumes: *Traitors* and *Places.* Launched in 2013 via crowdfunding, *Violator Union* is a dystopian series that follows a group of career criminals fighting an oppressive regime. Mills is both its creator and illustrator, sharing writing duties with coauthor Josephine Basch.

Mills is also the creator of *BoomTagX,* an action-adventure RPG video game under development with Mugen Studios. Like *Violator Union,* the game combines fantasy, combat, and a futuristic setting.

# MORAIS, DAVIANN

**(August 13, 1984– )**
- **Born in Miami, FL**
- **Florida International University, Elementary Education, 2007**
- **Artist and illustrator**
- **Published in *Comfort Food Zine***

Daviann Morais is a self-taught artist and illustrator. Her work has been published in a variety of contexts, including books, webcomics, and anthology zines.

Daviann Morais grew up reading Sunday funnies, X-Men, and Japanese manga. She gained inspiration from titles such as *Johnny Wander, Fungus Grotto, The Meek, Boondocks,* and *VIBE,* as well as the works of Josh Lesnick and the all-female Japanese manga artist group Clamp. After attempting a few comics in high school, she ended up focusing primarily on illustration until after she finished college.

Between 2008 and 2012, Morais published her first comic, a collaboration with a longtime friend, on the website PetiteSymphony.com. Called *Pet Symph*, it was a comedy slice-of-life comic about fan culture. She was later chosen to replace the artist for *Kickin' Rad*, a comic published on the same site.

"I DID A RECIPE COMIC ABOUT MY MOTHER'S CORNBREAD RECIPE! IT WAS A LOT OF FUN AND DEBUTED AT THE SMALL PRESS EXPO ALONGSIDE MANY OTHER FOOD-RELATED COMICS."

In 2013, Morais's art was published in Lauren Jordan's *Comfort Food Zine,* an anthology zine featuring comics and illustrations on the subject of food.

Daviann Morais's most personally meaningful creative work was in 2001, when she created illustrations for the Miami chapter of the National Association for the Advancement of Colored People (NAACP). Having done community service with the group throughout middle and high school, she was honored to provide illustrations for its 2001 awards ceremony.

Most recently, Morais's work was published in the 2015 *Women of Wisdom* project. She and other artists illustrated quotes from prominent women featured in the book.

Daviann notes that opportunities in the comics industry are expanding, especially for African Americans.

"I feel like compared to when I was young and there really wasn't much representation in comics I had seen or read outside

Image courtesy of Daviann Morais

of *The Boondocks* and some Marvel titles, there is a lot more now! If anything, there is definitely a lot more opportunities now than ever. I feel like in the past let's say four to five years, I've seen and met a lot of African American artists and writers in the field of comics."

As of 2017, Daviann continues to work on improving her artistic skills and achieving her personal and career goals.

---

### CREATIVE TIPS

Knowing that it can be challenging to get your name out there in the field of art and comics, especially for African Americans, Daviann Morais advises to keep at it and not be discouraged.

"Always ask others to give a look at your work. Criticism can hit hard, but sometimes it's good to see and hear things from another person's perspective. There are so many resources out there available to you, and even when things get hard, remember there is a whole community of writers and artists just like us."

---

# ODOM, YUMY

(June 5, 4545 S.K.Y.– )
- **Born in Brooklyn, NY**
- **Educator, writer, radio host, and convention founder**
- **Founder of the East Coast Black Age of Comics Convention**

Yumy Odom is the founder of the East Coast Black Age of Comics Convention. Occurring yearly since 2002, it is also home to the Glyph Comics Awards, the yearly award for excellence in comics by, for, or about people of color.

Yumy Odom's first exposure to comics came in the summer of 1975 while recovering from an arm injury. His mother brought him copies of Marvel titles *The Fantastic Four, The Avengers*, and *Hulk versus the Silver Surfer*. Already an avid consumer of ancient mythology like *Heru: The Avenger* and science-fiction programs like *Star Trek,* Odom quickly became a fan of the superhero genre.

Five years later, Odom began creating tales for his fictional Yumiverse with characters based on ancient figures. In 1982, Odom created a curriculum for summer youth programs, *Kemet & Komix in the Classroom,*

Image courtesy of Yumy Odom, artwork by Akinseye Brown

that used mythology, comics, and other media to improve student literacy. At this time, he also created the early versions of the forty-five characters that would comprise his property *Kham Chi: The Avenging Force*.

In the summer of 1986, Yumy Odom founded the nonprofit First World Komix, Incorporated. The aim of the company was to use ancient and contemporary myths to address human interconnectedness. At the same time, he continued developing the characters of the Yumiverse. Apadamax, based on the Nubian god Apedemak, was to be the Yumiverse's flagship character. He was joined by five principal characters, Karas, Raya, Kalia, Razanj, and Razaq, all Pan-African characters based on world mythologies.

In 1988, Odom relocated to Philadelphia and published *Kham Chi: The Avenging Force*. He also discovered a 1981 copy of *NOG*, by Turtel Onli, the father of the Black Age of Comics movement.

Between 1990 and 1992, Odom compiled a directory of producers/creators of Afrocentric comic characters and distributed the list among said persons. In those pre-internet days, Odom's aim was to develop an interconnected network of creators with shared interests.

Around 1998, Odom and comics historian Dr. William H. Foster III began discussing putting together a think tank based on Turtel Onli's Black Age concept. Their goal was to bring together interested people, be they illustrators, writers, or any other parties, to share ideas. The two discussed the idea with Onli in 2001 and set the apparatus in motion. Another year would pass before Odom, assisted not only by Foster, but also *Mama's Boyz* creator Jerry Craft and Omar Bilai, founder of the Museum of Black Superheroes, was able to bring the ECBACC into existence.

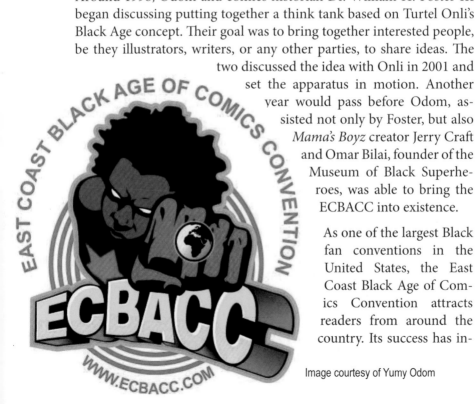

As one of the largest Black fan conventions in the United States, the East Coast Black Age of Comics Convention attracts readers from around the country. Its success has in-

Image courtesy of Yumy Odom

spired other convention founders, such as Joseph R Wheeler III of ON-YXCON, to create their own Afrocentric media conventions.

Yumy Odom also founded the Frator Heru Institute in Philadelphia, a nonprofit community-based education center that offers a range of classes on literacy, storytelling, and community organizing. It also supports community scholarship by providing resources for local scholars and entrepreneurs.

In the student workshops at ECBACC and Frator Heru alike, Yumy Odom's central concern is expanding the imagination. He wants students to move beyond simply creating Black versions of previously established white superheroes and superheroines and to create their own mythologies.

# ONLI, TURTEL

Turtel Onli is best known as the father of the Black Age of Comics, a movement he described as "comics products that are either owned, created, written or drawn for the African American aesthetic or perspective." He is also the author of several comic books, including *NOG: Protector of the Pyramides*. NOG, whose name stands for Nubian of Greatness, is widely considered to be the first Black Age superhero.

(January 25, 1952– )
- **Born in Chicago, IL**
- **School of the Art Institute of Chicago, BFA in fine art, MA in art therapy**
- **Artist, comic creator, and art teacher**
- **Originator of the Black Age of Comics movement**

As an ambitious high school graduate in 1970, Onli founded the Black Arts Guild to consolidate efforts of African American artists. Initially, Onli received little encouragement from his veteran artists, who warned him he had to pay his dues before he could significantly contribute to the field. He pressed on nonetheless, organizing touring exhibitions and publishing members' artwork.

After working as a therapy aide and paraprofessional, Onli opened the Helping Hand School for the Retarded (named before the shift to "intellectually disabled") and started attending the School of the Art Institute of Chicago with partial financial support from the Black Arts Guild. He also dabbled as a graffiti artist, although he quit that pursuit after getting in trouble with the law for an antidrug mural.

Upon his college graduation, Onli worked as a visual arts teacher in the Chicago Public Schools for more than two decades. During this time, he ran an after-school program in comic book art and publishing that led to the publication of a student-created anthology.

As the term "Afrocentric" was frequently met with discomfort among white art patrons, Turtel Onli coined a new term, "Rhythmistic," to describe his artwork. This combination of both primitive and futuristic elements first achieved mainstream success when, in 2007, one of his sculptures was featured on the front page of the *New York Times*.

Onli first introduced his concept of a Black Age of Comics in the early 1990s. In a 1993 editorial published in *Comics Buyer's Guide*, he noted that the few existing mainstream examples of Black superhero characters were often divorced from cultural and physical signifiers of Blackness in order to read as apolitical and "safe" to the white reading audience. "Curiously, we have the culturally oblivious black characters like *X-Men*'s Bishop or Storm who are long on presence but very short on cultural roots. Neither has nappy-kinky hair, brown eyes, or definite 'negroid' features. I guess the blacks in the 'X' universe have to be culture-neutral, powerful, exotic, and racially detached."

In 1993, Onli organized the first Black Age of Comics convention in Chicago. Held for four consecutive years, its success went on to inspire other Black Age of Comics conventions around the country. The largest, East Coast Black Age of Comics Convention, occurs annually in Philadelphia (see *Wheeler, Joseph R, III)*. Others take place in New York City, Los Angeles, Detroit, and Washington, D.C.

In 2005, Onli created a visual art exhibition honoring the work of his late grandfather and some of his own Rhythmistic paintings. It took place in the Center for the Visual and Performing Arts in Munster, Indiana. Some of his other major exhibitions include the group shows *Afrofuturism in the Visual Arts* at the Harriet Tubman museum and *AFRICOBRA:*

"MY POSITION IS THAT THE LACK OF PRESENCE IN TERMS OF 'BLACK COMICS' IS DUE TO THE FACT THAT BLACKS HAVE NOT FORMED SUCCESSFUL OR COMPETITIVE BLACK-OWNED AND -ORIENTED PUBLISHING CONCERNS. IT'S REALLY QUITE SIMPLE. NO BLACK COMICS COMPANY, NO BLACK COMICS."

- TURTEL ONLI, 1993

*Art and Impact* at the DuSable Museum of African American History. He currently runs his own comic company, Onli Studios, and continues to advocate for African American representation in the arts.

# ORMES, JACKIE

Jackie Ormes, née Zelda Mavin Jackson, was the first published female African American cartoonist. At the height of her career, her cartoons and comics reached more than a million readers across the nation through the Black press. Her comics, including *Torchy Brown*, *Candy*, and *Patty-Jo 'n' Ginger*, featured some of the

**(Aug. 1, 1911–Dec. 26, 1985)**
- **Born in Pittsburgh, PA**
- **Creator of *Torchy Brown in "Dixie to Harlem," Patty-Jo 'n' Ginger, Candy,* and *Torchy in Heartbeats***

earliest positive representations of Black women in comics, challenging the demeaning stereotypes of African Americans that were common in the mainstream press.

Zelda and her older sister, Delores, grew up outside of Pittsburgh in Monongahela, Pennsylvania. Zelda's natural ability as an artist brought her a position as arts editor on the 1929–30 Monongahela High School yearbooks. Here she demonstrated her earliest efforts as a cartoonist, with lively caricatures of her school's students and teachers on the yearbook pages. Ormes later acquired the nickname "Jackie," a shorter version of her maiden name.

After high school, Zelda Jackson was eager to begin her professional career. She applied to be a reporter for the *Pittsburgh Courier*, a weekly African American newspaper with national circulation. She was hired as a proofreader, with occasional opportunities to contribute articles.

While living in Pittsburgh, she met and married Earl Clark Ormes in 1931. They had a daughter, Jacqueline, in 1932, but the child died at age three due to a brain tumor.

After her daughter's death, Jackie Ormes continued to work part-time for the *Pittsburgh Courier*. In 1937, the paper began a one-year run of Ormes's *Torchy Brown in "Dixie to Harlem,"* making her the first African American woman to become a nationally published cartoonist. Her humorous comic strip portrayed Southern girl Torchy as she found stardom at the Cotton Club in a story that evoked the Great Migration.

Image courtesy of Professor W. Foster

Faced with economic challenges during the Great Depression, in 1938 the Ormeses left Pittsburgh to live with Earl's family in Salem, Ohio. In 1942, they moved to Chicago, where Earl Ormes worked in banking and in hotel management. He later managed the upscale Sutherland Hotel, one of few integrated hotels of the era. During this time, Jackie Ormes attended classes at the Art Institute of Chicago and did occasional reporting, briefly writing a social column for the *Chicago Defender*. After a seven-year break from cartooning, Ormes debuted her next work, *Candy,* which featured an attractive, wisecracking housemaid. The single panel cartoon ran in the *Defender* for four months in 1945.

In September 1945, Jackie released what would become her longest-running cartoon, *Patty-Jo 'n' Ginger.* This single-panel cartoon featured a fashionable college-educated woman, Ginger, and her opinionated younger sister, Patty-Jo. The comic featured gags about domestic life, while satirizing society and politics and protesting racial injustice.

Ormes often made her personal crusades public through the character of Patty-Jo. The outspoken little girl would sometimes admonish readers, "Did you VOTE Tuesday...?" or, "Find it in your pocket and your heart to join the march," referring to the March of Dimes that fought infantile paralysis.

"Shucks — Let's go price Atom bombs —
They haven't outlawed **them** yet!"

Image courtesy of Nancy Goldstein

The success of *Patty-Jo 'n' Ginger* led to the creation of the first upscale African American doll, Patty-Jo, made by the Terri Lee doll company in 1947. The doll has now become a desirable collector's item.

During the late 1940s, Jackie and Earl Ormes mixed with Chicago's African American elite, socializing with the leading political figures and entertainers of the time and contributing time and money to social activist organizations such as the Urban League. She produced charitable fashion shows, took part in arts functions, served on housing boards, and volunteered at election polls in her South Side community.

Ormes's politics, which fell decidedly to the left and were apparent to even a casual reader of her cartoons and comics, eventually led to her investigation by the FBI during the McCarthy era. These investigations extended from the 1940s through the mid-1950s.

Following the success of *Patty-Jo 'n' Ginger*, Ormes created a full-color romance-themed reboot of the Torchy character in *Torchy in Heartbeats*. Now reimagined as a mature, independent woman, Torchy challenged racism, violence against women, and environmental injustice.

Image courtesy of Nancy Goldstein

*Torchy in Heartbeats* also included a cut-out paper doll with an extensive, fashionable wardrobe in another nod to positive self-representation for young Black girls and women.

Jackie Ormes retired in 1956 to dedicate time to her husband and to volunteer work. She was a founding member of the DuSable Museum of African American History in Chicago. She also served as a board member of the South Side Community Art Center and on housing boards, and continued to produce charitable fashion events in South Side Chicago. In 1976, her husband, Earl Ormes, passed away. Ormes continued drawing regularly until the onset of rheumatoid arthritis. She passed away in December 1985, leaving behind a significant artistic and cultural legacy.

Jackie Ormes's posthumous honors include induction into the National Association of Black Journalists' Hall of Fame in 2014. She is also the namesake of the Ormes Society, an artists' collective that provides networking and promotion for Black women in the comic book industry.

# ORR, ERIC

Eric Orr is the creator of *Rappin' Max Robot*, the first hip-hop comic. After beginning his career as a graffiti artist in 1978, he was one of the first street artists to develop an iconic character, Robot Head, which became an iconographic shorthand for his work.

(1959– )
- **Born in the Bronx, NY**
- **School of the Visual Arts, Art Studies League**
- **Artist and comic creator**
- **Author of *Rappin' Max Robot***

In 1982, he met and collaborated with the renowned fine artist Keith Haring. The two collaborated on numerous works in the New York City Subway system, resulting in greater recognition of Orr's work in the street art community.

After studying art at the School of Visual Arts and the Art Studies League, Orr began working as a graphic designer and commercial artist. He produced imagery for musicians such as Masters of Ceremony, Afrika Bambaataa, and Jazzy Jay, the latter of whom was instrumental in the founding of Def Jam Recordings. Orr later served as art director for Jazzy Jay's label Strong City Records.

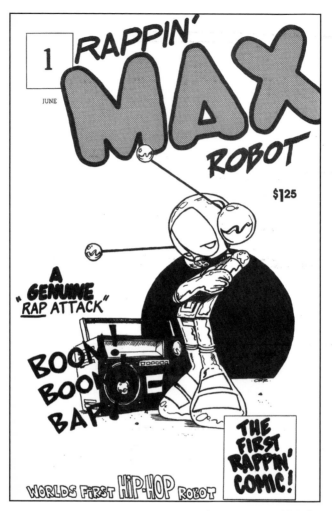

Image courtesy of Eric Orr

In 1986, Orr refined Robot Head into the independently published *Rappin' Max Robot*. Written entirely in rhyme, it follows the eponymous robot character around his daily life in New York City. The comic also included current news in the hip-hop community, such as record release dates and shows, and a guest art section populated by other graffiti artists.

Orr wrote, drew, and distributed the twelve-page, black-and-white comic himself. Published with the financial help of both Orr's family and friends and Keith Haring, the initial print run of five hundred copies sold out by summer of 1986. The first issue was later featured in *Rap Masters* magazine.

Orr took time off from his art in the 1990s to raise a family, returning to full-time production by the early 2000s. Since then, his art has gone on to grace numerous New York art galleries, including the Schomburg Center's Latimer Edison Gallery and WallWorks New York gallery. It has taken him as far as New Zealand, where he taught children's art workshops. Closer to home, he assisted in the creation of a street mural for the benefit of the Children's Aid Society and is a frequent Comic-Con attendant in both New York and San Diego.

As of 2017, he was still creating, working from his Hunts Point studio. Copies of *Rappin' Max Robot* are housed in the Cornell University Library's Hip Hop Collection. It was later the first hip-hop comic book to be included in Columbia University's archive of rare books and manuscripts.

# PASSMORE, BENJAMIN SCOTT

Benjamin Passmore is the author of *DAYGLOAYHOLE*, a postapocalyptic adventure comic, and *Your Black Friend*, a single-issue comic about race and racism in the United States. In 2017, *Your Black Friend* was nominated for an Eisner Award for Best Single Issue.

**(Aug. 25, 1983– )**
- **Born in Great Barrington, MA**
- **Savannah College of Art and Design, BFA in sequential arts, 2009**
- **Comic creator and artist**
- **Author of *Your Black Friend* and *DAYGLOAYHOLE***

Passmore knew that he wanted to create comics for a living from an early age. In the Black comic book characters Spawn and Venom, he found stories that reflected his own experiences. He was particularly interested in Venom, who, in oscillating between a weakened white Symbiote and an aggressive Black antihero, provided him with an artistic metaphor for his personal struggles as a biracial person.

Growing up as a biracial child in rural Massachusetts, Passmore spent a significant amount of time alone walking through the woods and exploring abandoned buildings. These personal experiences of isolation and seclusion would later translate into major themes in his artwork.

Early on, Passmore struggled as a student and was often placed in classes for students with learning disabilities. His mother, Karin Joy Passmore, advocated strongly for her son's education. Once the school discovered that some of his problems in the classroom stemmed from being unable to see the chalkboard, Passmore was prescribed Ritalin and reading glasses. While these relieved some of his learning barriers, Passmore still felt trapped in the K–12 educational system. After two years at his local high school and two at a residential reform school, he attended the Savannah College of Art and Design (SCAD), graduating in 2009.

> DAYGLOAYHOLE IS "A PSYCHEDELIC POST-APOCALYPTIC ADVENTURE COMIC ABOUT MISANTHROPY, OLD PUNKS, GENTRIFICATION, TV FACED MONSTERS, ANARCHISM, ART THEORY, [AND] LAME LITERARY REFERENCES."

At SCAD, Passmore created two collective zines and created a political comic strip, *We Think For You*, which regularly ran in the college newspaper. In one incident, the SCAD administration reprimanded him for his zine's political commentary and criticism of the school's policies. Passmore was undeterred, however, and continued to use comics as a medium for tackling important social debates.

From 2010 to 2013, Passmore was the editor of a New Orleans–based anarchist journal. He was also a firsthand witness to the political and corporate corruption that shaped the city in the aftermath of Hurricane Katrina. These influences later took shape in Passmore's 2012 comic, *DAYGLOAYHOLE*.

In this work, the main character, a middle-aged Black man, grapples with economic hardship, loneliness, and greed. The complexity of the character was central in Passmore's development of *DAYGLOAYHOLE*, as Passmore wanted the audience to both sympathize with the pathetic character and hold disdain for his piggishness. For Passmore, too often Black characters are one-dimensional and overly "polished for the white gaze." This overcompensation dehumanizes Black characters, as it neglects to fully explore the very real personal complications that confront Black Americans. As he sees it, Black Americans are as complicated as anyone else, and therefore their fictional characters should reflect those same complications.

While living in New Orleans, Passmore became active in the punk anarchist scene and teamed up with punk cartoonist Otto Splotch. From here, Passmore's drawings extended beyond his own comics, and he began designing promotional materials for local bands, authors, and your black friend doesn't really like your white friends, they wear dashikis and express their undying enthusiasm for the "Black Lives Matter Movement." your black friend thinks wannabe politicans hijacked the BLM, but your white friends ignore him, your white friends are really bummed-out by negativity.

Your white friends compliment your black friends lips, skin and hair. He gets shit from his own black friends about his messy hair. He knows that your white friends would love that anecdote, it would seem like secret information to them.

Your white friends recommend a lot of black authors to your black friend and he's starting to feel like they're trying to "out black" him,

Image courtesy of Ben Passmore

publishing houses such as Crescent City Comics and Silver Sprocket. He also helped organize the New Orleans Comics and Zine Festival, an annual event that showcases the work of local artists and provides free creative workshops for children and adults.

In 2016, Ben Passmore published *Your Black Friend*, which is "a letter from your black friend to you about race, racism, friendship and alienation." Listing it as one of the best comics of 2016, *Comics Beat* reported, "The explosions of discussions on systemic racism and inequalities have become so prominent as to be unavoidable. *Your Black Friend* explores the conflict of those caught in it." With bold, arresting artwork, the eleven-page comic follows the thoughts of a Black man who silently witnesses racist interactions and reflects whether to engage with them.

At the core of much of Passmore's work is commentary on political, social, and economic issues. With his comics, he works to expand popular understanding of both philosophical ideas and current events. He is also a contributing cartoonist at *The Nib*, a publication focusing on political commentary, essays, and journalism in the sequential art format.

# PRIEST, CHRISTOPHER

**(1961– )**
- **Born in Queens, NY**
- **New York School of Media Arts**
- **Comics writer and editor**
- **Writer for *Black Panther*, *Spider-Man*, and *Power Man and Iron Fist***

In 1978, while studying journalism at the New York School of Media Arts, Christopher Priest (born James Christopher Owsley) earned an internship at Marvel Comics and, by 1979, became the first African American editor in the history of modern comics.

After a stint as assistant editor on Marvel's *MAD* magazine imitator *Crazy* (1979), Priest transitioned to a longtime collaboration with his mentor, Larry Hama, on Robert E. Howard's *Conan the Barbarian* comic books. With the publication of *The Falcon* limited series in November of 1983, he then became the industry's first African American writer ever assigned to a monthly title. The character of the Falcon, Captain America's African American friend, has since received a worldwide audience through the Avengers movie franchise and the recent Netflix live-action series *Luke Cage* and *Iron Fist*.

In 1985, at age twenty-four, Christopher Priest assumed control of Marvel's flagship Spider-Man franchise. He later became the first African American editor and writer at DC Comics in 1990.

Priest has also created compelling versions of Deadpool, Spider-Man, Wolverine, Thor, the Hulk, Green Lantern, Wonder Woman, and the Ray. The first act of the 2005 movie *Batman Begins* is based on Priest's work on *Batman* (*Batman* #431). In *Batman: The Hill*, the caped crusader becomes the focus of community outrage when a Black teen steals the Batmobile only to be accidentally killed in a car accident.

The lasting accomplishment of this first phase in Priest's writing career is his run on *Power Man and Iron Fist*. One of the high points on the title was "The Daughter of the Dragon King" storyline, where the frailty, courage, and irony of the characters' lives showcased Priest's sense of humor and drama.

In the mid-1990s, Priest transitioned to freelance work. Along with Dwayne McDuffie, Denys Cowan, Michael Davis, and Derek T. Dingle, he helped create the Milestone Comics universe (see *Cowan, Denys*). Although Priest withdrew from the effort before the contract took effect, his vision and voice are apparent in many of the characters and stories, especially *Icon and Rocket, Static Shock, The Shadow Cabinet,* and *Blood Syndicate*.

This landmark accomplishment also changed Priest's writing, as evidenced in the 1998 *Black Panther* series. Lauded by media outlets ranging from *Entertainment Weekly* to *The Village Voice,* Priest transformed T'Challa, the king of the African nation of Wakanda, into one of the most powerful and dangerous characters in the Marvel Universe. The opening narrative arc, "The Client," laid out a mystery about the murder of a child in Brooklyn, while a refugee crisis threatened Wakanda's borders. The Black Panther had to solve the murder, prevent a civil war, and, ultimately, steal the Devil's soul in order to prevail.

Well ahead of its time, the series struggled with sales, but editorial support kept it afloat for five years. Blending humor, politics, and economics with the conventions of the superhero genre, Priest laid the foundation for the kinds of cinematic narratives that have shaped recent Marvel films and television shows. Moreover, Priest's writing attracted a dedicated audience of writers, artists, and scholars engaged with Afrofuturism.

Besides his many professional accomplishments, Priest has also helped launch the careers of many industry legends, including Marvel chief creative officer Joseph Quesada, Top Cow creator Marc Silvestri, legendary comics writer and novelist Peter A. David, award-winning cartoonist and writer Kyle Baker, cutting-edge illustrator Mark Beachum, and many others, all of whom began their careers in Priest's DC or Marvel office.

When office politics prompted rumors that "Owsley was planning to fire all the white guys and replace them with black guys," Priest pointed out that these freelancers were his friends, and his office was the main place within Marvel where they felt welcome. On any given payday, it wasn't unusual to find talent such as Ron Wilson, Trevor Von Eden, Michael Davis, Cowan, Bright, Beachum, Dwayne Turner, James Fry, Keith Williams, Josef Rubinstein, and Bob Layton (both of whom were white, but nonetheless included), and many others crowded into Christopher Priest's (then Jim Owsley's) tiny office at the end of the hall, sharing stories amid strains of Earth, Wind, and Fire from his stereo. There were usually a pile of artist portfolios along with coats and hats piled in a beach lounge chair in the corner next to a fake potted palm. These portfolios typically belonged to creators of color who used Priest's office as their point of entry.

In 2001, Priest launched PraiseNet.Org, an online Christian ministry consisting of hundreds of essays deconstructing modern Christianity with an emphasis on contextual criticism of the African American church. He has published collections of those essays on his Amazon Kindle store, along with a collection of prose novels. He was formally ordained in 2006, serving as a Baptist pastor for a number of years.

After a long absence due mostly to publishers offering him only characters of color to write (Priest is repeatedly quoted as saying he wants to be known as a writer, not a "Black" writer), Priest returned to monthly comics writing with the relaunch of DC Comics' *Deathstroke* in the summer of 2016. In January 2017, Priest and former Milestone partner Denys Cowan reunited (along with an uncredited Reginald Hudlin) for "Chicago," published in *Deathstroke* #11. In this story, mothers of Chicago gun violence victims pool their money to hire the eponymous assassin to exact revenge against the killers of their children. "Chicago" elicited great controversy for Priest, Cowan, and DC Comics, prompting ethical concerns over a white character brutally murdering dozens of Black young men in the pretext of an antiviolence story and stirring accusations of the creators and publisher exploiting an ongoing tragedy for commercial purposes. "Chicago" was discussed in the *Chicago Sun-Times, Washington Post,* on NPR, and in other national media.

Christopher Priest's careful, critical engagement with questions of social and racial justice foreshadowed the rise of contemporary writers like Ta-Nehisi Coates and Chimamanda Ngozi Adichie. His life and work place him in the company of the best writers of any genre in the last forty years.

# RANDOLPH, KHARY

Khary Randolph's past projects include properties such as *Spider-Man*, *X-Men*, *Hellboy*, *Teenage Mutant Ninja Turtles*, *The Boondocks*, *Black*, *Tech Jacket*, and *Teen Titans*. He has also collaborated with industry icons such as Stan Lee, the former chairman of Marvel Comics, and creator of *Spider-Man*.

> (January 19, 1979– )
> - **Born in Boston, MA**
> - **School of Visual Arts, BFA in cartooning and illustration**
> - **Illustrator, comic creator, and character designer**
> - **Creator of Mosaic, an African American Marvel character**

Khary Randolph's mother taught her son to read by sharing comics with him. While he continued reading comics throughout his childhood, he was not driven to create them himself until he discovered Image Comics in 1993. The founders of the imprint were comic book writers and illustrators who believed creators should maintain the rights to their works. Inspired, the thirteen-year-old Randolph decided to one day become a comic book creator.

In 1996, Randolph moved to New York City to study at the School of Visual Arts. During his studies, Randolph interned at the New York offices of DC Comics, where he learned the business and production sides of the industry. "It's not always pretty," he noted, "but it's real, and after four years of high-minded art school thinking, reality is exactly what you need if you want to be a true professional."

Lawrence Christmas of Fantascope hired Randolph in 2000, right after his graduation, and taught Randolph to use programs like Adobe Illustrator, Photoshop, and Flash. Randolph remained with Fantascope as a Flash animator until the internet crash of 2001, when he was laid off. Within a few weeks, the September 11 attack on the World Trade Center caused an economic spiral. Left with limited options, Randolph took a job in a candy factory.

By 2003, Randolph's comic book career had resumed. Robert Kirkman, creator of *The Walking Dead* (2003– ), published Randolph's first professional work in *Inkpunks Quarterly* (2001). Subsequently, comics illustrator Skottie Young called Randolph for help with *Spider-Man: Legend of the Spider-Clan* (2002). When Young asked Randolph to take over the series, Randolph initially refused. At the time, he had a salaried position drawing children's books for Kenn Viselman Productions (*The Teletubbies*). However, Randolph quickly realized that working for a publisher like Marvel would fulfill his childhood aspirations, and minutes later, Randolph called Young back to accept the *Spider-Clan* offer.

> "I PUT MY ALL INTO EVERYTHING I DO. I HAVE LOVE FOR ALL OF MY PREVIOUS PROJECTS BUT I CAN'T NAME A 'GREATEST HIT' BECAUSE I HONESTLY DON'T THINK THAT THING HAS HAPPENED YET."

From 2003 onward, Randolph continued to work in the comics industry. By 2015, he had drawn hundreds of comics, accruing additional credits in the advertising and animation industries. He provided character design for 4Kids Entertainment and The CW Network and produced a fan favorite *Heroes For Hire* poster in collaboration with fellow artist Emilio Lopez (2013).

In 2016, Randolph received the opportunity to create a canonical African American Marvel character in the tradition of Black Panther, Storm, and Blade. In April 2016, Marvel introduced Mosaic, a superpowered antihero, cocreated by Randolph and writer Geoffrey Thorne. This marks one of few instances in which a Black creative team has created a Black Marvel character with a stand-alone series from inception.

Randolph wrote, "It's an amazing opportunity of course and I'm honored to add on to a legacy of great characters. At the end of the day, my biggest goal is to create a character that feels real and isn't a caricature of a stereotype. Mosaic, like anyone else is a complex individual – he's capable of great things but comes with his share of faults. I think that's all of us. It's my job to translate that onto the page and hopefully create something that resonates with the public and outlives my run.... I think it's any creator's goal to create something that becomes bigger than them. The fact that he is a black man is just the icing on the cake."

Khary Randolph has lived in New York since 1996.

# RICHARDSON, AFUA NJOKI

Afua Njoki Richardson, of Choctaw Indian and African American heritage, is best known for the original series *Genius*, and for her illustration work on Marvel's *World of Wakanda*. A talented musician as well as an illustrator, she performs under the alias Docta Foo.

**(April 25, 1980– )**
- **Born in New York, NY**
- **Juilliard School**
- **Illustrator, writer, and musician**
- **Illustrator of *Genius* and *World of Wakanda***

Afua Richardson attended the Laguardia High School for the Performing Arts and went on to study classical flute at the Juilliard School, a performing arts conservatory considered to be one of most elite musical institutions in the world. Despite her prestigious training in the performing arts, she comes from humble beginnings. Both poor and occasionally displaced throughout her childhood, she struggled with poverty and at first did not see a place for herself in the comic industry.

Image courtesy of Afua Richardson

While working a series of temporary office jobs, Richardson taught herself Adobe Photoshop during her lunch breaks. She continued to perform as well, playing classical, jazz, and hip-hop with larger bands; touring as a background singer; and acting in small Broadway productions. During this period, Richardson was frequently the only illustrator amongst groups of performing artists. Taking advantage of the exposure, she began to design graphics, album covers, and other promotional materials for various projects.

Richardson started studying the work of other illustrators and attending as many comic book conventions as she could afford. Through connections made on the convention circuit, Richardson earned her first comic illustration opportunity in 2004, publishing a quarterly comic book under the alias Lakota Sioux.

In 2006 she began work on *Genius*, a comic about the fraught relationship between law enforcement and communities of color. Set in Los Angeles, it features a young Black woman named Destiny Ajaye who uses her tactical abilities to revolt against a repressive police force. Originally accepted as the winner of Top Cow's Pilot Season, *Genius* was finally published in 2014 as a six-issue miniseries. Its publication

Image courtesy of Afua Richardson

coincided with the militarized police occupation of Ferguson, Missouri, prompting numerous media discussions of its uncanny prescience.

The series's coauthor, Marc Bernardin, wrote on Twitter: "The six years between the *Genius* Pilot Season issue release and the miniseries dropping [last week] felt like an eternity. But now, it feels like the world was making us wait for just the right time. When the hunger for female leads would reach a tipping point. When the hunger for diversity on and behind the comics pages would reach a tipping point. And, sadly, when the devaluation of black youth would reach a tipping point."

*Genius* went on to be nominated for six Glyph Awards.

Afua Richardson is a true Renaissance woman. She is an accomplished illustrator and a musical innovator who continues to perform for live audiences even as she blazes a trail as one of a handful of women who are regularly published as visual artists in the mainstream comic book industry.

# RICHARDSON, JASON

Jason Richardson is the founder of several events and fan conventions in Philadelphia, including the J1 Music Fest and J1-Con. His media company, J1 Studios, bills itself as an "entertainment hub for geeks," offering media news and reviews as well as original comics, novels, and music.

(August 17, 1978– )
- **Born in Philadelphia, PA**
- **Comic publisher, event founder, and public speaker**
- **Founder of J1 Studios**

Growing up in West Philadelphia, Richardson developed a love of comic books and video games. When his mother gave him a set of video games, he was inspired to create board games in the same style. Upon the purchase of their first computer, Richardson then began creating computer games on floppy discs. With each game he made, Richardson would hand-make an instruction manual and cardboard casing with cover art, then sell them to children and adults in the neighborhood. He also frequently talked them into subscribing to his handmade magazine for tips and tricks.

After a falling-out with family members over his unorthodox creative drive, Richardson was forced to live on the streets and was eventually taken in by the Wheeler family. After obtaining his GED, he studied at several schools, including Delaware County Community College,

Image courtesy of Jason Richardson

Montgomery Community College, and the Katharine Gibbs School, reuniting with his mother along the way. He then left Katharine Gibbs to attend the Art Institute of Philadelphia to learn animation. Unfortunately, even with a GPA of 3.8, the tuition costs were out of reach. Richardson was forced to leave the institute and earn his living as a graphic designer.

With his newfound income, Richardson was able to start his company, J1 Studios, in 2006. Its first published comic was a biblical action fantasy, *Angel Savior*, that told the story of how Adam, Eve, Cain, and Abel become the Four Horsemen of the Apocalypse. As the popularity of *Angel Savior* increased and audiences demanded a comic featuring his company mascot, J1, as well, he knew he needed help.

In 2008, Richardson expanded his operations and brought on a team of new creators. He also wrote and illustrated several more comics, including *Super Bounty J1*. The same year, he founded the J1-Music Fest in Philadelphia and married his wife, Danae Whitley. He later founded the J1 Cosplay Prom, a prom for all ages that allows people to embrace their nerdy side by attending in character. In 2012, he founded Philadelphia's largest anime convention, J1-Con.

Among his many accomplishments, Richardson is also one of the hosts of the geek radio show *Black Tribbles*, which took home a 2014 Geek Award for Streaming Media Project of the Year. In 2014, he won the Philly Geek Awards' Geek of the Year; in 2015, J1-Con was nominated for Philly Geek's Event of the Year.

Richardson continues to build his brand and inspire youth by speaking at schools around the country. By sharing his story, he illustrates to children – especially children of color – that they too can succeed in careers that people tell them are out of reach.

# ROBINSON, JIMMIE LEE, JR.

Jimmie Robinson has published original comics series with Image Comics for over twenty years. He has written and illustrated numerous comics, including *Amanda and Gunn, Bomb Queen, Power Lines*, and *The Empty*.

> **(August 22, 1963– )**
> - **Born in Oakland, California**
> - **Comic creator, writer, and artist**
> - **Creator of *Amanda and Gunn, Bomb Queen*, and *The Empty***

After attending art magnet programs from elementary through high school, Robinson graduated at age sixteen. He later married at the age of twenty-one, had a daughter, and then divorced within two years. After his divorce, he became a single parent and put his art career on hold, although he was involved in a number of creative industries, including work as a commercial artist for Sears, Roebuck.

Once his daughter was older, Robinson moved into full-time comic creation. In 1993, he founded the independent company Jet Black

Image courtesy of Professor W. Foster

Graphiks, which published eight issues of his independent comic *Cy-berZone*. Beginning in 1996, he also created comics for Image Comics, including the sci-fi series *Amanda and Gunn* (1997), hospital drama *Code Blue* (1998), children's series *The Adventures of Evil and Malice* (1999), and *Avigon* (2000). *Amanda and Gunn*, which was based on his first comic, *CyberZone*, is also notable for featuring the first Black lesbian superhero in comics.

Robinson's more recent titles include *Bomb Queen* (2006), a satire of politics, popular culture, and superhero genre tropes; *The Empty* (2015), an adventure story set on a dying planet; and *Power Lines* (2016), his first comic to discuss issues of race and diversity. In *Power Lines*, a poor Black teenage boy develops superpowers that only work in an upper-class white neighbourhood, while a middle-aged white woman discovers powers that only work in his. As the characters take on superhero roles in each other's communities, they learn about people they had previously stereotyped.

While Robinson was initially hesitant to write a book about race, he wanted to contribute to the growing number of uniquely Black narratives in comics. He premised the book both on his experience growing up in Oakland and on his research on geographical class and race divisions.

Besides his comics, Robinson has also contributed art to the Comic Book Legal Defense Fund, a nonprofit that defends the First Amendment rights of comics professionals, and the Hero Initiative, a nonprofit that provides grants to comics creators in need. In 2015, Jimmie Robinson received Comic-Con International's (CCI's) Inkpot Award for his contributions to the comics industry. He also served as a judge for CCI's Eisner Spirit of Retailer Award and has spoken at numerous conventions around the United States.

## ROBINSON, STACEY

Afrofuturist artist Stacey Robinson is one half of the pseudonymous art collective Black Kirby, which re-creates mainstream comics with Black protagonists.

Robinson's first commissioned artwork was the album art for jazz vibraphonist Stefon Harris & Blackout's *Urbanus* (2009). In that early piece he exhibited many of the hallmarks of his later style, drawing heavily on juxtaposed textures, photography, and bright color palettes. For Castle's *Gasface*

**(March 24, 1972– )**
- **Born in Albany, NY**
- **Fayetteville State University, BA, 2012**
- **State University of New York, MFA, 2015**
- **Artist, designer, and professor**
- **Cocreator of Black Kirby project**

Image courtesy of Stacey Robinson

(2012), he employed line-ink figural illustrations inspired by comics cartooning.

As a graduate student at the State University of New York (SUNY), his professors challenged him to dig deeper into the themes of Black freedom and resistance that permeate his work. His resulting thesis, "Binary ConScience" explored W. E. B. Du Bois's concept of double consciousness, adaptation, and survival under colonial rule.

During his time at SUNY, Robinson also developed his most successful ongoing project, a collaboration with artist John Jennings called Black Kirby. Black Kirby – a play on the name Jack Kirby, one of the most prolific and influential comic book artists of the twentieth century – takes viewers into spaces where the familiar is skewed and the overwhelmingly white history of superhero comics is put on full display. Fusing Black history and social justice activism with comic art, it imagines alternative timelines where Black heroes and villains are the cornerstone of American popular culture. For example, in one popular Black Kirby image, perennial Marvel Comics villain Galactus is remade as "Mo'Blacktus" (2012); in another, the Incredible Hulk becomes recast as "The Unkillable Buck" (2012). In 2014, Black Kirby – along with writer Tan Lee, a pseudonym for Damian Duffy – released its first book, *Kid Code: Channel Zero*, with Rosarium Publishing.

Robinson has exhibited and lectured widely, becoming a mainstay in the Black Speculative Arts Movement and Afrofuturist community. His work is held in permanent collection at a number of American colleges and universities, including Jackson State University, Virginia State University, Brigham Young University, Bucknell University, Lehigh University, and Northeastern University. In addition, examples of Robinson's work are held in the world-renowned research collection at the Schomburg Center for Research in Black Culture in Harlem, New York.

A teacher as well as a professional artist, he has taught art, graphic design, and comics at a range of institutions. As of 2017, he was an assistant professor of graphic design at the University of Illinois, Urbana–Champaign.

# SANDERS, Y.

Yvette Sanders is a contemporary comic artist and illustrator. She is the creator of *Possessed* and the cocreator (with writer Ellen Goodlett) of the short comics "Single Serving" and "William's Last Words."

**(April 4, 1982– )**
- **Born in New York, NY**
- **School of Visual Arts**
- **Comics artist and illustrator**
- **Creator of *Possessed***

Growing up in a mixed household and a predominantly Haitian and West Indian neighborhood, Sanders interacted mostly with other people of color as a child. Around 1985, she began reading comics based on her favorite cartoons, like *Fraggle Rock* and *Hugga Bunch*. Sanders often drew with her grandfather, who told her about the racism he experienced during the Great Depression, when Cambria Heights was a more Italian neighborhood.

Watching Marvel's 1992 *X-Men* cartoon series inspired her to pick up the corresponding comic series. While reading, Sanders was confused by how the character Psylocke was drawn and colored, as she didn't realize the character was ethnically Japanese. According to a 2016 interview, Sanders thought she was "just a yellow woman" and compared the coloring technique to how Black Barbies from her childhood were created: "They were just [regular] Barbies dunked in brown."

Sanders began to notice how other comic characters of color were illustrated and began creating her own characters by redrawing the X-Men. Using the art of Chris Bachalo and Joe Madureira as a base, she created superpowered mutants that were Black, Latino, queer, and predominantly female.

As a student at LaGuardia High School, Sanders gravitated away from American comics and began reading more character-driven stories with female protagonists, like Japanese manga and Wally Lamb's novel *She Comes Undone*. She also began to incorporate manga drawing styles into her art. However, at the time, LaGuardia teachers discouraged students from pursuing comics, saying that it was "not real art."

During her senior year at the School of Visual Arts, Sanders started to sell fan art at anime conventions. She later teamed up with her classmate Ivory McQueen to create an erotic comic collection, which later developed into their independent publishing company, Sin Comix. In 2007, Sanders and McQueen self-published *PiL* (Psychos in Love), a twenty-page comic about a shy girl who would do anything to impress her crush, even commit murder.

In their early years attending anime conventions, Sanders and McQueen couldn't help but notice that they were one of few Black creators present. In later years, however, the number of Black artists increased visibly.

In 2011, Sanders started attending conventions that focused more on American comics. A year later, she attended the first Black Comic Convention in Harlem, New York. The same year, Sanders wrote and drew *Possessed*, a short comic about four girls looking for ghosts in a New Orleans hotel. The comic won a Blue Dot Award at the Art Students League of New York.

A year later, she and writer Ellen Goodlett created "Single Serving," an eight-page comic about a speed-dating event for cannibals. It was published in the 2013 anthology *Girls Night Out: The Way Love Goes* by Amy Chu. In 2015, Sanders and Goodlett teamed up again to create "William's Last Words," which was inspired by the disappearance of Manic Street Preachers' Richey Edwards. It appeared in Red Stylo and Action Lab Media's Harvey Award–nominated *27, A Comic Anthology*. The same year, Sanders worked with writer Obioma Ofoego to create an educational digital comic about Sojourner Truth. The comic was featured in the United Nations Educational, Scientific and Cultural Organization's (UNESCO's) Women in African History series.

In 2016, Sanders released *MTA Sketch Series*, a portrait collection of various subway commuters in New York City. She also drew a cover for Regine Sawyer's *Ice Witch #1* and an interior illustration for Michael Vincent Bramley's comic book, *Sherbet*.

*27, A Comic Anthology* © Red Stylo Media. Writer: Ellen Goodlett

# SAWYER, REGINE

Sawyer is the founder of Women in Comics Collective, an artists' collective that promotes the work of female creators and encourages literacy through comics.

Sawyer was surrounded by the arts from an early age. Her mother, a painter, encouraged her to read widely and deeply. Sawyer's father

- **Born in Queens, NY**
- **Founder of Women in Comics Collective**
- **Comic writer, manager, and entrepreneur**
- **Founder of Women in Comics Collective**

fostered her love of comics by reading the Sunday comics section to her and her brother each week. From age nine onward, Sawyer was determined to make it in the comic book industry. She even once convinced her mother to call the office of John Romita Jr., the head of Marvel Comics at the time, to inquire if he wanted to purchase any of her characters.

In 2006, Sawyer met Rob Taylor, the owner of independent comic company Superhuman Works, and began working for him as an editor. After a year at Superhuman Works, she founded her own company, Lockett Down Productions, and published two comics, *The Rippers* and *Eating Vampires*.

In 2012, Ray Felix, the executive director for Bronx Heroes Comic Con, asked Sawyer to host a panel on women in the comic industry. At the panel, she met numerous female comic creators, editors, and publishers, such as Alitha E. Martinez, an Afro-Latina artist who has done penciling work on a number of big-name titles, including *Black Panther, Fantastic Four*, and *X-Men*. Hearing the stories of Martinez and the other panelists inspired Sawyer to create a space designed for women within the comics industry. That same year, she founded the Women in Comics Collective, or WinC.

Through the Women in Comics Collective, Regine Sawyer spotlights hundreds of women artists, writers, animators, and self-publishers and helps them succeed in the larger comic book industry. The collective also hosts workshops, panels, and traveling art exhibitions. In 2015, WinC hosted its first convention, the Women in Comics Con, in New York City. It has also appeared at conventions including the East Coast Black Age of Comics Convention, New York Comic Con, and Denver Comic Con.

# SCOTT, ADRIAN (AGE)

- **Born in Oakland, CA**
- **Artist, author, and teacher**
- **Creator of *Won and Phil: Hip Hop Heroes***

Age Scott is the creator of the independent comic *Won and Phil: Hip Hop Heroes*, which is widely considered the longest-running embodiment of hip-hop culture in comics. Its longevity distinguishes it from Eric Orr's short-lived *Rappin' Max Robot*, which in 1986 became the first hip-hop-influenced comic in print.

Image courtesy of Age Scott

Citing musicians such as Boogie Down Productions' KRS-One and Public Enemy's Chuck D. as inspiration, Age Scott draws on 1980s and '90s hip-hop culture to create *Won and Phil: Hip Hop Heroes*. It was first published in 1993 and remains in production on a sporadic basis. Remaining defiantly anticommercial for decades, *Won and Phil* acts as a counterpoint to oversimplified representations of hip-hop culture. It also reflects Scott's frustration with the state of contemporary hip-hop music, in particular its ubiquitous use in advertising.

From 1993 onward, Age Scott has published his material through small presses to maintain creative control of his work. He also serves as his own marketing executive by promoting his work firsthand at comic book conventions along the Pacific Coast. In 2013, *Won and Phil* became available as a weekly webcomic.

Besides his work as an independent artist, Age Scott is also a youth art teacher with the Mount Diablo Unified School District in California. He is the author of several other comics, including *SuperHood*, *Tales of Hip-Hop Horror*, *Age Page*, and *Hood Magazine*.

# SHEARER, THADDEUS "TED"

**(Nov. 1, 1919–Dec. 26, 1992)**
- **Born in May Pen, Jamaica**
- **Art Students League of New York, 1940**
- **Cartoonist**
- **Creator of *Quincy***

Ted Shearer was the creator of *Quincy*, a syndicated comic strip about growing up in New York City. It ran from 1970 until Shearer's retirement in 1986.

Ted Shearer's parents moved to Harlem, New York, when Ted was a small child. While still in elementary school, he met and studied under the mentorship of pioneering African American cartoonist E. Simms Campbell. He sold his first cartoon to the *New York Amsterdam News*, a Harlem-based weekly newspaper serving the African American community of New York City, at the age of sixteen.

Shearer received a scholarship to the Art Students League of New York, where he studied from 1938 to 1940 at night, while working as a gallery assistant to curator Edith Halpert during the day.

In the late 1930s, Shearer created his first effort at a regular comic strip, a family strip called *The Hills*. It was published in the *Afro-American* newspaper chain as a nearly full-page feature and was syndicated to other newspapers via Continental Features.

Shearer's first single-panel gag strip, *Every Tub*, a slice-of-life humor strip, debuted in 1940 but was short-lived. In 1942, he began to produce two somewhat more successful regular single-panel comics for the *Amsterdam News*. The first was *Around Harlem*, a humorous and more "mature" cartoon about the nightlife and social lives of young people in Harlem. *Next Door*, another single-panel cartoon, was more family focused in its humor and less unique to life in Harlem. It ran slice-of-life gags about children, society, the workplace, and other aspects of modern life. He also contributed art to magazines such as *Click*, *Swank*, and *Collier's* during this time, and exhibited his art at the 1939–40 World's Fair in Queens, New York.

In 1942, Shearer enlisted and served in the public-relations section of the 92nd Infantry Division of the US Army, a segregated unit made up of African American soldiers. It was the only American unit of its kind to see European combat. Nicknamed the "Buffalo Soldiers," the division also produced a magazine called *The Buffalo*, for which Shearer drew cartoons alongside fellow Black cartoonist Ray Henry and served as art director.

During his time in the military, Shearer also contributed to the military newspaper *Stars and Stripes*, as did many other distinguished cartoonists of the day, such as Morrie Turner of *Wee Pals*, Mort Walker of *Beetle Bailey*, and Pulitzer Prize–winning editorial cartoonist Bill Mauldin. He also continued to create *Around Harlem* and *Next Door* on a weekly basis. *Around Harlem* was discontinued in 1944. *Next Door*, the significantly more popular of the two cartoons, was syndicated in dozens of papers and ran until 1953.

By the end of his service, Shearer had attained the rank of sergeant and was honored with a Bronze Star for his service, the only one of its kind awarded in his division.

With the end of the war, Shearer went back to work as a magazine and newspaper illustrator, contributing art to many national magazines, such as the *Saturday Evening Post* and the *Ladies' Home Journal*. He also continued his studies, this time attending Pratt Institute from 1946 to 1947.

Shearer married attorney Phyllis Wildman in 1945. They would have two children: son John and daughter Kathleen. Later in her career, Phyllis would go on to become the deputy commissioner of social services for Westchester County, New York.

In 1953, Shearer was hired to model for a Lucky Strike cigarette ad campaign targeted toward African Americans. It showed Shearer taking a break from a busy day at work, his drafting table in the background. The ads appeared in the *Afro-American* chain of newspapers, where many of his cartoons also appeared.

Shearer took a job with the world-famous advertising agency Batten, Barton, Durstine & Osborn (BBDO) as a television art director in 1955. During his tenure at BBDO, he worked on major national ad campaigns for brands like Betty Crocker and won several awards. He also continued to draw cartoons for a variety of different outlets, including the *Amsterdam News*.

After fifteen years at BBDO, King Features hired Shearer to draw a nationally syndicated comic strip, *Quincy*. Quincy was a humorous, family-oriented strip about the title character, a young Black boy living with his grandmother and little brother in Harlem, New York. While it had a racially diverse cast of characters and was written with awareness of social issues, it did not often feature overt discussion of race or other politically charged statements. *Quincy* ran from 1970 until Shearer's retirement in 1986.

Beginning in 1978, Shearer published a series of children's books called Billy Jo Jive, which he cocreated with his son, John Shearer. John wrote the series, while Ted contributed art. Billy Jo Jive was about a young Black boy detective who solved a variety of mysteries over the course of five books. The series was adapted into animated segments for *Sesame Street* as well as a longer animated feature in 1979.

Ted Shearer died in 1992, at age seventy-three, from cardiac arrest.

# SIMMONS, ALEXANDER

**(June 1, 1952– )**
- **Born in New York, NY**
- **Comic writer, convention organizer, and actor**
- **Author of *Blackjack* and founder of Kids Comic Con**

Alexander Simmons has worked in the comic industry since 1969. A man of many talents, he has created original stories, written for major comics titles, and founded a youth comic convention, Kids Comic Con.

In 1969, Simmons met writer Don McGregor at an after-hours party at the Comic Arts Convention in New York. They collaborated on a comic, *Detectives, Inc.*, which McGregor wrote and Simmons drew, and self-published it for the following year's convention. This was Simmons's first comic.

In 1970, shortly before Simmons graduated from high school, his mother had a health crisis and a few months later was admitted to a nursing home. At age eighteen, Simmons was on his own. He worked at a number of jobs, including selling encyclopedias, while he built a career as an actor. In the early 1980s, he performed in a musical based on Al Capp's comic strip *Li'l Abner*. There he met his future wife, Lorraine Walker, who was designing props for the show. They were married in 1988 and had three children: Matthew, Gavin, and Lena.

Simmons returned to New York in 1985 and worked for the book packager Mega-Books, which produced the popular Nancy Drew, Hardy Boys, and Bobbsey Twins series. While he started out there as an office worker, he soon began participating in editorial meetings, eventually writing a number of books for the company under a pseudonym.

In the early 1980s, Simmons began writing his creator-owned comic, *Blackjack*. A fan of old movies from the 1930s and 1940s, he created a Black main character, Arron Day, along the lines of the dashing heroes of the earlier movies. While Black actors had always been minor characters in those films, Arron Day took center stage. The first *Blackjack* story was never published, however, because Simmons's mentor, DC editor Dick Giordano, pointed out that the supposedly globe-trotting character never left New York City. Simmons went back to the typewriter and came up with *Blackjack: Second Bite of the Cobra*. DC originally intended to publish the comic, but dropped it after management changes led to a shift in direction.

Simmons then took it to several other publishers, including Eclipse Comics and Harris Comics, without success. Thinking perhaps the story was flawed, Simmons showed *Blackjack* to several colleagues. Their consensus was that the story was good, but it was not attractive to big publishers both because the main character was Black and had no superpowers, and because the stories were set in the past. Simmons then decided to self-publish with help from a financial backer. He hired Brazilian artist Joe Bennett (Benedito José Nascimento) to create the art. *Blackjack: Second Bite of the Cobra* was finally published in 1996.

Simmons worked with several artists on the second Blackjack story, *Blackjack: Blood and Honor*. Issue #1 was published in 1997, issue #2 in 1998, and a 104-page graphic novel was published in 1999. More than a decade later, Simmons worked with artist Tim Fielder to publish *Blackjack: There Came a Dark Hunter* in 2015.

Simmons has also written Blackjack short stories and novelettes. In 2002, *Blackjack* was featured in a crossover with the *Tarzan* newspaper comic strip.

Besides his original stories and comics, Alexander Simmons has contributed to several major comic series, including *Batman, Archie*, and *Scooby-Doo*. In 2001, at the suggestion of Joe Illidge, *Batman* editor Denny O'Neil asked Simmons to design a new Black superhero for the Batman universe. Simmons responded with Orpheus, a stage performer who was galvanized by the injustices he saw when on tour and resolved to fight them. The character featured prominently in the five-issue miniseries *Batman: Orpheus Rising*.

Although Simmons planned more Orpheus stories, O'Neil had moved on by the time the miniseries was finished. After appearing in several more issues, Orpheus was killed by the character Black Mask in *Batman: War Games*.

Simmons began writing for Archie Comics in 2008 and created a number of story arcs, including "World Tour!" "New Kids Off the Wall," and "The Cartoon Life of Chuck Clayton," starring Archie's most prominent Black character. In 2011, he wrote "Campaign Pains," in which President Barack Obama and vice presidential candidate Sarah Palin come to Riverdale.

Simmons has also contributed stories to two anthologies, *African-American Classics, Graphic Classics Volume 22*, and *The World's Finest Comic Book Writers and Artists Tell Stories to Remember*.

In addition to his writing work, Simmons taught at the New York Film Academy and led writing and acting workshops for students of all ages. Around 1998, concerned that the comics industry was leaving its original audience behind, Simmons set up a children's section at Wizard World Comic Con in Chicago. A few years later he introduced a similar section at the East Coast Age of Black Comics convention in Philadelphia. In 2007, he produced the first Kids Comic Con at Bronx Community College. It was planned as a small, one-time event, but after journalist Calvin Reid spotlighted it in *Publishers Weekly*, it ended up drawing more than seven hundred attendees.

Since then, Simmons has organized Kids Comic Con as an annual event. While the main convention takes place in the Bronx, he has also brought scaled-down versions to a number of other cities, including Buffalo, New York; Miami, Florida; and Dakar, Senegal.

# SIMS, GUY A.

Guy Sims is the chief writer of the *Brotherman* series and the author of *Living Just a Little*, *Revelation*, and *The Cold Hard Cases of Duke Denim*. He also wrote the graphic novel adaptation of Walter Dean Myers's young adult novel *Monster*.

Sims's earliest inspiration as a writer came from his father, whose audio recording of Richard Wright's *Black Boy* captivated him. His first publication was a short story that appeared in his middle school newspaper. He continued to write in high school and beyond, often setting his stories in his home city of Philadelphia.

**(March 24, 1961– )**
- **Lincoln University, BS in human services, 1983**
- **Arcadia University, MSEd in educational leadership, 1989**
- **National University, MA in human behavior, 1994**
- **University of Northern Iowa, EdD, 2003**
- **Writer and educator**
- **Wrote *Brotherman* and adapted Walter Dean Myers's *Monster***

In 1984, Sims wrote the first children's book about Kwanzaa. Called *The Kwanzaa Kids Learn the Seven Principles*, the book was a collaborative effort with Sims's brother, artist and illustrator Dawud Anyabwile. The next year, Sims would author *The Kwanzaa Handbook*, again the first publication of its kind. Six years after their initial collaboration, Sims and Anyabwile collaborated on the *Brotherman* comics series (see *Anyabwile, Dawud*).

Beginning in 2013, Sims began publishing the series *The Cold Hard Cases of*

Image courtesy of Professor W. Foster

*Duke Denim* with its first title, *Hold'em Close*. He released four more volumes over the next three years.

In 2015, Guy Sims adapted Walter Dean Myers's award-winning novel *Monster* to the graphic novel format. Again illustrated by Dawud Anyabwile, it was a faithful retelling of the 1999 novel, which told the story of a teenager awaiting trial for murder and robbery. Sims's adaptation met with similar acclaim to the original, receiving a Coretta Scott King Honor selection, an ALA Best Book award, and a National Book Award nomination.

Besides his work as a writer, Guy Sims is also an educator of thirty years. In 2013, he assumed the office of assistant to the president for equity, diversity, and inclusion at Bluefield State College.

In 2016, Sims received two major writing awards, the Junior Library Guild Selection Award for *Monster* and the Glyph Award for Best Story for *Brotherman: Revelation*.

# SMITH, JULIANA "JEWELS"

**(Aug. 2, 1981– )**
- **Born in Foster City, CA**
- **University of California, Riverdale, BA in sociology, 2003**
- **University of California, San Diego, MA in ethnic studies, 2008**
- **Comics writer**
- **Creator of (H)afrocentric**

Juliana "Jewels" Smith is the writer and creator of the character-driven independent comic *(H)afrocentric*. Illustrated by Ronald Nelson with colors and lettering by Mike Hampton, it follows two mixed-race siblings, Naima and Miles Pepper, as they navigate life at the fictional Ronald Reagan University.

*(H)afrocentric* was first inspired by Smith's experience as a young educator in community colleges. In a 2017 interview, she said, "While I was teaching a class on the prison industrial complex at Laney College in Oakland, California, I needed a tool to break down the complexities of the prison system. I explored an unconventional resource: a series of comic books, *The Real Cost of Prisons Comix*."

Her success using *The Real Cost of Prisons Comix* led her to begin regularly using comics in the classroom to discuss difficult social issues. She soon started using original comics as well, covering everything from gentrification to racism and popular culture. These comics developed into *(H)afrocentric*. The main characters of *(H)afrocentric*, Naima and

Image courtesy of Juliana "Jewels" Smith

Miles, are modeled after Juliana Smith and her brother, Darren Smith. The title refers to the protagonists' mixed-race (black and white) heritage as well as to the comic's tagline, "Because it's hard being Afrocentric in a Eurocentric world."

Smith credits Aaron McGruder's *The Boondocks* as an inspiration, stating, "The topics, the crass humor, and the subject matter all had a deep impact on my initial writing."

Smith received the first annual Excellence in Comics and Graphic Novels Award at the African American Library and Museum of Oakland. In 2016, she received the Glyph Award for Best Writer for her work on *(H)afrocentric* Volume 4. She also speaks publicly about using comics to address social justice and gender equity.

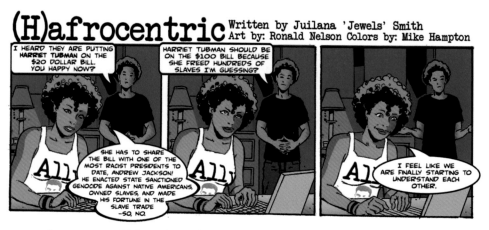

Image courtesy of Juliana "Jewels" Smith

# STELFREEZE, BRIAN

- **Comic artist and illustrator**
- **Created *Batman* cover art and illustrated *Black Panther* (2016)**

Brian Stelfreeze is a twenty-year veteran of the comics industry, with art credits ranging from *Batman* to *X-Men*. He is the art director of 12 Gauge Comics, an independent comics publisher, and the cofounder of Gaijin Studios, a now-defunct artist collective. In 2015, he joined National Book Award winner Ta-Nehisi Coates to produce Marvel's revival of *The Black Panther*.

Brian Stelfreeze's first professional work was in 1988, when he collaborated with writer Julie Lee Woodcock on the sci-fi miniseries *CyCops*. The series lasted one year, with Stelfreeze returning to magazine and trade publication work after three issues.

In 1991, Stelfreeze cofounded Gaijin Studios with Cully Hamner and Karl Story. Based in Atlanta, Georgia, it was the longest-running freelance comic art collective in the United States. Over its nineteen years, its roster of talent included artists such as Adam Hughes, Jason Pearson, Dave Johnson, Tony Harris, Georges Jeanty, and Laura Martin.

Concurrent with the founding of Gaijin Studios, Brian Stelfreeze began a long-standing relationship with DC Comics. For more than twenty years, he created covers for the *Batman* comic series and its spin-offs, from *Batman: Legends of the Dark Knight* in 1989 to *Batman: Arkham – Two-Face* in 2015.

Besides his work with DC Comics, Stelfreeze has produced art for several other major comic book companies, including Image, Marvel,

BATMAN                                          Image courtesy of BOOM! Studios

and Dark Horse. Some of his previous titles include *X-Men Unlimited* (1993), *The Heretic* (1996), *X-Men Extra* (1997), *DC Universe Holiday Bash* (1997), *Domino* (2003), and *Gun Candy* (2005). He is also art director for 12-Gauge Comics, an action- and crime-focused independent publisher that first launched in 2004 as an imprint of Image Comics. Its debut series, *The Ride,* was the top-selling black-and-white comic of 2004. After reaching sustained success, the company severed its ties with Image Comics in 2009. It continues to publish titles such as *The Boondock Saints* and *Plastic.*

In 2015, Marvel Comics chose Brian Stelfreeze as the artist for *The Black Panther.* Originally created by Stan Lee and drawn by Jack Kirby, the Black Panther was the first Black superhero in mainstream comics. The story of a heroic king ruling over a technologically advanced African country rich in natural resources was controversial for its time. As a result, the series has undergone sporadic dormancy since its inception, with brief reincarnations such as a run in the late 1990s to early 2000s authored by Christopher Priest (see *Coates, Ta-Nehisi* and *Priest, Christopher*). The 2016 revival of *The Black Panther* drew major media interest and strong sales.

In 2016, Brian Stelfreeze released an art book with Boom! Studios, *The Signature Art of Brian Stelfreeze.*

# TAYLOR, WHITNEY

**(May 22 1984– )**
- **Born in Denville, NJ**
- **University of California, Los Angeles, education**
- **Boston University, MA in public health**
- **Author of *Wallpaper* and *Ghost Stories***

Whitney "Whit" Taylor is a self-taught artist who has been active since 2011. Along with her many self-published comics, her work has been featured in numerous comic anthologies as well *The Nib* and *The Comics Journal.*

Taylor works as a reproductive health educator while making comics in her spare time. Her comics touch on a wide variety of subjects, from humor to nonfiction and slice-of-life. While her early work was primarily autobiographical, her later comics frequently deal with issues such as race, politics, and women's health. Her 2015 comic for *The Nib, The Myth of the Strong Black Woman,* addressed how the societal perception of Black women as psychically strong helps deter them from seeking mental health care. In 2016, she followed it up with *Finding Your Roots*, a discussion of the role Black women's hairstyles play in both self-acceptance and the culture at large.

As a female artist, she has experienced routine sexism in the comics industry, such as inappropriate comments, harassment, and condescension. As a Black artist, she faces additional challenges getting her work published: since many of her comics deal with the Black experience, potential publishers have at times rejected them for being unmarketable. She deals with this prejudice by self-publishing the bulk of her work.

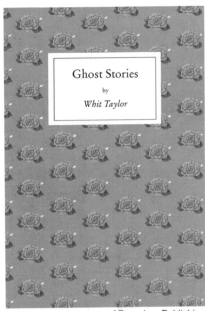

Image courtesy of Rosarium Publishing

In 2016, Whit Taylor self-published *Wallpaper,* a short-form comic about her grandmother's failing health. Each spread featured an intricate wallpaper or macro-view illustration on the right side and text on

"AS AN AUTOBIOGRAPHICAL CARTOONIST, BEING BLACK HAS HAD A TREMENDOUS INFLUENCE ON WHAT I WRITE ABOUT. IT'S ALSO BEEN A JUMPING-OFF POINT FOR OTHER STORIES THAT DEAL WITH CULTURE AND SOCIETY. I'VE ALWAYS WANTED TO BE A CARTOONIST WHO ADDRESSED THE DIFFICULT TOPICS AND CONVERSATIONS WE OFTEN IGNORE, AND I THINK I'VE SUCCEEDED IN THAT SO FAR.

"AS FOR MY IMPACT ON OTHER BLACK PEOPLE, I CAN SAY THAT I'VE HAD MANY PEOPLE, PARTICULARLY WOMEN, REACH OUT TO ME TO TELL ME ABOUT HOW MY WORK HAS CLICKED WITH THEM BECAUSE IT'S REFLECTED THEIR FEELINGS IN SOME WAY. MY COMICS HAVE BEEN EFFECTIVE IN NOT JUST REACHING BLACK PEOPLE, BUT OTHERS WHO MAY NOT HAVE UNDERSTOOD CONCEPTS SUCH AS CULTURAL APPROPRIATION."

- WHITNEY TAYLOR

the left. As comics critic Rob Clough wrote on *High-Low*, "The story is really about the ways in which certain details are important to children on an emotional level that adults simply don't perceive.... Concealing an emotionally complex story in a simple package is what gives this mini its punch."

In fall of 2017, Rosarium Publishing was scheduled to release Taylor's graphic novel *Ghost Stories*, which depicts "three hauntings" – the ghosts of past selves and past relationships – "in different forms."

Whit Taylor is a frequent attendant at Black comic conventions, where she sells her work and provides advice and encouragement to budding artists, especially "younger girls who have an interest in drawing and making comics." She has also spoken in several panels, including Constructing the Self at Boston Comics Workspace; Autobiography, Identity, and Self-Reflection in Comics at Interference Archive; and Why Comix? Drawing the World You Want to See at Northeastern University.

Taylor's awards include a 2012 Glyph Rising Star Award for her debut comic, *Watermelon*, and a 2015 Notable Comic recognition from Best American Comics for *The Anthropologists*. She has also received numerous nominations from the Ignatz Awards, Glyph Awards, Autostraddle, and Slate.

# THOMAS, BRANDON

(January 24, 1980– )
- **Born in San Diego, CA**
- **Illinois Wesleyan University**
- **Comic writer**
- **Cocreator of *The Many Adventures of Miranda Mercury***

Brandon Thomas is the cocreator of *The Many Adventures of Miranda Mercury*, an independent comic about a Black female adventurer. Prior to publishing his creator-owned series with artist Lee Ferguson, he worked as a freelance writer for DC, Marvel, Dynamite Entertainment, and Arcade Comics. His credits include work on *Robin*, *Nitrogen*, *Spider-Man: Unlimited*, *Fantastic Four*, *Voltron*, and *X-Force*.

Thomas's father, a voracious reader, took his son to his first comic book shop in 1992. Trips to the comics shop soon became a weekly occurrence for both father and son. However, another six years would pass before Thomas realized he too could write comics.

In 2001, Thomas began the long-running online column *Ambidextrous,* a comics news review. He intended to use the column to break into writing for the major comic book publishers. An early champion came in the form of Mark Millar, who, when Marvel was looking for untested writers, pointed the company in Thomas's direction. In 2003, Thomas scripted the *Youngblood: Genesis* miniseries. The next seven years involved sporadic scripting work for Marvel as well as other freelance titles. His first ongoing series was at Dynamite Comics, where he worked on *Voltron* and *Voltron: Year One,* both based on the 1980s American adaptation of the anime series *Beast King GoLion.*

The year 2005 marked a crossroads in Thomas's career. He was frustrated after having spent years trying to break into the larger companies with little to show for his efforts. He wanted to create his own series rather than working on someone else's characters. Joining with Lee Ferguson, an artist with whom Thomas had previously collaborated, the two developed the character Miranda Mercury.

As untested creators with an original character doubly stigmatized as both a woman and a person of color, the pair met with repeated rejections. Finally, *Miranda Mercury* found a home with Archaia Comics in 2008. The comic saw publication in August 2011, subsequently receiving four Glyph Award nominations. It also made the list for the Young Adult Library Service Association's Twenty-Five Great Graphic Novels for Teens as well as the *Library Journal's* Twenty-Five Graphic Novels for Black History Month.

Thomas hoped that *The Many Adventures of Miranda Mercury* would help lead to a greater number of female lead characters in comics and encourage more female creators to enter the industry. He sought to create a complex, developed, original character that was not going to be a victim in her own story. Miranda Mercury is resourceful and determined, with a strong sense of justice and integrity.

In 2016, Thomas followed *Miranda Mercury* with *Horizon,* a science-fiction series published by Image Comics. The comic focused on another female lead, Zhia, whose team of extraterrestrial soldiers arrives on Earth to stop what they have been told is a planned invasion of their own planet. *Horizon* Volumes 1 and 2 were published in 2017.

Brandon Thomas lives and writes in San Diego, California.

# THOMAS, PAMELA

**(1962– )**
- **Born in Newark, NJ**
- **City College of New York, BFA 1996**
- **Museum curator and historian**
- **Cofounder of the Museum of Uncut Funk**

Pamela Thomas is the cofounder of the Museum of Uncut Funk, an online museum celebrating 1970s-era Black culture.

In 2000, Pamela Thomas opened the Eclectic Connection Fine Art Gallery with partner Loreen Williamson in Summit, New Jersey. Both women were longtime cartoon and comic art collectors: Williamson collects art from major animation studios like Disney and Warner Brothers, and Thomas has been acquiring Black comics from the 1970s since 1997. Having identified an untapped market, Thomas and Williamson reached out to private collectors and art galleries to collect and display animation art featuring African American characters.

The gallery saw moderate success, but the attacks on September 11, 2001, devastated both the community and the business. Faced with a need to adapt to the changing landscape, Thomas and Williamson curated their inventory, bought a domain, and started the online Museum of Uncut Funk.

The Museum of Uncut Funk celebrates 1970s Black culture and the contributions and legacies of black icons. While some of the online exhibitions feature artifacts from their collection, others discuss important aspects of Black history. For instance, the Vintage Black Heroes and Vintage Black Heroines exhibitions feature the first Black heroes and heroines to appear in comic strips in the 1950s through the 1970s. A rare find from this collection are several *Torchy Brown in Heartbeats* and *Torchy's Togs* comic strips by Jackie Ormes, the first African American woman cartoonist in the United States.

In addition to comics, the museum also houses animation art from the first *Fat Albert* cartoon special in 1969, before the series aired in 1972; a Booker T. Washington commemorative silver half dollar coin from 1946; and 1970s Blaxploitation movie posters from all over the world.

While the museum itself is entirely virtual, portions of the material collection travel around the country for display. These traveling exhibitions feature a unique timeline of Black history firsts. *Funky Turns 40: Black Character Revolution* is one such exhibit. Premiering at the Schomburg Center for Research in Black Culture, it features animation art of the first positive Black animated characters to appear on television in 1970s Saturday morning cartoons and specials. The *Funky Turns 40* exhibit has traveled to six states in total, and at the time of this printing will be on display at a seventh.

While many established museums are trying to build their online presence, the Museum of Uncut Funk is ahead of the curve, allowing visitors to browse their collections for free twenty-four hours a day, seven days a week. It has been entirely self-funded to date, including the purchase of all the artifacts in the collection, the development and maintenance of the website, and the funds for traveling exhibitions. It is also a member of the Association of African American Museums.

Besides serving as museum curator and cofounder, Pamela Thomas was also the Glyph Comics Awards chair from 2011 to 2016. As of 2017, she lived and worked in Newark, New Jersey.

## THOMPSON, BART ALEX

Bart Thompson has been active in the comics industry since 1992, when he founded Approbation Comics. He is the author of numerous comics titles, including *Vampires Unlimited, Chaos Campus: Sorority Girls vs. Zombies, ChiSai,* and *Hass.*

Early on in Thompson's career, he hoped to write and direct television shows and movies. However, comic books like *The Maxx,* scripted by William Messner-Loebs and written and illustrated by Sam Keith, inspired him to pursue comics instead.

**(September 20, 1978– )**
- **Born in Los Angeles, CA**
- **Comics writer, letter artist, and publisher**
- **Founder of Approbation Comics**
- **Creator of *Chaos Campus, ChiSai* and *Hass***

In 1992, Thompson founded Approbation Comics in Louisville, Kentucky, bringing together like-minded creators to publish independent graphic novels and artwork. Between 1992 and 1996, Thompson wrote, drew, lettered, and distributed ashcan (promotional) copies of his work. These early copies would give birth to the *Vampires Unlimited* series and later on *The Metamutoids* (then known as *The New York Creatures*). At the time, Thompson had a small following of about thirty people started by local fans, which then expanded via the Pen Pals section of *Wizard* magazine. Thompson also traded publications with other in-

Image courtesy of B. Alex Thompson

die creators, learning to network and getting insight into the nuts-and-bolts of comic creation. As time progressed, he further expanded his readership by improving his artistic skills and developing the nuances of his characters and storylines.

In 2002, Thompson made his official debut with the full color comic series *Vampires Unlimited: Shades of Things to Come*. Told against a backdrop of New York City goth life, the story depicts humans who have been genetically altered into vampires. Also during that time, Thompson created *Chaos Campus: Sorority Girls vs. Zombies*, which details the survivalist tactics of three sorority girls determined to save their community from the zombie apocalypse. Thompson planned for the series to have sixty issues and also began work on a movie adaptation.

In 2005, Thompson began working as a professional writer, letterer, and editor with previously established companies such as Dead Dog Press, Alias Enterprises, and Arcana Studios. Also in 2005, Thompson debuted *ChiSai*, a sci-fi thriller about a young woman looking for revenge after her life was left in shambles. Other notable works include *Flesh for the Unborn* (2013), *The Vessel* (2013), *Southern Hospitality* (2013), and the 2014 graphic novel *Hass*, which was nominated for two Glyph Awards the same year.

In addition to his self-published work at Approbation Comics, Thompson writes and coauthors comics for both Arcana Comics and Lion Forge. At Arcana Comics, he wrote *Amour* (2006), *Lethal Instinct* (2005), and *Blood, Shells & Roses* (2010). At Lion Forge, he contributed to the digital series *Catalyst Prime* (2013). In 2017, he contributed to the *Love Is Love* anthology published by IDW Publishing and DC Entertainment. In 2017, Thompson was working on writing the three-issue miniseries *F.O.R.C.E.* for CrownTaker; that same year, he lettered John Ward's *Don't Save the Girl*, also for CrownTaker.

As of this writing, Thompson lived in Southern California, where he continued to create new comics and screenplays. He also acts in horror films, where he is billed as B. Alex Thompson.

# TROTMAN, SPIKE C.

Spike Trotman is the author of *Templar, Arizona*, an alternate history webcomic set in a fictional Arizona town. She is also the founder of Iron Circus Comics, an independent comics publisher in Chicago.

(November 18, 1978– )
- **Born in Washington, DC**
- **Spelman College, studio art, 2000**
- **School of the Art Institute of Chicago**
- **Cartoonist and publisher**
- **Creator of *Templar, Arizona***

Trotman knew from a young age that she wanted to work in comics. After graduating from Spelman College, a historically Black college in Atlanta, she then attended the School of the Art Institute of Chicago, taking a qualifying year to prepare for a master's degree. While there, she found that her sensibilities clashed with those of her teachers. The faculty discouraged her more realistic drawing style and attempted to move her from comics to abstract art. Trotman finished the qualifying year but did not go on to complete her master's.

Trotman remained in Chicago and continued to work on her craft. Turning her skills into a career proved to be a challenge at first, however. She believed her style and interests were a poor fit for the traditional comics industry, with its focus on adolescent male readers. Rather than creating comics for the superhero audience, she wanted to discuss relationships and culture, and to work in neglected genres like erotica. She decided to try self-publishing online, which at the time was widely viewed with skepticism.

For comics artists, the internet created a way to reach an audience without the need for a publisher or direct seller. However, it also involved giving the comic away for free. Early webcomics tried a number of methods to create revenue, like advertising, subscription services, or asking for donations. Trotman first tried the subscription method.

In 2003, Trotman launched *Sparkneedle*. She collaborated on the comic with Matt Sheridan, whom she would marry in 2004. *Sparkneedle* was published on Girlamatic, an early comic subscription site, making Trotman one of the earliest comic artists to use the internet as a primary means of publication. Her work caught some attention due to its experimental method of telling a story using only pictures. She also created the comic *Lucas and Odessa* for the same website.

Her work gained traction when she launched the online serial comic *Templar, Arizona* in 2005. The comic took place in an alternate history, focusing on a number of subcultures in a fictional Arizona town. Stories focused on groups like ancient religions and survivalist cults and featured a diverse cast of characters. True to Trotman's interests, *Templar* told stories about relationships, culture, and romance. Its unique dialogue and characterization found praise among other independent cartoonists and fans of independent comics.

She self-published the first collection of *Templar, Arizona* in 2007, creating Iron Circus Comics, a label that would eventually grow to become the biggest comics publisher in Chicago. In time, Iron Circus Comics began to publish graphic works by other creators in genres like fantasy, science fiction, horror, and erotica. Trotman found success by focusing on comics and creators typically ignored by mainstream publishers, particularly comics created by women. A commitment to inclusivity and representation helped Iron Circus Comics, and Spike Trotman, have an impact on the independent comics scene.

In 2012, she revived the erotica anthology series *Smut Peddler*, first published by Johanna Draper Carlson and Trisha L. Sebastian in 2003. *Smut Peddler* was unique in that it featured erotica targeted toward women, an audience ignored by most media outside of prose. Trotman

## TEMPLAR, ARIZONA.

4 – Trouble Every Day.

Image courtesy of Spike Trotman

saw an opportunity to reach an untapped market using stories she herself loved, so she reached out to Carlson and Sebastian. They gave her permission to take control of the title and assisted in editing.

Besides targeting stories toward a female audience, *Smut Peddler* also required that all creative teams involved have at least one woman. The stories featured a wide range of characters, ranging from traditional straight relationships to gay, bisexual, or polyamorous ones, as well as science-fiction or fantasy themes. Trotman funded *Smut Peddler* through Kickstarter, a crowdfunding platform that allows audiences to pledge money toward creative projects. The campaign proved to be a success, leading to multiple *Smut Peddler* anthologies published under the label in 2014 and 2016.

Iron Circus Comics continues to grow, and Spike Trotman continues to create new avenues for creators. In an industry that discouraged the work she wanted to read and create, Spike Trotman managed to carve out a place for herself and open the way for others to follow.

# TURNER, MORRIE

(Dec. 11, 1923–Jan. 25, 2014)
- **Born in Oakland, CA**
- **Cartoonist and educator**
- **Creator of *Wee Pals***

Morrie Turner was the creator of *Wee Pals*, the first comic strip with a multiethnic cast. As both the first openly Black cartoonist to be syndicated in the white mainstream press and the author of an influential and beloved comic strip that ran for nearly fifty years, he holds a prominent place in comics history.

Morrie Turner was born in Oakland, California, the youngest of four sons. The Turners' working-poor neighborhood was multiethnic: African American, Chinese, Japanese, Portuguese, Greek, Mexican, Jewish, and white. While the Chinese were commonly referred to by a negative term, Nora Spears Turner forbade her children from using it. As a Pullman porter, James Turner was frequently away from his family. Mrs. Turner ran a household where schoolwork, church, and dignity were valued, and the artistic interests of her youngest son were encouraged.

Morrie Turner was determined to become a cartoonist by the age of seven. During the Depression, materials were scarce, so Turner drew on paper that he begged from the butcher with stubs of pencils and crayons. When he was the first to reach the newspapers, the family knew that they would be covered with tracing and the margins filled with doodles.

Image courtesy of Kheven LaGrone

While in elementary school, Turner created a four-page weekly newspaper called *Neighborhood Nooz*, featuring illustrations of his friends and neighbors alongside their latest sports statistics and tidbits, which he proudly sold for five cents. He excelled creatively but struggled academically throughout school. At Lowell Junior High School, he practiced nuanced techniques of crosshatching and feathering after a Spanish teacher loaned Turner a book on James Montgomery Flagg – the illustrator of the World War I Uncle Sam recruitment poster declaring "I Want You" – and suggested working with pen and ink. Hungry for advice, Turner wrote to Milton Caniff, whose *Terry and the Pirates* was one of his favorites, for advice on becoming a cartoonist. The reply was a six-page typed letter, single spaced.

Turner was also influenced by two prominent Black cartoonists: E. Simms Campbell and Ollie Harrington. Turner was impressed by Campbell's distinct inking style, which he knew from the Black press. He also recognized Campbell's work from covers of *Esquire*. The idea that white readers were unaware that the artist was Black interested him. The realism and dignity that Ollie Harrington brought to his characters in the Black press also left a lasting impression on Turner.

The racial harmony Turner felt in childhood was disrupted at the end of junior high school. That year, he was elected class secretary, a position that required a graduation speech. Turner was disheartened when he was never approached about the tradition, and more so when the girl who ran against him appeared on stage instead. At McClymonds High School, Turner was invited to illustrate for the newspaper, *Warriors,* until the reputation of his brothers as the "Fighting Turners" got him into trouble by association. His father insisted on a fresh start, and Turner transferred to Berkeley High School. Before graduating in 1942, everything changed. He went on a first date with the love of his life, Letha Mae Harvey. Then, December 7, 1941, marked the attack on Pearl Harbor and America's entry into World War II. Turner witnessed sudden, divisive intolerance toward his Japanese neighbors. He was further unsettled when they were removed to a detention camp.

In 1943, Morrie Turner was drafted. Although he was a pacifist, Turner intended to become a pilot and was sent to Biloxi, Mississippi, for training. On his way, he enjoyed visits with his mother's family and abhorred the segregation so prevalent in the South. Caught up in newfound experiences, Turner arrived to training late and ultimately did not pass the final day of testing. He rejoined the 477th Bombardment Group, part of the Tuskegee Airmen, at Godman Air Force Base in Kentucky and was ultimately assigned to Special Services for his talents as an artist. Working for the military newspaper *Stars and Stripes* under the guidance of established Arkansas-based cartoonist Greeley Hall and other professional cartoonists, Turner had his first teachers. An empathetically bumbling character named Rail Head became Turner's first published cartoon, and he was elated.

At the end of World War II, Turner returned to Berkeley where he proposed to and married Letha Mae Harvey. In 1947, their son Morrie Jr. was born, the same year Turner earned his first freelance check for cartooning. He took a job as a desk clerk for the Oakland Police Department, which allowed time for freelancing and correspondence courses in cartooning and marketing. Talking with Letha Turner became integral to Turner's process, and they discussed ideas for cartoons and marketing strategies. Communicating by mail was the key to avoiding

Image courtesy of Professor W. Foster

discrimination and maintaining a viable freelance career for Turner. With his wife's assistance, Turner submitted work to industrial publications, trade journals, and national publications, including *Baker's Helper*, *True*, *Argosy*, *Extension*, *Better Homes & Gardens*, *The Saturday Evening Post*, and *Collier's*. When *Negro Digest* (later rebranded *Black World*) began to regularly purchase cartoons by "Morrie" in 1961, Turner's artistic career hit a new stride.

*Negro World* published essays, prose, and poetry by the likes of Dr. John Henrik Clarke, Amiri Baraka, Ishmael Reed, and Abbey Lincoln. "Humor in Hue" was their one-page cartoon section. Turner was finally welcome to create cartoons that not only depicted but addressed race in the United States, and he rose to the occasion. In one cartoon, a bemused well-dressed Black patient informs his Black psychotherapist, "I just can't seem to smile like my ancestors used to do." In another, a Black psychotherapist informs a Black patient wearing a Nazi uniform, "Your case is destined to make psychiatric history!" Children were also a catalyst for humor. In a November 1961 cartoon, a Black child stands dripping in white paint as a white friend says happily, "Now Mother won't forbid our playing together!" In another, two Black children in white hoods wonder why their father is so upset when they play bogeyman.

In 1962, Turner's life mission came into focus when he received a job to illustrate for *Mississippi Educational Advance*, a notoriously segregationist newsletter for white teachers. As he cashed the job's paycheck directly to the NAACP, Turner was formulating a comic strip with a diverse cast that would reach readers of all races. In 1963, *Dinky Fellas*, with a small cast of all-Black characters, was published in the *Chicago Daily Defender* and weekly in the *Berkeley Post*. Attempts to market to the white press were met with rejection, and Turner reworked the strip with a confluence of inspirations: Dr. Martin Luther King, Jr., whose message was pervasive; advice from comedian Dick Gregory, whom he had met earlier that year; and a burgeoning friendship with *Peanuts* cartoonist Charles Schulz, whom he met at gatherings of the Northern California Cartoonist and Gag Writers where Turner was the first Black member. *Dinky Fellas* later became *Wee Pals*, with a multiethnic cast of astute elementary school children, also representing physical impairment. The strip's diversity – which Turner lovingly called "Rainbow Power" – became the championing theme of Turner's lifelong work. Nipper – a Black boy with eyes always hidden by a Confederate hat – was named after comedian Nipsey Russell and was the most controversial character. In the first strip, Nipper carried a Confederate flag to match his hat, and a coolheaded Randy remarked with the punch line, "Obviously

American History is not a required subject of the Kindergarten Class." After reading about the Civil War and nearly ditching the hat for good, Nipper concludes that "we pardon in the degree that we love." In a later interview, Turner shared that the hat is "forgiveness."

At the recommendation of the editor of the *Berkeley Gazette*, Lew Little, who ran his own San Francisco syndication, decided to take a chance on Turner's work. When *Wee Pals* entered national syndication on February 15, 1965, it was the first comic strip with a multiethnic cast, and Morrie Turner was the first openly Black cartoonist to be syndicated in the white mainstream press. In a brief article published in *Negro World*'s May 1965 issue titled "'Morrie' Moves Up," Turner's mainstream success was applauded, although there was cause for concern that the cartoonist would leave the publication. Crediting *Negro World* as the origin of *Wee Pals*, Turner reassured the readership that mainstream success would not stop him from contributing to "Humor in Hue."

By the mid-1960s, Turner had sold thousands of gag comics to dozens of publications and was finally able to sustain a living from cartooning. With his wife, Letha – then employed as a government clerical worker – in the role of business manager, Turner resigned from the Oakland Police Department and entered his dream career full time. *Wee Pals* quickly became nationally celebrated. Honors followed, and his engagements increased. The Women's Anti-Defamation League awarded Turner with the 1965 Humanitarian Award. After nomination by the *Tribune* and the *Los Angeles Times*, he was awarded the 1966 National Conference of Jews and Christians Brotherhood Award. In April 1966, the *Negro Digest* reported that Turner was developing an integrated army strip for the *Chicago Defender* called *Dogbert*. In 1967, the National Cartoonist Society invited Morrie Turner to join five other cartoonists on an intensive four-week tour of Vietnam with the USO. Turner drew thousands of cartoons on the rear and front lines. During the deeply impacting experience, a lifelong bond was formed with Bil Keane, creator of *Family Circus*, who would call Turner on the day Barack Obama was elected the forty-fourth president of the United States.

The 1968 assassination of Dr. Reverend Martin Luther King, Jr. changed Turner's career. The number of papers who purchased *Wee Pals* for daily publication skyrocketed – a bittersweet fact that saddened Turner even in old age. *Wee Pals* readership was in the millions, and soon cartoonist friends such as Charles Schulz and Bil Keane would make efforts to diversify their strips by introducing Black characters. Letha Turner countered her sadness by initiating a coloring book project to highlight

## LITT YOUNG AND COMPANION

For the art exhibit *I Am America: Black Genealogy Through the Eye of An Artist*,
Morrie Turner portrayed Litt Young. Litt Young is the great-great grandfather of
the exhibit's curator/creator, Kheven LaGrone. Image courtesy of Kheven LaGrone

achievements of African Americans. Combing history books and creating mini-biographies for each entry, Mrs. Turner was lead researcher on their *Black and White Coloring Book* published by Troubador Press in 1969. They continued collaborating on a historically informative weekly installment of *Wee Pals* called *Soul Corner*. In 1969, the first of many collections of *Wee Pals* was published. The introduction written by Charles Schulz concludes, "Morrie is a credit to his profession and I am proud to have him as a friend."

Turner received a humanitarian award from the B'Nai Brith Anti-Defamation League of Philadelphia in 1968–69 and the Northern California Award of Merit in 1969. When he received an invitation to serve on the 1970 White House Conference on Children as the vice chairman of the Child Development and Mass Media Section, Turner could not refuse. He worked alongside Fred Rogers and Joan Ganz Cooney, cocreator and producer of *Sesame Street*, and their team of writers and editors. Upon his return, Turner worked with ABC to develop *Kid Power*, which ran on ABC Saturday mornings in 1972–73.

Turner's focus was staying in touch with children. Teaching, going into classrooms to conduct "chalk talks," and library engagements were essential. When NAACP program director Aileen O. James asked him to collaborate on a Back to School/Stay in School project, Turner was elated. A two-booklet series, one offered pointers to parents about being supportive to students, and the other focused on "Power to the Pupil."

Image courtesy of Kheven LaGrone

In December 1987, Turner was inducted into the California Public Education Hall of Fame for his work with the NAACP. Throughout the 1990s and 2000s, Turner continued working on *Wee Pals*, on his own or with assistance. He gave presentations, attended comic conventions, exhibitions, and more. In 2000, the Cartoon Art Museum presented Turner with the Sparky Award, named after Charles Schulz. In 2003, when the National Cartoonists Society honored Turner, his friend and colleague Bil Keane was on stage to present him with the Milton Caniff Lifetime Achievement Award. In the early 2000s, Heaven Sent Productions created a short documentary called *Keeping the Faith with Morrie Turner*. Turner was honored at the San Diego Comic-Con both in awards and on panels: in 1981, he was given an Inkpot Award, and in 2012 he was given the Bob Clampett Humanitarian Award.

Morrie Turner's creative partner and wife, Letha Turner, died in 1994. At the time of his death in 2014, Turner was still working on *Wee Pals*, which had graced the pages of newspapers for more than forty-eight years. He is survived by his son, Morrie Jr., grandchildren, and scores of fans.

# WALKER, DAVID F.

David Walker is the writer for several prominent DC and Marvel titles, including the 2016 reboot of *Power Man and Iron Fist*. He is also a pop culture critic and documentarian, focusing on the Blaxploitation and kung fu films of the 1970s.

> (Dec. 1, 1968– )
> - **Filmmaker, author, journalist, and comic book writer**
> - **Writer of *Shaft* graphic novel adaptation**

Much of David Walker's early work was in journalism, film, and essays that analyzed pop culture. Although he later went on to teach and speak at various institutions of higher learning, Walker dropped out of college multiple times. Most of his skills were self-taught and earned through years of effort and collaboration.

In 2004, he combined his passion for filmmaking and pop culture analysis and created the documentary *Macked, Hammered, Slaughtered, & Shafted*, which explored the role that blaxploitation film has played in pop culture and racial politics.

Some of the essays and analyses he has written were collected into *Becoming Black: Personal Ramblings on Racial Identification, Racism, and Popular Culture*, published by Drapetomedia in 2013. In these essays, Walker confronted not only the overall role that pop culture plays in the construction and understanding of race and racism, but also investigated his own personal media obsessions and how they impacted his understanding of himself, his race, and the world around him. His young adult novel *Super Justice Force* was also published in 2013.

Although Walker had written comics before, including one on which his 2007 short film *Black Santa's Revenge* is based, he published few for wider audiences until 2012. In December of that year, he released *Number 13* through Dark Horse Comics. Walker then went on to write *The Army of Dr. Moreau* for MonkeyBrain Comics, which hit shelves in

October 2013. With these books, Walker broke into the industry that had fascinated him for so long.

In December 2014, Dynamite Comics published *Shaft #1*, written by Walker, with art by Bilquis Evely. While the miniseries was only six issues long, it helped draw attention to both Walker and Evely's talents. Walker did more than just contribute scripts: he lettered the pages and created playlists that were carefully curated to capture the tone and arc of each issue. He also became the first person to write a John Shaft novel besides the character's creator Ernest Tidyman, with the permission of Tidyman's widow, Chris Clark. That novel, *Shaft's Revenge*, was available digitally to people who purchased issues of the *Dynamite* miniseries.

This first run on *Shaft* earned significant critical acclaim. It was nominated for the first-ever Dwayne McDuffie Award for Diversity in Comics in 2015, along with *Ms. Marvel*, *The Shadow Hero*, *Hex11*, and the webcomic *M.F.K.* While *M.F.K.* won the award, *Shaft* went on to claim the Glyph Award for Story of the Year.

All six issues were collected into a trade paperback titled *Shaft: A Complicated Man*. It garnered enough interest that Walker returned to the character for four more issues, which were published in 2016 as *Shaft: Imitation of Life*.

2015 also marked the beginning of Walker's collaboration with two of the largest comic book publishers. That summer, DC Comics launched a new group of titles under the DCYou initiative, including one written by David Walker, *Cyborg*. Victor "Cyborg" Stone is one of the most recognizable Black comic book characters, thanks in no small part to the *Teen Titans* cartoon series, but Walker's take on the character was intentionally more mature. Cyborg tackled issues of race, identity, privilege, and disability with the same kind of attention to detail and understanding of intersectionality that Walker had demonstrated in his essays and *Shaft*. Although he only contributed to the first nine issues, Walker prominently featured Black characters who were skilled scientists with nuanced relationships. It was a far more in-depth take on the cape-and-cowl comic book than is common.

In early 2016, Marvel's *Power Man and Iron Fist* hit the shelves. With his study of both blaxploitation films and kung fu movies, David Walker was the ideal writer for the series. Working with Sanford Greene, he created a book that retained its distance from the *Civil War II* movie later that year, which was derided by both fans and critics for its treatment of another well-known Black character, James "Rhodey" Rhodes, aka War Machine.

That same year, Walker added two more Marvel books to his name. First was *Nighthawk*, about a Black vigilante hero attempting to combat both crime and corrupt cops and politicians in Chicago. With art by Ramon Villalobos, *Nighthawk* was a new take on the Marvel character that had originally been part of the *Supreme Power* books, a Batman corollary bathed in violence but specifically and especially aware of racial justice. When *Nighthawk* was canceled after five issues, many fans objected that Marvel hadn't promoted or marketed the book enough to help it succeed, suspecting the publisher found it too confrontational about race and police brutality in a politically volatile year.

The second title was *Occupy Avengers*. Calling on imagery from the Occupy Wall Street and other populist protests, *Occupy Avengers* was supposed to answer the age-old question of who polices those with superpowers, especially when they put civilians in danger. It was the first time that Walker was at the helm of a book that was not led by a Black character, with Clint "Hawkeye" Barton at the center.

In *Becoming Black,* Walker recounts a story about the actor Joe Brown in which Brown asked him, "What is black?" In the essay, Walker admits to continuing to struggle to answer that question. He has continued to ask himself, and his readers, that same question over and over again, using comics to confront intersectional issues of identity and justice and encouraging everyone to find their own answers.

As of 2017, David Walker was based in Portland, Oregon.

# WHALEY, DEBORAH E.

Deborah Whaley is the author of the first academic treatment of Black women in comics, the 2015 book *Black Women in Sequence: Re-inking Comics, Graphic Novels, and Anime*. An associate professor of American studies and African American studies at the University of Iowa, she publishes critical work on comics and pop culture in a range of settings.

- **Born in Wheat Ridge, CO**
- **University of California, Santa Cruz, BA in American studies, 1993**
- **California State University, MA in American studies, 1996**
- **University of Kansas PhD in American studies, 2002**
- **Visual artist, curator, author, and professor**
- **Author of *Black Women in Sequence: Re-inking Comics, Graphic Novels, and Anime***

Deborah Whaley initially set out on a very different path from the one she eventually chose. After her high school graduation, she intended to move to New York to study fashion design. However, she had such a revelatory experience in an English college-level course, taught by a professor who lauded her talent for writing, that she decided to pursue American studies as an academic. "It is amazing how one person believing in you and mentoring you can change the trajectory of your life," she said.

As an undergraduate at the University of California, Santa Cruz, she developed an interest in the intersection of American culture, Black culture, visual arts, and feminism. Her research there focused on social movements, sororities in popular culture, and Afrofuturism in film. She also served as a teaching assistant to her American studies professor Michael Cowan, an unusual feat for an undergraduate. She credits both Cowan and instructor Ann Lane with encouraging the research on sororities that led to her first book, *Disciplining Women: Alpha Kappa Alpha, Black Counterpublics, and the Cultural Politics of Black Sororities* (2010).

Deborah Elizabeth Whaley

**BLACK WOMEN IN SEQUENCE**

Re-inking Comics, Graphic Novels, and Anime

Image courtesy of University of Washington Press

Later, while working on her master's under Leila Zenderland, Whaley continued research on independent Black cinema and popular cinema, at which point her work took on a theoretical lens.

From 2001 on, Whaley held a number of academic positions and earned multiple honors and awards, ultimately building toward a position as associate professor of American studies and African American studies at the University of Iowa in 2007. Her courses include studies of film and popular culture, focusing on comics and other media as cultural disruptors.

In 2011, her article "Black Cat Got Your Tongue? Catwoman, Blackness, and the Alchemy of Postracialism" was published in the *Journal of Graphic Novels and Comics*. Using the 2004 *Catwoman* film as a lens through which to discuss the representation of female comic book characters in multimedia, it was later incorporated into *Black Women In Sequence*.

In *Watching While Black: Centering the Television of Black Audiences*, edited by Beretta Smith-Shomade (2012), Whaley contributed a chapter called "Graphic Blackness/Anime Noir: Aaron McGruder's *The Boondocks* and the Adult Swim." It discusses the interaction of comic strips with cultural and historical events, using Aaron McGruder's *The Boondocks* as an example. She further discussed this theme in a foreword for the 2013 exhibit *Toonskin*, curated by Kenya Robinson.

> "I AM COMMITTED TO HOW A COMPLEX UNDERSTANDING OF HISTORY AND CULTURE CAN ALLOW ACTION UPON BETTER WAYS OF BEING AND LIVING TOGETHER IN THE WORLD."

"Visual art is very powerful, as is the written word. When you put the two together in the form of sequential art, magic happens. In dealing with topics related to identity and inequality, sequential art engages multiple aspects of cognition and recognition. Topics that are difficult and challenging have an ability to reach a larger audience through popular culture in general, but a graphic novel, for example, is something that is read, re-read, [and] studied...."

In *Black Women in Sequence,* Whaley discusses the evolution of Black female characters in comics, starting with the first Black female superhero, The Butterfly, in 1971. It features detailed examinations of the work of Black female comic creators such as Jackie Ormes and Barbara Brandon-Croft as well as analyses of Black female characters in a range of media. As the first academic treatment on the impact of Black women on the art form, it is a significant contribution to the field of comics criticism.

In her published work and university courses alike, Deborah Whaley uses an interdisciplinary framework to analyze American culture and advance the cause of social justice.

# WHEELER, JOSEPH R, III

**(Sept. 9, 1975– )**
- **Born in Atlanta, GA**
- **Pratt Institute, foundation studies**
- **Atlanta College of Art, BFA**
- **Actor, film writer, producer, convention founder, and artist**
- **Founder and president of ONYXCON Convention**

Joseph R Wheeler III is the founder and president of the Atlanta-based ONYX-CON, a convention focusing on the African diaspora in popular culture. It celebrates diverse media in many forms, including video games, film, books, comics, and collectibles.

Growing up in the 1970s during the heyday of hip-hop and Black cinema, Joseph R Wheeler III fell in love with comics and popular culture at an early age. His first work was *The Aftermath Saga: Eve Marse*, a postapocalyptic epic featuring African American heroes and monster film themes. Looking back on this early work, he said, "In places the drawing could have been stronger, but it was my first and it was full of heart."

In 2009, Joseph III founded ONYXCON, the largest African American fan convention in the Southeast. It was inspired by other Black media–focused conventions such as the East Coast Black Age of Comics convention, the National Black Arts Festival, and the Motor City Black Age of Comics. He said, "I always knew, 'If I build it, they will come.' Atlanta showed up and showed love in 2009 and ever since."

Besides his work in arts infrastructure and organization, Joseph R Wheeler III is also a professional artist. His art has been featured in the *International Review of African American Art* from Hampton University. He was also shown at a number of museums, such as the Hammonds House Museum, the Tubman Museum, and the Schomburg Center of Harlem.

Joseph III feels that his largest contribution to Black popular culture after ONYXCON is his large-scale work the *United African Confederation ANKH* or *UAC-ANKH*. He describes it as "a salute to the history of major and minor characters played by thespians of direct African descent on *Star Trek*." Completed in 2013, it was featured in a solo exhibition at the Atlanta Aviation Community Cultural Center in 2015.

As a trailblazer for African Americans in the field of art and comics, Joseph III believes that the future is extremely bright for others like him.

Illustration by Marcus Williams, image courtesy of Joseph R. Wheeler III

As of 2017, Joseph III continued to work in the art field. Besides his work with ONYXCON, he was also an arts instructor and art therapist for youth and aging populations.

> *"A GREAT DEAL OF LIFE, LOVE, AND STRUGGLE GOES INTO THE DEVELOPMENT OF COMIC BOOKS AND RELATED MEDIA WHETHER BOOKS, FILMS, GAMING, COSPLAY, OR WHATEVER. ALL OF THESE ARTS ARE BEING LOVED AND SHARING A RENAISSANCE IN BLACK TOGETHER. INDEPENDENT CREATORS ARE GETTING PRESS AND BRINGING VOICES THAT NEED A PLATFORM. THAT IS BEAUTIFUL!"*
>
> *- JOSEPH WHEELER III*

# WHITE, CANAAN

(1977– )
- Born in St. Joseph, MO
- Artist and illustrator
- Illustrator of *The Harlem Hellfighters* and *Uber*

Caanan White is the illustrator of *The Harlem Hellfighters* and *Uber*, two historical comics about World War I and II. *The Harlem Hellfighters*, written by Max Brooks, tells the true story of the 396th Infantry, an all-Black regiment that, despite returning from World War I as heavily decorated war heroes, faced discrimination and prejudice at home. *Uber*, by Kieron Gillen, is a more fantastical rendering of World War II, featuring weaponized German soldiers called Ubermensch.

Both books feature graphic scenes of carnage and violence. Regarding their extreme content, White admits, "I'm not a lover of gore, so my first reaction was, 'This is insane!" But then, I understood this is war and war is very ugly in all its facets." He painstakingly researches the setting of his books and avoids glorifying combat in his illustrations.

Calling *The Harlem Hellfighters* "a stunning work of historical recovery," Maureen Corrigan at NPR wrote, "It's not pretty, but the 'in your face' style of *The Harlem Hellfighters* is suited to dramatizing a crucial part of American history that hasn't been thrust forcefully enough into our collective faces."

Caanan White grew up in the 1990s inspired by artists such as Jim Lee, Marc Silvestri, Brett Booth, and Michael Turner. His resulting art style is a mix of different influences, with bold shadowing and cinematic layouts.

His other works include *Anna Mercury Artbook: The New Ataraxia Mission* (Avatar Press), *Absolution: Rubicon* (Avatar Press), *Ghosting*

Image courtesy of Caanan White

(Platinum Studios Comics), *Gravel: Combat Magician* (Avatar Press), *R.R.H.* (Devil's Due/1First Comics), and *Ptolus: City by the Spire* (Dabel Brothers/Marvel). Most recently, he collaborated with writer Jay Longino on an urban kung fu story called *The Son of Shaolin.*

## CREATIVE TIPS

When working on a large job, White advises "not to perfect every page, but rather, improve with the next one."

"I think the biggest thing is staying on schedule.... It doesn't mean I slack off, but I do my best to learn from my mistakes and keep rolling."

# WILLIAMS, MAIA "CROWN"

- **Entrepreneur, convention founder, and chef**
- **Founder of MECCAcon**

Maia "Crown" Williams is the CEO and founder of MECCAcon, the Midwest Ethnic Convention for Comics and Arts. Since 2013, MECCAcon has convened creators and fans of color in Detroit to celebrate multicultural comics, films, and art. She is also the cofounder of the Black Speculative Arts Movement, a convention celebrating Afrofuturism in the United States and abroad.

A successful entrepreneur in a variety of different disciplines – she is a small business manager as well as an executive sous chef – Maia Williams first became interested in Black comics thanks to her teenage son. Taking note of his love of comics and *Static Shock*, an animated show featuring a young Black male protagonist, she sought out books that would reflect his culture and heritage. In the process, she learned about the Black comics community, which impressed her with its history and sense of solidarity.

Despite Detroit's large African American population, it was not yet home to a Black comics convention along the lines of Pittsburgh's East Coast Black Age of Comics Convention. After several years of helping organize other conventions, she decided to create one to fill that niche herself.

Image courtesy of N. Steven Harris

MECCAcon was first held in October of 2013. In recent years, the event has been held in September at the Detroit Public Library. The convention includes more than fifty vendors, an international film festival, workshops, classes, Q&A panels, and demonstrations. While primarily celebrating African American contributions to comics and art, it features creators from various other cultures as well.

SHE ENJOYS SEEING "CHILDREN REACT TO BEING IN A VENUE FILLED WITH COMICS THAT LOOK LIKE THEM ... ONE OF THE GREATEST FEELINGS ON THIS REALM. IT WARMS ME EVERY TIME WITH EVERY FACE."

While the work that goes into MECCAcon – collecting vendors, creating programs, marketing, and scheduling – is intense, Williams believes the results are worth the effort.

In addition to her work as a convention organizer, Williams also works to address the objectification of women in comics and the underrepresentation of Black superheroes. She also promotes independent comics such as *Brotherman*, which feature protagonists of color more often than those from mainstream publishers.

Aside from MECCAcon, Williams curates art installations, jazz and reggae concerts, hip-hop ciphers, and open mics. She is a cofounder with Dr. Reynaldo Anderson of the Black Speculative Arts Movement. This convention centers on Afrofuturism, Black comics, art, and cooperative economics and is held at colleges and universities across the United States and abroad.

With her conventions, Maia Williams aims to show children that "heroes come in many backgrounds, many hoods, many planets, and many suburbs too." She hopes that the children who attend MECCAcon leave inspired to develop their talents and create new art.

## WIMBERLY, RONALD

(April 28, 1979– )
- Born in Washington, DC
- Comics writer and artist
- Author of *Prince of Cats*

Ronald Wimberly is a comics artist who specializes in penciling and inking. Besides his work on numerous titles for Marvel and DC Comics, he is the author of an original graphic novel, *Prince of Cats*, and numerous short-form comics published in The Nib, *The New Yorker*, and Stela.

In 1997, Wimberly moved from Rockville, Maryland, to Brooklyn to attend Pratt Institute. Although he did not graduate from Pratt, he was a member of Static Fish, the school's comics club, as a student. While there, he began work on the ninja action story *GratNin* (short for "Gratuitous Ninja"), which was later published in Dark Horse's *Strip Search* anthology. In 2004, Wimberly was the penciler, inker, and colorist of the short story "Overdose," written by James MacDonald, which appeared in the 2004 anthology *Metal Hurlant #14: The Zombies That Ate the World*.

In 2005, Wimberly did his first work for the DC imprint Vertigo Comics as the penciler and inker of *Lucifer* #58, written by Mike Carey. That same year, he created the covers for the five-arc miniseries *John Constantine – Hellblazer Special: Papa Midnite* and was the penciler and inker for *Swamp Thing* #19. All three titles were collected in graphic novel format in 2006. In 2007, he was the penciler and inker for *Deadman* #11 and #12.

Wimberly was the artist for Percy Carey's graphic memoir *Sentences: The Life of MF Grimm*, published in 2007 by Vertigo. As a child, Carey was a member of the cast of *Sesame Street* who later gained fame as a hip-hop MC under the name MF Grimm. His career was cut short when he was shot during a drug deal and paralyzed from the waist down, but he eventually made a comeback as a music producer. *Sentences* won two Glyph Awards in 2008, for Story of the Year and Best Cover, and was nominated for the 2006 Eisner Award for Best Reality-Based Work.

Wimberly's next graphic novel was the authorized adaptation of Ray Bradbury's 1962 novel *Something Wicked This Way Comes,* a horror story about two teenage boys who encounter strange phenomena at a sinister carnival. The book was published by Hill and Wang in 2011.

The following year, Vertigo published Wimberly's original graphic novel *Prince of Cats*, a postmodern deconstruction of Romeo and Juliet that places Tybalt and other supporting cast members at the forefront and sets the conflict in a world informed by 1980s New York street culture. The characters speak in iambic pentameter throughout, mixing Elizabethan English with contemporary imagery, and settle their grudges with sword duels. A new edition was published by Image in 2016.

In 2013, Wimberly wrote and drew a set of four comic strips titled *Calvin & Johnson* for the athletic apparel company Nike and the advertis-

Image courtesy of Ronald Wimberly

ing agency Wieden & Kennedy. The comics feature Detroit Lions wide receiver Calvin Johnson and rapper P. Diddy, who is Johnson's alter ego in the story. The comics ran on Nike's Football Facebook page.

Wimberly continued to work on monthly comics for a variety of publishers. He penciled and inked a two-part *She-Hulk* story, "Blue," which ran in *She-Hulk* #5 and #6 in 2014, and he has contributed covers and other artwork for a number of other Marvel comics. He also was the penciler for the first issue of *Black Dynamite*, published by IDW Publishing in 2013.

In 2015, Wimberly's short comic "Lighten Up" ran on the comics journalism website The Nib. In it, he describes his experience as a colorist working on Marvel's *Wolverine & The X-Men* #10, when an editor asked him to lighten a character's skin tone. Throughout the comic, Wimberly uses the hexadecimal codes for different hues as he discusses the social concept of race and its intersection with art. "Lighten Up" was shared and discussed widely on social media and comics sites.

Wimberly has also had several short comics appear in *The New Yorker* magazine, including "Ten Years After," about the gentrification of New Orleans after Hurricane Katrina, and "The Lot," about a small radio station that broadcasts out of a shipping container in a vacant lot in Brooklyn.

Wimberly returned to *GratNin*, his early comic, in 2016, reworking it in a different format for the mobile comics site Stela. Stela presents comics as a vertical sequence, rather than the standard panel-by-panel comics format, on the theory that the vertical scroll is a more natural experience for mobile phone users.

Wimberly has contributed to a number of anthologies, including *Meathaus: S.O.S.* (2008), *Occupy Comics* #1 (2013), *Little Nemo: Dream Another Dream* (2014), *Strange Sports Stories* #2 (2015), *Attack on Titan Anthology* (2016), and *The CBLDF Presents Liberty Annual* (2016). In 2007 he was penciler, inker, and colorist for a story "The Stain," written by Joshua Dysart, which appeared in *MySpace Dark Horse Presents* #15. He also worked on the multicreator comic *Prophet* and helped create the DMC Universe featured in musician Darryl McDaniels' comics imprint Darryl Makes Comics.

Outside of comics, Wimberly worked at Titmouse Studios in 2012 as a character designer for the Adult Swim series *Black Dynamite: The Animated Series*.

Ronald Wimberly's work has been exhibited in Paris, Tokyo, and New York. He has also earned several artist residencies, including the Maison des Auteurs in Angouleme, France, in 2014 and 2015 and the Columbus Museum of Art and the James Thurber House in 2016. In addition to his given name, Wimberly also goes by "D-π" or "D-pi" on social media.

# WOODS, ASHLEY A.

(Oct. 15, 1985– )
- Born in Chicago, IL
- International Academy of Design and Technology, film and animation, 2007
- Illustrator, comic creator, and writer
- Illustrated *Niobe: She Is Life*

Ashley Woods is an artist best known for her work on Amandla Stenberg's *Niobe: She Is Life*. She has contributed art to numerous comics projects, including the superhero comic *Black* and Rosarium Publishing's anthology *Artists against Police Brutality*.

Artistic inspirations such as Brian Stelfreeze (Marvel Comics's *Black Panther and Domino* miniseries), Hideo Kojima (*Metal Gear* game series), and Satoshi Kon (*Paranoia Agent* anime series) were important influences on Woods's artwork, as were her interest in video games and in studying Japanese.

Raised on the South Side of Chicago, Woods chose a career in comics after being exposed to a few Marvel comics given to her by her mother.

Top row (l - r): John Crawford, Tamir Rice, Eric Garner, Michael Brown, Cary Ball Jr., Amadou Diallo
Bottom row (l - r): Tanisha Anderson, Miriam Carey, Yvette Smith, Rekia Boyd, Aiyana Stanley-Jones

Image courtesy of Ashley Woods

As an artist, she began her career by self-publishing her action-fantasy comic series, *Millennia War*, while attending the International Academy of Design and Technology in Chicago. After earning her degree, Woods traveled to Kyoto, Japan, where she presented her work in a gallery showcase called *Out Of Sequence*.

When Woods returned to the United States, her comic book work was included in the 2010 compilation *Black Comix: African American Independent Comics Art and Culture*, edited by Damian Duffy and John Jennings, a coffee-table book that is used in college courses nationwide and internationally. Woods's artwork has also been featured in social and political spaces such as Rosarium Publishing's 2015 comic anthology *Artists against Police Brutality*, in which her work honors recent victims of police violence. The anthology addresses critical issues such as the criminal justice system, civil rights, and police brutality in prose and comics form.

In 2015, Woods joined the team of Hunger Games actor Amandla Stenberg and Stranger Comics to work on *Niobe: She Is Life*, a comic that tells the coming of age story of Niobe Ayutami, an orphaned wild elf teenager in a fantasy world. *Niobe: She Is Life* is the first nationally distributed comic with a Black female writer, artist, and protagonist. The groundbreaking work was wildly successful, with the first issue selling more than 10,000 copies during its launch.

Ashley Woods also created a variant cover of *Black* (Black Mask Studio, 2016), by Kwanza Osajyefo, Tim Smith, and Jamal Igle. This politically engaged comic posits a world where only Black people have superpowers. Her other artistic projects include creating the cover art for the *Black Comix II* anthology; illustrating the second issue of *Dziva Jones*, an ongoing independent series created and written by Aminah Armour; and working with New Arab Media on a postapocalyptic book featuring a female Saudi heroine, Latifa. She has also contributed to the sci-fi action comedy *Baaaaad Muthaz* (Rosarium Publishing) and the comic anthology *Past the Last Mountain*.

Woods is a frequent attendant at comic book and video game conventions across the country. At Comic-Con International in San Diego, she spoke on the panel "Black Comix Returns: African Independent Comic Publishing." She also participated in a panel with comics artist and writer LeSean Thomas (*The Boondocks, Black Dynamite, Legend of Korra*) at the Black Comix Arts Festival in San Francisco. She has also been featured in several popular culture publications, including *Afropunk* magazine (2015), the comics news site Black Girl Nerds (2015), Bleeding Cool (2015), and the #BlackComicsChat podcast.

During a time in which both women and people of color are underrepresented in comics, Woods evolved, pushed boundaries, and created firsts in the medium.

# YO, ONJENA

- **Born in Abilene, TX**
- **Dartmouth College, environmental engineering and economics**
- **Writer, comics editor, and designer**
- **Cofounder of Carbon-Fibre Media**

Onjena Yo is an independent comics editor and the cofounder of Carbon-Fibre Media. She has collaborated on several projects with Grey Williamson, the author of *Val-Mar, Prince of the Damned* and *The Legend of Apollo.*

Onjena Yo's parents met in Kunsan, South Korea, while her father was enlisted in the US Air Force. Her mother, South Korean, and father, African American, moved to the United States together in 1976. Yo's upbringing instilled her with cultural pride and respect for working-class struggles, which have in turn influenced her creative perspective.

Although she would not actually read a comic book until adulthood, Yo was first exposed to them by watching her older brother draw popular comic characters. In 2008, she met veteran comic book artist Grey Williamson, who introduced her to *The Dark Knight Returns.* At the time, Williamson – who had worked in comics since 1988, and was one of the few Black comic book artists to draw for all the major companies

Image courtesy of Onjena Yo

– was developing independent comics projects *Val-Mar, Prince of the Damned* and *The Legend of Apollo*. Adept at organizing and editing, Yo began to work with Williamson on his projects.

"[I WRITE] TO EMPOWER CHILDREN AND OUR INNER CHILD. I WANT KIDS TO SEE ALL OF THEMSELVES ... FLAWED, IMPERFECT BUT GROWING."

The two formed the company Carbon-Fibre Media, based in Brooklyn, as a platform for their work.

Yo edited the first two books of *Val-Mar, Prince of the Damned*, which debuted in fall 2015 and early 2016, respectively. Inspired by her collaborations with Williamson, and fueled by a need to counter the chronic lack of diversity in popular culture, Yo also developed and launched her own creative project in 2011: O'BOTs. The O'BOT is a template for creative expression: a cylindrical figurine in a defiant stance, adorned with a heart on its chest, that can be customized to fit any character. With a cast of original characters, as well as O'BOTs that represent real people, Yo communicates messages of compassion through comics and social media.

In 2012, Yo developed the Multinational Patriot Flag & Blog Series, in which she customizes flags to represent multinational identities. She wrote, "As a child, I remember watching my father quietly replace our flag each time it was stolen from our porch by our 'neighbors.' I listened to my mother who taught us to assimilate for success but not be a 'typical American.' To this day, I am still conflicted when expressing my 'patriotism.'" With her flag series, she encourages individuals to honor both their personal and cultural journeys.

In 2014, Onjena Yo began actively promoting diversity in children's literature. In a 2016 blog post on Carbon-Fibre Media titled "OUR AMERICA: And how are the children?" Yo cited a study by the Cooperative Children's Book Center at the University of Wisconsin–Madison and asked, "Seriously, animals/trucks have the same level of representation as Blacks, Asians, Pacific Islanders, Latinxs and Native Americans combined?" She then shared links to more than forty groups promoting creators of color and diversity in media.

Through Carbon-Fibre Media and social media, Yo advocates for independent artist communities and promotes artists and organizers who combat anti-Blackness.

# AFTERWORD

## by Christopher Priest

I remember an autumn morning on Madison Avenue in 1978 when I suddenly realized, to my horror, that I was, literally, skipping to work. Working at Marvel Comics was, for me, a surreal experience, as I'd been taught by a well-meaning and dearly beloved mother to lower my career sights and life expectations. At age seventeen I'd applied for a high school internship at Marvel without believing, even for a minute, that I'd actually be considered. I then went to the interview without believing, for one moment, that I'd be chosen.

I found myself in competition with a reception area full of aspiring artists, portfolios in hand. I was a writer and had brought along a dreadful high school comics project that I had written and drawn.

In the intervening years I've discovered most managers tend to replicate themselves, choosing to hire people who reflect qualities the managers value in themselves; someone who reminds them of, well, them. This is perhaps the most insidious feature of institutionalized racism, the fact that it hides itself even from many who unknowingly practice it. These managers weren't excluding Black applicants, they were hiring applicants who reminded them of themselves.

Through several cycles of hiring and promotions, a workforce can and often does become creatively and ontologically tone deaf. Worse, nobody even realizes anything is wrong. Facts, therefore, arrive as accusations where no accusal or even criticism is intended. Facts such as, in Marvel's nearly eighty-year history, no African American has ever been assigned regular writing duties to *Superman* or *Batman*. Facts like comics with Black protagonists routinely sell fewer copies than comics with white protagonists. If I say these things out loud, I am accusing somebody of something, but, wait, I'm really not. I am stating facts – things nobody noticed because we've all hired ourselves. So it surprised me a great deal when Jim Shooter, Marvel's editor in chief, selected me, a nearsighted black kid who could not possibly be less like himself. Shooter, and at Shooter's behest, Stan Lee, sat with me one-on-one, teaching me the business of comics and elements of writing and sequential art.

At age seventeen, I felt prepared to learn the business but had not thought about or prepared myself for the fact that every office, everywhere on the planet, is a political environment. My schooling equipped me with nouns and verbs and tools applicable to my trade, but not even one word of advice for navigating through the ignis fatuus culture of presumed liberals – people who can be and often are the most pernicious racists of all because their intellect and liberal leanings tell them they are beyond racism. That's a dangerously arrogant presumption. We are all racial and subject to tribalism.

Image courtesy of Stanford Carpenter

In those days, Marvel was an irreverent frat house not unlike *Mad Men*'s Sterling Cooper ad agency (in fact, the Season One set of *Mad Men* looked almost exactly like seventies-era Marvel). There was bawdy language. There were racist jokes, sexist jokes. People rubbed my head for good luck and mocked me for having "black hands" after repeatedly Xeroxing Gene Colan's elegant and amazing art for Marv Wolfman's *Tomb of Dracula*.

In those early days, I was focused only on finding ways to stay at Marvel beyond my internship. My life's philosophy has always been to concentrate on the goal and not get sidetracked by hardships, challenges, or distractions along the way.

It never occurred to me that I was the first African American to be hired on staff as well as the first African American hired as a full-time comics series writer in the industry's history. To be honest, neither distinction meant much to me. I wasn't there to make history, I was there to make comics.

I wanted, and still want, to be just another guy on a level playing field competing for writing and editorial slots. I viewed and still view the race thing as an incredible distraction and annoyance; my having become the Radioactive Man because of all of the self-replication done in the industry. This is the reality of the market we produce for: selling relationships. Our market, our audience, consists largely of existing (mostly white male) fans of the medium and we are in the business of selling ongoing relationships with characters they have grown to love.

However, for many Blacks, he is not Superman so much as he is Super-WhiteMan. Many comics shop retail displays are unknowingly hostile to Blacks and Black culture. It is a kind of violence, these stores – many of which present the appearance of bunkers, their windows papered over with white iconic characters leaping and jumping and zapping. There's no sign on the window that reads WHITE POWER, but the sensibility is implied: these are power fantasies for whites. White power fantasies.

Pooh anem ain't trying to go into these places where Blacks are whispered about and followed not so much because they are Black but because they are new, because they are not regulars, so there is this awkward tribal introduction where the retail staff tries to bridge that gap. But, to many Blacks, surveillance is surveillance, and this awkwardness feels one step away from a police call, handcuffs, and Rodney King.

I don't present myself as a Black writer, dashiki and Kente cloth Kufi. I'm just another guy who wants to write comics. For many editors, however, "Black" is the first quality that pops to mind when my name appears on a list. And, just as often, those eyes continue to glide down the list because "Black" and, for example, Wonder Woman, don't usually free associate. But I wrote a great *Wonder Woman*. I enjoyed writing *Wonder Woman*.

Marvel made huge headlines for hiring noted *Atlantic* columnist Ta-Nehisi Coates to write *The Black Panther*. With due respect to Mr. Coates, that really didn't impress me. If you want to impress me, hire this brilliant young writer Coates to write *Superman*.

I don't believe writing or art assignments should be offered on the basis of gender or race. A Russian female writer is totally capable of writing a dynamic *Luke Cage* comic. It's not about gender or race, it's about talent and research. It's about committing to the character, learning the character's voice, and becoming master of that specific universe. A writer writes.

Hiring minority talent to write minority books is not progressive, it's Replicant thinking – Replicant Theory. I'd be eager to read a Coates-written Superman not because Coates is Black but because Coates really is that good.

Some will ask why an encyclopedia of Black comics needs to exist. Ta-Nehisi Coates is why. David Walker is why. Pioneers like Orrin Cromwell Evans, John Terrell, George J. Evans Jr., Billy Graham, Keith Pollard, Ron Wilson, Trevor Von Eden, Denys Cowan, ChrisCross is why. "If we're going to chronicle the collective history of comics," *Lion Forge* editor in chief Joseph Illidge told me regarding this project, "these milestones cannot be excluded." Yet, in many if not most of the self-congratulatory anniversary histories written about Marvel, DC, and other publishers, these notable firsts are obviously missing. I believe this is less about racism than it is about tone-deafness; nobody thinks anything is wrong. If the choice not to highlight these persons was deliberate, if someone dismissed these landmarks as unimportant or even irrelevant, that's a Replicant mindset. *We alone are the baseline "normal,"* this mindset asserts. *Nobody cares who the first black editor was, or who the first female artist was.*

Yes they do. Ramona Fradon matters. Jan Duursema matters. Every step this industry has taken to evolve from white men in ties to what it is swiftly becoming multicultural in a very real sense, is significant; most especially to the consumer base to which these publishers sell.

Now here's my bifurcated convolution: I want to be thought of as a writer, not a "Black" writer. But I also consider my being the first Black writer and editor in modern comics (Marvel 1978, DC 1990) to be significant and larger than myself. The omission of those historical highlights from the publishers' colorful histories makes them look small and tends to cast aspersions where none should be. I seriously doubt the omissions were capricious. They were, instead, most likely the tone-deaf narrow thinking of Replicants. Everything Is Okay. Thus, the cloud of racist suspicion is self-created and the goodwill such volumes were created to project is needlessly undermined.

So, here we are: a handy reference for any future Ain't We Great historical anthologies. Based upon what the business looks like now, I have to believe future AWG volumes will – must – include significant cultural milestones routinely omitted from the Replicant works. I'm sure many a researcher will reach for this volume because no other exists.

I have such a deep and inexplicable affection and admiration for Dr. Sheena Howard that I must impose guardrails on the bowling lanes to keep my adoration from being misinterpreted. She is immediately infectious, a happy Borg Queen injecting everyone with this serious, positive Afrocentric vibe. Meshell Ndegeocello thumpin' that Fender is Howard's soundtrack: "Ain't it great to be Black today?!" I can write (and in fact have written) a volume about the porcupine interactions between Black men and Black women, but Dr. Howard is incredibly easy to talk to and share with and learn from.

I am continually surprised to meet young African American women who have an interest in comics. I find this incredibly puzzling as, when I was twenty- or even thirtysomething, the mere mention of comic books would be enough to earn you The Look, that thing Black women do to emasculate men with their eyes. You really don't want to know what the good Doctor can do with hers. It's possible she may well be the single most delightful woman on the planet.

Image courtesy of Juliana "Jewels" Smith

Which takes nothing away from her academic chops or her edgy sense of humor, which she wields like a machine gun at a bank heist. All I really remember about the writers summit where we met was her smile and the hotel charging everybody's room to my credit card.

I'm honored and a little embarrassed by the very kind portrait she creates of this very ordinary aging comics geek. Thank you, Dr. Howard, for just being you.

CHRISTOPHER PRIEST

June 2017

# FURTHER READING

Here is a short list of books that I recommend for those interested in the history of comics. I hope it can serve as a resource for readers interested in learning more about the politics of comics, the history of Black people in comics, and theories of representation.

Brown, Jeffrey A. (2001). *Black Superheroes, Milestone Comics, and Their Fans.* Oxford: University Press of Mississippi.

Duncan, Randy, and Matthew J. Smith (2015). *The Power of Comics: History, Form, and Culture.* London: Bloomsbury Academic.

Foster, William H., III (2005). *Looking for a Face Like Mine.* Waterbury, CT: Fine Tooth Press.

Goldstein, Nancy (2008). *Jackie Ormes: The First African American Woman Cartoonist.* Ann Arbor: University of Michigan Press.

Heer, Jeet, and Kent Worcester (2004). *Arguing Comics: Literary Masters on a Popular Medium.* Oxford: University Press of Mississippi.

Howard, Sheena, and Ronald L. Jackson II (2013). *Black Comics: Politics of Race and Representation.* New York: Continuum

Inge, M. Thomas (1990). *Comics as Culture.* Oxford: University Press of Mississippi.

Jennings, John, and Damian Duffy (2010). *Black Comix: African American Independent Comics, Art, and Culture.* New York: Mark Batty Publisher.

Mcallister, Matthew H., Edward H. Sewell, Jr., and Ian Gordon (2001). *Comics and Ideology.* New York: Peter Lang Publishing.

Pustz, Matthew J. (1999). *Comic Book Culture: Fanboys and True Believers.* Oxford: University Press of Mississippi.

# SELECT BIBLIOGRAPHY

The URLs listed in the following citations are correct as of the time of publication. Please note that they are subject to change.

## Baker, Matt

Amash, Jim, and Eric Nolen-Weathington, eds. *Matt Baker: The Art of Glamour*. Raleigh, NC: TwoMorrows Publishing, 2012.

Hadju, David. *The Ten-Cent Plague: The Great Comic Book Scare and How It Changed America*. New York: Picador, 2009.

Howard, Sheena C., and Ronald L. Jackson II, eds. *Black Comics: Politics of Race and Representation*. London: Bloomsbury Academic, 2013.

Jackson, Tim. *Pioneering Cartoonists of Color*. Jackson: University Press of Mississippi, 2016.

Jones, William B., Jr. *Classics Illustrated: A Cultural History, with Illustrations*. Jefferson, NC: McFarland & Company, 2001.

Ringgenberg, Steven, and Joseph V. Procopio. *The Lost Art of Matt Baker: The Complete Canteen Kate*. Silver Springs, MD: Picture This Press, 2013.

## Bell, Darrin

Bell, Darrin. "Darrin Bell: Editorial Cartoons for the Washington Post Writers Group." Accessed August 31, 2016. http://darrinbell.com/.

## Billingsley, Ray

Billingsley, Ray. "Ray Billingsley." http://www.billingsleyart.com/Main-Page.html.

King Features Corporation. "Curtis by Ray Billingsley." http://kingfeatures.com/comics/comics-a-z/?id=Curtis.

Otfinosky, Steven. *African Americans in the Visual Arts (A to Z of African Americans)*. New York: Facts on File, 2011.

## Brandon, Brumsic

Jackson, Ester Cooper, with Constance Pohl, eds. *Freedomways Reader: Prophets in Their Own Country*. New York: Basic Books, 2001.

Katz, Harry, ed. *Cartoon America: Comic Art in the Library of Congress*. New York: Harry N. Abrams, 2006.

Knauer, Christine. *Let Us Fight as Free Men: Black Soldiers and Civil Rights (Politics and Culture in Modern America)*. Philadelphia: University of Pennsylvania Press, 2014.

## Broadnax, Jamie

Broadnax, Jamie. "About BGN." Accessed August 24, 2016. https://blackgirlnerds.com/about-bgn/.

### Campbell, Bill

Alverson, Brigid. "Rosarium Bets on Multicultural Novels and Comics." *Publishers Weekly*. February 20, 2015. https://www.publishersweekly.com/pw/by-topic/industry-news/publisher-news/article/65665-rosarium-bets-on-multicultural-novels-and-comics.html.

Anderson, Porter. "Rosarium's Faces of Diverse Publishing: 'Get Out of Our Way.'" *Publishing Perspectives*. January 24, 2017. https://publishingperspectives.com/2017/01/rosarium-publishing-diversity-multiculturalism/.

### Campbell, E. Simms

Bontemps, Arna. *We Have Tomorrow*. Boston: Houghton Mifflin, 1945.

Brown, Sterling. *Southern Road*. Boston: Beacon Press, 1932.

Jackson, Tim. *Pioneering Cartoonists of Color*. Jackson: University Press of Mississippi, 2016.

King Features Syndicate. *Famous Artists & Writers of King Features Syndicate*. New York: King Features Syndicate, 1949.

Merrill, Hugh. *Esky: The Early Years at Esquire*. New Brunswick, NJ: Rutgers University Press, 1995.

Simms Campbell, E. *The WWII Era Comic Art of E. Simms Campbell: Cuties in Arms & More Cuties in Arms*. Darke County, OH: Coachwhip Publications, 2012.

### Chambliss, Julian

Chambliss, Julian C., William Svitavsky, and Thomas C. Donaldson. *Ages of Heroes, Eras of Men: Superheroes and the American Experience*. Newcastle upon Tyne, UK: Cambridge Scholars Publishing, 2014.

Chambliss, Julian C., William Svitavsky, and Thomas C. Donaldson. *Assemble: Essays on the Modern Marvel Cinematic Universe*. Jefferson, NC: McFarland & Company, 2017.

### Commodore, Chester

Chester Commodore Papers, "Guide to the Chester Commodore Papers, 1914–2004," Chicago Public Library, Carter G. Woodson Regional Library, Vivian G. Harsh Research Collection of Afro-American History and Literature.

Jackson, Tim. *Pioneering Cartoonists of Color*. Jackson: University Press of Mississippi, 2016.

Nelson, Stanley, dir. *The Black Press: Soldiers without Swords*. DVD. PBS, 1998.

Otfinosky, Steven. *African Americans in the Visual Arts (A to Z of African Americans)*. New York: Facts on File, 2011.

### Craft, Jerry

Craft, Jerry. "Jerry Craft: Children's Book Author and Illustrator." Jerrycraft.net.

### De La Cruz, Sharon

De La Cruz, Sharon. "LinkedIn Profile: Sharon De La Cruz." Accessed November 1, 2016. https://www.linkedin.com/in/sdlcruz.

De La Cruz, Sharon. "Uno Seis Tres: The Works of Sharon Lee De La Cruz." http://unoseistres.com/.

Milosheff, Peter. "Bronx Graffiti Artist Sharon De La Cruz Teams Up With Calvin Klein." *The Bronx Times.* April 17, 2013. http://www.bronx.com/news/Art/2814.html.

"The Digital Citizens Lab." Accessed November 7, 2016. http://www.digitalcitizenslab.com/.

Whitehead, Kim. "Sharon De La Cruz, Artist and Activist from The POINT, Honored for Community Work in The Bronx." *New York Daily News.* February 23, 2012. http://www.nydailynews.com/new-york/bronx/sharon-de-la-cruz-artist-activist-point-honored-community-work-bronx-article-1.1026377.

WYSK. "Women Talk: 10 Questions With Miss 163 … Art Meets Activism." September 20, 2012. http://womenyoushouldknow.net/women-talk-10-questions-with-miss-163-art-meets-activism/.

### Evans, Orrin Cromwell

Christopher, Tom. "Orrin C Evans and the Story of All Negro Comics." 2002. http://www.tomchristopher.com/comics3/orrin-c-evans-and-the-story-of-all-negro-comics/.

Friedman, Drew. *More Heroes of the Comics: Portraits of the Legends of Comic Books.* Seattle: Fantagraphics, 2016.

Gateward, Frances, and John Jennings. *The Blacker the Ink: Constructions of Black Identity in Comics and Sequential Art.* New Brunswick, NJ: Rutgers University Press, 2015.

"Orrin C. Evans, Journalist, 68: Veteran Black Reporter in Philadelphia Is Dead." *New York Times.* August 8, 1971.

"The Press: Ace Harlem to the Rescue." *Time.* July 14, 1947.

### Fitzgerald, Bertram

Christopher, Tom. "Bertram Fitzgerald and the Golden Legacy Series of Black History Comics." 2004. http://www.tomchristopher.com/comics/bertram-a-fitzgerald-and-the-golden-legacy-series-of-black-history-comics/.

Kleefeld, Sean. "Bertram A. Fitzgerald." February 28, 2011. http://www.kleefeldoncomics.com/2011/02/bertram-fitzgerald.html.

Stromberg, Fredrik. *Black Images in the Comics: A Visual History.* Seattle: Fantagraphics, 2003.

### Gay, Roxane

Collins, Ellie. "Who Is Roxane Gay? Get to Know the Feminist Critic Who Just Became One of Marvel's First Black Women Writers." Comics Alliance. July 22, 2016. http://comicsalliance.com/roxane-gay-world-of-wakanda/.

Gustines, George Gene. "Marvel's World of Wakanda Will Spotlight Women, on the Page and Behind It." *New York Times.* July 22, 2016.

### Gibbs, Shawneé and Shawnelle

Gibbs, Shawneé and Shawnelle. "Fashion Forward." Reel Republic: TV/Film/Animation. Accessed August 16, 2016. http://www.reelrepublic.com/Projects.html.

Pruitt, Sharon Lynn. "The Gibbs Sisters Are Storytelling Superheroes." Oxygen. November 9, 2016. http://www.oxygen.com/blogs/the-gibbs-sisters-are-storytelling-superheroes.

### Gill, Joel Christian

Barlow, Rich. "Forgotten African American Stories, Told in Comic Books." BU Today. April 16, 2015. https://www.bu.edu/today/2015/african-american-comics/.

Gill, Joel Christian. "Let's Get Rid of Black History Month." *Huffington Post.* February 10, 2015. http://www.huffingtonpost.com/joel-christian-gill/lets-get-rid-of-black-history-month_b_6655356.html.

NPR Staff. "'Strange Fruit' Shares Uncelebrated, Quintessentially American Stories." National Public Radio. February 14, 2015. http://www.npr.org/sections/codeswitch/2015/02/14/384947485/strange-fruit-shares-uncelebrated-quintessentially-american-stories.

Purdy, Megan. "Comics as History: Discussing Joel Christian Gill's 'Strange Fruit.'" Comics Alliance. August 17, 2015. http://comicsalliance.com/joel-christian-gill-strange-fruit/.

### Grant, Shauna

"Bubbly Princess Love Pon with Shauna J. Grant." Interview by Greg Anderson-Elysee (Griotvine interview). The Outhousers. September 22, 2016. http://www.theouthousers.com/index.php/features/136305-bubbly-princess-lovepon-with-shauna-grant-griotvine-interview-3.html.

Grant, Shauna. "Princess Love Pon." https://www.princesslovepon.com.

### Grant, Vernon

Grant, Betsy. *The Adventures of Point-Man Palmer in Vietnam.* Mineral Point, WI: Little Creek Press, 2014.

Absolute Astronomy. "Vernon Grant." 2017. Absoluteastronomy.com (webpage no longer available).

### Guillory, Robb

Hannon, Blake. "'Chew': John Layman, Rob Guillory Talk 'Family Recipes,' Savoy, Poyo." *Los Angeles Times.* November 11, 2013. http://herocomplex.latimes.com/comics/chew-john-layman-rob-guillory-talk-family-recipes-savoy-poyo/.

Harper, David. "The Life and Times of the Modern Comic Book Artist." Multiversity Comics. May 28, 2014. http://www.multiversitycomics.com/longform/the-life-and-times-of-the-modern-comic-book-artist/.

Rawls, Alex. "Robb Guillory Prepares for the Last 'Chew.'" My Spilt Milk. January 5, 2016. http://myspiltmilk.com/rob-guillory-prepares-last-chew.

### Harrington, Ollie

Brunner, Edward. "'This Job Is a Solid Killer': Oliver Harrington's Jive Gray and the African American Adventure Strip." *Iowa Journal of Cultural Studies* 6 (2005): 36–57.

Dolinar, Brian. *The Black Cultural Front: Black Writers and Artists of the Depression Generation.* Jackson: University Press of Mississippi, 2012.

Harrington, Oliver W. *Why I Left America and Other Essays.* Jackson: University Press of Mississippi, 1993.

Inge, M. Thomas, ed. *Dark Laughter: The Satiric Art of Oliver W. Harrington.* Jackson: University Press of Mississippi, 1993.

### Harris, Steven

Hayashi, William. "Master Artist N. Steven Harris." Podcast. *Genesis Science Fiction Radio Series*. November 22, 2013.

"Live Streaming Interview with Artist/Writer N.Steven Harris." By Marc Torres. Podcast. *It Came from the Radio*. July 29, 2015. https://www.youtube.com/watch?v=Nx-cvb-czxN0&index=5&list=PLzk6S0Nw93B9ATsbM8V0p1beua8u8p7y_.

Morrell, Marc. "Voltron Comic Book Artist N. Steven Harris and Jacob Chabot." Podcast. *Let's Voltron*. September 13, 2016.

### Hendricks, Paul

Contributor interview with Jerry Craft. N.d.

### Hollingsworth, Alvin

Hadju, David. *The Ten-Cent Plague: The Great Comic Book Scare and How It Changed America*. New York: Picador, 2009.

Holtz, Allen. "Ink-Slinger Profiles: A. C. Hollingsworth." Stripper's Guide. February 12, 2012. http://strippersguide.blogspot.com/2012/02/ink-slinger-profiles-ac-hollingsworth.html

Howard, Sheena C., and Ronald L. Jackson II, eds. *Black Comics: Politics of Race and Representation*. London: Bloomsbury Academic, 2013.

Jackson, Tim. *Pioneering Cartoonists of Color*. Jackson: University Press of Mississippi, 2016.

Lewis, Samella. *African American Art and Artists*. Berkeley: University of California Press, 2003.

Parfrey, Adam. *It's a Man's World: Men's Adventure Magazines, the Postwar Pulps*. Port Townsend, WA: Feral House, 2003.

Schelly, Bill. *Man of Rock: A Biography of Joe Kubert*. Seattle: Fantagraphics, 2008.

PBS. *History Detectives*, 2011, season 9, episode 4. Public Broadcasting Service. Aired July 12, 2011.

### Holloway, Wilbert

Holtz, Allen. "Ink-Slinger Profiles: Wilbert Holloway." Stripper's Guide. February 13, 2012.

Howard, Sheena C., and Ronald L. Jackson II, eds. *Black Comics: Politics of Race and Representation*. London: Bloomsbury Academic, 2013.

Jackson, Tim. *Pioneering Cartoonists of Color*. Jackson: University Press of Mississippi, 2016.

Stevens, John D. "Reflections in a Dark Mirror: Comic Strips in Black Newspapers." *The Journal of Popular Culture* 10, 1 (1976): 239–244.

### Hudlin, Reginald

Costello, Brannon. "Christopher Priest's Black Panther, Jack Kirby's Black Panther, and the Question of 'Black Comics'." The Hooded Utilitarian. February 4, 2014. http://www.hoodedutilitarian.com/2014/02/christopher-priests-black-panther-jack-kirbys-black-panther-and-the-question-of-black-comics/.

# Igle, Jamal

Contino, Jennifer M. "E-I-E-I-Igle." *Sequential Tart*. Accessed August 2, 2011. http://www.sequentialtart.com/archive/apr00/igle.shtml.

Dallas, Keith. "Firestorm Artist Jamal Igle Signs Exclusive Contract with DC Comics." Comics Bulletin. January 10, 2006. http://www.comicsbulletin.com/news/113693793893595.htm.

Igle, Jamal. "Why I'm Walking Away From Characters I Don't Own." 13th Dimension. December 1, 2015. http://13thdimension.com/why-im-walking-away-from-characters-i-dont-own-by-jamal-igle/.

## Illidge, Joseph

Fomich, Nikolai. "A Career of Milestones: Joseph Illidge Talks Hardware, Batman, Diversity, and Verge Entertainment." Bleeding Cool. July 17, 2014. https://www.bleedingcool.com/2014/07/17/a-career-of-milestones-joseph-illidge-talks-hardware-batman-diversity-and-verge-entertainment/.

"Interview: Joseph P. Illidge on the Intersections of Comic Books." By J. Skyler. Comicosity. August 22, 2013. http://www.comicosity.com/interview-illidge-intersections/.

## Jackson, Jay

Jay, Allen. "Ink-Slinger Profiles by Alex Jay: Jay Jackson." Stripper's Guide. December 15, 2015. http://strippersguide.blogspot.com/2015/12/ink-slinger-profiles-by-alex-jay-jay.html.

## Johnson, Ariell

Cineas, Fabiola. "I Love My Job: Amalgam Comics and Coffeehouse Owner Ariell Johnson. May 15, 2017. http://www.phillymag.com/business/2017/05/15/ariell-johnson-amalgam-comics-coffeehouse-philadelphia/.

Hitt, Tarpley. "Philly Comic Shop Awarded $50,000 to Open More Doors." *Philadelphia Inquirer*. Updated June 18, 2017. http://www.philly.com/philly/entertainment/geek/amalgam-comics-ariell-johnson-knight-foundation-50000-20170618.html.

Scott, Sydney. "#BlackGirlMagic: Comic Book Store Owner Ariell Johnson Will Appear on 'Iron Man' Cover. October 26, 2016. http://www.essence.com/culture/comic-book-ariell-johnson-iron-man-cover.

Rosen, Judith. "A Glimmer of Hope for Black-Owned Bookstores." Publishers Weekly. February 19, 2016. https://www.publishersweekly.com/pw/by-topic/industry-news/bookselling/article/69460-a-glimmer-of-hope-for-black-owned-bookstores.html

## Johnson, Mat

CBR Staff. "Johnson Tells the Unknown Origin of 'Hellblazer's' Papa Midnite in New Mini." Comic Book Resources. February 2, 2005. http://www.cbr.com/johnson-tells-the-unknown-origin-of-hellblazers-papa-midnite-in-new-mini/.

Cox, Tony, and Johnson, Mat. "Searching For Black Utopia ... In Antarctica." National Public Radio. August 17, 2011. http://www.npr.org/2011/08/17/139706474/searching-for- black-utopia-in-antarctica.

"Writer Mat Johnson On 'Loving Day' and Life as a 'Black Boy' Who Looks White." Interview by Terry Gross. *Fresh Air*. National Public Radio. June 29, 2015. http://www.npr.org/2016/09/16/494234198/writer-mat- johnson-on-loving-day- and-life-as-a-black-boy-who-looks-white.

## Louis, Mildred

"Comic Creator You Should Know: Mildred Louis." Interview by Jamie Broadnax. Black Girl Nerds. September 30, 2015. https://blackgirlnerds.com/comic-creator-you-should-know-mildred-louis/.

"Drawn to Comics: Talking to Mildred Louis about How 'Agents of the Realm' Is a Love Letter." Interview by Mey Valdivia Rude. February 16, 2016. https://www.autostraddle.com/drawn-to-comics-talking-to-mildred-louis-about-how-agents-of-the-realm-is-a-love-letter-328008/.

"Mildred Louis Recruits Her 'Agents of the Realm' for Kickstarter." Interview by Steve Morris. Comics Alliance. February 9, 2016. http://comicsalliance.com/mildred-louis-agents-of-the-realm-kickstarter/.

## Magruder, Nilah

Alverson, Brigid. "Webcomics World." *School Library Journal* 62, 4 (2016): 36–42.

Cavna, Michael. "M.F.K. Cartoonist Nilah Magruder in Shock After Winning First Dwayne McDuffie Diversity Award." *Washington Post.* March 1, 2015.

Magruder, Nilah. *A Year of Marvels: September Infinite Comic #1.* Marvel Comics Publications. September 7, 2016.

Magruder, Nilah. Personal interview by Donnalyn Washington. September 1, 2016.

Phillips, Jevon. "Magruder and M.F.K. Win the Dwayne McDuffie Diversity Award." *Los Angeles Times.* March 1, 2015.

## Mance, Ajuan

"Ajuan Mance." Black Past. October 27, 2016. http://www.blackpast.org/contributor/mance-ajuan.

Macy, Jon. "Spotlight on Ajuan Mance." Interview by Jon Macy. Prism Comics. October 27, 2016. http://www.prismcomics.org/spotlight-on-ajuan-mance/.

Mance, Ajuan. "About the Blogger." Black On Campus. November 6, 2006.http://www.blackoncampus.com/about-2/ (website no longer available).

Mance, Ajuan. "Mills College CV." Mills.edu. October 27, 2016. https://www.mills.edu/academics/faculty/eng/amance/amance_cv.php.

Sloan, Louise, and Shirin Chen. "1001 Black Men." Brown Alumni Magazine. http://www.brownalumnimagazine.com/content/view/4337/32/.

## Martinbrough, Shawn

Martinbrough, Shawn. "Bio." 2017. Shawnmartinbrough.com/bio/.

## McGruder, Aaron

"Aaron McGruder Biography." IMDB. http://www.imdb.com/name/nm1412298/bio.

## Mills, Shawna

"Shawna Mills: Creating Violator Union." Interview by Takeia Dunlop. Spray Paint and Ink Pens. June 4 2013. https://spraypaintandinkpens.com/2013/06/04/shawna-mills-creating-violator-union/.

### Odom, Yumy

"About ECBACC, Inc." ECBACC.com/wordpress4/about/.

### Onli, Turtel

"Interviews: Turtel Onli." By Rebecca Zorach. Never the Same. 2012. https://never-the-same.org/interviews/turtel-onli/.

Onli, Turtel. "Black Age of Comics." *Comic Buyer's Guide.* February 26, 1993.

### Ormes, Jackie

Goldstein, Nancy. *Jackie Ormes: The First African American Woman Cartoonist.* Ann Arbor: University of Michigan Press, 2008.

Norris, Kyle. "Comics Crusader: Remembering Jackie Ormes." NPR. July 29, 2008. http://www.npr.org/templates/story/story.php?storyId=93029000.

Whaley, Deborah Elizabeth. *Black Women in Sequence: Re-Inking Comics, Graphic Novels, and Anime.* Seattle: University of Washington Press, 2015.

### Passmore, Benjamin

Arrant, Chris. "An Open Letter of Racism From 'Your Black Friend.'" Newsarama. March 7, 2017. https://www.newsarama.com/33477-an-open-letter-on-racism-from-your-black-friend.html.

Passmore, Ben. "Benjamin Passmore Is Creating Comics!!!" Patreon. https://www.patreon.com/daygloayhole.

Passmore, Ben. "D A Y G L O A Y H O L E." http://daygloayhole.tumblr.com/.

### Randolph, Khary

"Khary Randolph Talks About His Love of Comics." The Comic Archive. April 10, 2015. https://www.youtube.com/watch?v=RUaBf8buIfY.

Riesman, Abraham. "Meet Mosaic, Marvel's New Body-Jumping Antihero." Vulture. June 20, 2016. http://www.vulture.com/2016/06/mosaic-marvel-randolph-thorne.html.

Schiach, Kieran. "Marvel Unveils New 'Mosaic' Character with Ongoing by Geoffrey Thorne And Khary Randolph." Comics Alliance. June 20, 2016.http://comicsalliance.com/marvel-mosaic-geoffrey-thorne-khary-randolph/.

### Richardson, Jason

Dagnelli, Christina. "Top Summer Conventions Held in Philadelphia." CBS Philly. June 6, 2016. http://philadelphia.cbslocal.com/top-lists/top-summer-conventions-held-in-philadelphia/.

J1 Studios. "J1 Con: Philadelphia's #1 Anime Convention." J1 Studios: The Entertainment Hub for Geeks. www.j1studios.com.

### Robinson, Jimmie

Robinson, Jimmie. "Robinson's Biography, Resume and Trivia." www.jimmykitty.com.

### Sanders, Y.

Goodlett, Ellen, and Y. Sanders. "Single Serving." *In Girls Night Out: The Way Love Goes,* ed. Amy Chu. Alpha Girl Comics, 2014.

Goodlett, Ellen, and Y. Sanders, "William's Last Words," in 27, *A Comic Anthology*, ed. Enrica Jang. Action Lab Entertainment, 2015.

## Scott, Age

None cited

## Shearer, Ted

Otfinosky, Steven. *African Americans in the Visual Arts (A to Z of African Americans)*. New York: Facts on File, 2011.

Reynolds, Moira Davison. *Comic Strip Artists in American Newspapers, 1945–1980*. Jefferson, NC: McFarland & Company, 2003.

## Sims, Guy

Kirkus Reviews. "Monster: A Graphic Novel." *Kirkus Reviews*. July 22, 2015. https://www.kirkusreviews.com/book-reviews/walter-dean-myers/monster-sims/.

## Smith, Juliana

Browntourage. "2 Great Authors in Conversation Repping Black Women." Browntourage. March 28, 2014.

The Establishment. "'(H)Afrocentric' Comic Strip Comes to The Establishment." The Establishment. August 21, 2016. https://theestablishment.co/h-afrocentric-comic-strip-comes-to-the-establishment-8959a270bb03.

Smith, Juliana. "Meet the Creators." (H)afrocentric. Accessed June 8, 2017. https://hafrocentric.com/about/.

## Thomas, Pamela

Museum of Uncut Funk. "Welcome to the Museum of UnCut Funk: International. Intergalactic." http://museumofuncutfunk.com/.

O'Brien, Kathleen. "From Shaft to Fat Albert, NJ Duo Preserves 1970s Black Pop Culture." NJ Advance Media for NJ.Com. February 4, 2016.

## Thompson, B. Alex

Thompson, B. Alex. "Approbation Comics." Approbation Comics. Accessed August 8, 2016. http://www.approbationcomics.com/.

## Turner, Morrie

Chang, Jeff. *Who We Be: The Colorization of America*. New York: St. Martin's, 2014.

Ericsson, Mary Kentra. *Morrie Turner: Creator of "Wee Pals."* Chicago: Childrens Press, 1986.

Harvey, R. C. "Morrie Turner: To Say the Name Is Both Eulogy and Tribute." *The Comics Journal*. 2014. http://www.tcj.com/morrie-turner-to-say-the-name-is-both-eulogy-and-tribute/.

Turner, Morrie. *Wee Pals*. New York: Signet, 1969.

## Walker, David

Betancourt, David. "What Marvel Canceling Nighthawk Means to Superheroes of Color." *Washington Post*. September 8, 2016. https://www.washington-post.com/news/comic-riffs/wp/2016/09/08/what-marvel-canceling-night-hawk-means-for-superheroes-of-color/.

McNally, Victoria. "*Ms Marvel, Shaft*, and Others Nominated for the Dwayne McDuf-fie Award for Diversity." The Mary Sue. February 19, 2015. http://www.themary-sue.com/dwayne-mcduffie-prize-finalists/.

Rosberg, Caitlin. "David F. Walker Talks *Shaft, Cyborg*, and a Changing Industry." The A.V. Club. July 22, 2015. http://www.avclub.com/article/david-f-walker-talks-shaft-cyborg-and-changing-ind-222118.

Walker, David F. "BadAzz Mofo." Posted on July 1, 2016. http://www.badazzmofo.com/.

Walker, David F. *Becoming Black: Personal Ramblings on Racial Identification, Racism, and Popular Culture*. Portland, OR: Drapetomedia, 2013.

Walker, David F. "The David Walker Site." http://thedavidwalkersite.com/bio/.

## Whaley, Deborah

"Deborah Whaley." The University of Iowa College of Liberal Arts and Sciences. https://clas.uiowa.edu/american-studies/people/deborah-whaley.

Howard, Sheena C. Author interview, October 18, 2016.

"Interview: Re-inking Black Women in Comics with Deborah E. Whaley." By Paul Lai. Multiversity Comics. December 4, 2015. http://www.multiversitycomics.com/interviews/deborah-e-whaley-interview/.

Whaley, Deborah Elizabeth. *Black Women In Sequence: Re-inking Comics, Graphic Novels, and Anime*. University of Washington Press, 2015.

## Wheeler, Joseph R., III

"ONYXCON." http://www.onyxcon.com/.

## White, Caanan

Corrigan, Maureen. "'Bintel Brief' and 'Hellfighters': American Stories, Pow-erfully Illustrated." National Public Radio. April 17, 2014. http://www.npr.org/2014/04/17/301028267/bintel-brief-and-hellfighters-american-stories-power-fully-illustrated.

"Uber: Caanan White Talks about Rendering the Superrealities of War and Kieron Gillen's OMG Moments." Interview by Mike Seifert. Bleeding Cool. February 9, 2013. https://www.bleedingcool.com/2013/02/19/kieron-gillens-uber-canaan-white-talks-about-rendering-the-superrealities-of-war/.

Wang, Hansi Lo. "The Harlem Hellfighters: Fighting Racism in the Trenches of WWI." National Public Radio. April 1, 2014. http://www.npr.org/sections/codeswitch/2014/04/01/294913379/the-harlem-hellfighters-fighting-racism-in-the-trenches-of-wwi.

### Williams, Maia "Crown"

"Interview with Maia 'Crown' Williams, Founder of #Meccacon." By Ari Limbrick. Geek Girl World. September 19, 2015. http://geekgirlworld.com/2015/09/13/interview-with-maia-crown-williams-founder-of-meccacon/.

### Woods, Ashley

Johnston, Rich. "New Talent at Marvel Comics: Ashley A Woods." Bleeding Cool. August 26, 2015. https://www.bleedingcool.com/2015/08/26/ashley-a-woods-tapped-for-marvel-comics/.

Johnston, Rich. "Amandla Stenberg's Comic, Niobe: *She Is Life*, Comes to Stores in November." Bleeding Cool. August 20, 2015. https://www.bleedingcool.com/2015/08/20/amandla-stenbergs-comic-niobe-she-is-life-comes-to-stores-in-november/.

### Yo, Onjena

Yo, Onjena. "MULTINATIONAL PATRIOT FLAG & BLOG SERIES: American? But How Can That Be? You Are Brown." Carbon-Fibre Media. https://www.carbon-fibre.me/patriot/multi-national-patriot-flag-series-american-but-how-can-that-be-you-are-brown.

# INDEX

# ABOUT THE AUTHORS

Sheena C. Howard is associate professor of communication at Rider University. Howard is an award-winning author, including a 2014 Eisner Award for her coedited book, *Black Comics: Politics of Race and Representation*. She is also the author of *Black Queer Identity Matrix* and *Critical Articulations of Race, Gender, and Sexual Orientation*.

Howard has appeared in the *Washington Post* and on NPR, ABC, PBS, and other networks and in documentaries as an expert on popular culture, race, politics, and sexual identity negotiation. In 2016, she directed, produced, and wrote the documentary *Remixing Colorblind*. She also has bylines in *The Huffington Post*, *Curve* magazine, the *Philadelphia Inquirer*, and more.

**Henry Louis Gates, Jr.** is the Alphonse Fletcher University Professor and director of the W. E. B. Du Bois Institute for African and American Research at Harvard University. He is the author of sixteen books, including *Life Upon These Shores: Looking at African American History, 1513–2008* and *Tradition and the Black Atlantic*, and has made twelve documentaries, including *Finding Your Roots, Black in Latin America*, and *Looking for Lincoln*. He is also the editor in chief of *The Root*, a daily online magazine. He is the recipient of fifty-one honorary degrees and numerous awards. In 1981, he was a member of the first class awarded "genius grants" by the MacArthur Foundation, and in 1998, he became the first African American scholar to be awarded the National Humanities Medal. He was named to *Time's* 25 Most Influential Americans in 1997, to *Ebony's* Power 150 list in 2009, and to *Ebony's* Power 100 list in 2010 and 2012. *The Henry Louis Gates, Jr. Reader*, a collection of Professor Gates's essays, was published in 2012.

**Christopher James Priest** is a critically acclaimed novelist and comic book writer. Priest is the first African American writer and editor to work in the comic book industry. His groundbreaking *Black Panther* series was lauded by *Entertainment Weekly* and *The Village Voice*. *Static Shock,* which Priest cocreated with Milestone Media, Inc., has become the first nationally syndicated African American superhero animated series, and the first act of 2005's *Batman Begins* was largely based upon Priest's *Batman* comic book work. Priest has also written and recorded numerous songs and served as producer and sideman for various bands and choirs, and has developed many properties for Hollywood, including projects with former BET president Reginald Hudlin (producer of *Django Unchained*), Hamm & Kitchens, Inc. (Tim Burton *Batman* films), Edward R. Pressman Productions Inc., and Eddie Murphy Productions. He currently serves as a Baptist pastor in Colorado Springs, where he founded PraiseNet Electronic Media in 2001. Priest is a four-time American Advertising Federation Addy Award winner for graphic and web design. His most current comics work was the hit series *Quantum and Woody* from Valiant Entertainment, and a trio of *Green Lantern* novels from iBooks/Simon & Schuster.

FULCRUM